WITHDRAWN
UTSA LIBRARIES

The Protestant Challenge to Corporate America
Issues of Social Responsibility

Research for Business Decisions, No. 69

Richard N. Farmer, Series Editor

Professor of International Business
Indiana University

Other Titles in This Series

No. 63 *What Auditors Should Know About
        Data Processing*   Donald L. Dawley

No. 64 *Federal Intervention in the Mortgage
        Markets: An Analysis*   Douglas Hearth

No. 65 *Accounting Distortions and the Consistency
        of Firms' Performance Measures*   Kenneth M. Harlan

No. 66 *The Impact of Taxes on U.S. Citizens
        Working Abroad*   Ernest R. Larkins

No. 67 *Distribution Channel Strategy for
        Export Marketing: The Case of Hong
        Kong Firms*   T.S. Chan

No. 68 *Internal Accountability: An
        International Emphasis*   Wagdy M. Abdallah

No. 70 *Strategies of the Major Oil Companies*   William N. Greene

No. 71 *Industrial Cooperation between Poland
        and the West*   John Garland

No. 72 *Asian Business in Transition*   W. Chan Kim

The Protestant Challenge to Corporate America
Issues of Social Responsibility

by
Roy W. Morano

UMI RESEARCH PRESS
Ann Arbor, Michigan

Copyright © 1984, 1982
Roy William Morano
All rights reserved

Produced and distributed by
UMI Research Press
an imprint of
University Microfilms International
A Xerox Information Resources Company
Ann Arbor, Michigan 48106

Library of Congress Cataloging in Publication Data

Morano, Roy W.
   The Protestant challenge to corporate America.

   (Research for business decisions ; no. 69)
   Revision of thesis—New York University, 1982.
   Bibliography: p.
   Includes index.
   1. Industry—Social aspects—United States. 2. Church and industry—United States. I. Title. II. Series.
HD60.5.U5M66 1984   658.4′08   84-8514
ISBN 0-8357-1592-2

This book is dedicated to my wife, Hope, who not only patiently encouraged me year after year, but made sure that I had all the necessary time to complete this study. This was not always easy for a Long Island commuter with a full-time position with a major American corporation (American-Standard, Inc.) in New York City. The greatest tribute to her success as wife and mother is reflected in the attainments of her family. All received her unselfish inspiration and encouragement to complete a project once it was undertaken.

Contents

List of Tables   *ix*

1 Introduction   *1*
   The Problem
   Research Questions
   Definitions
   Delimitations of the Study
   Implications of the Problem
   Review of Related Literature
   Methodology
   Organization of the Study

2 Protestant Activism in the 1970s: Shareholder Resolutions, Boycotts and Other Contacts—The Social Issues Involved   *29*
   Introduction
   The Social Concerns
   Statistical Summaries of the Issues
   Shareholder Resolution Activism, 1970 to 1979
   Boycotts
   Other Direct Contacts

3 Business Responses to Protestant Activism in the 1970s   *123*
   Business Challenged in the 1970s Over Social Responsibility
   Increasing Criticisms of Business in the 1970s
   The "Project for Corporate Responsibility" Provides a Model
   Business Response: Openly Critical of the Tactics of Church Activists
   Business Response: Reaffirmation of the Classical or Traditional Position

Business Response: Moderate View of Business Toward Corporate Social Responsibility
Specific Responses of Business to Shareholder Resolutions
Business Policy Modifications in Response to Pressures on Social Issues

4 Summary and Conclusions *163*

5 Observations: The Transnational Corporations *189*

Notes *193*

Bibliography *217*

Index *233*

List of Tables

1. Protestant Sponsored or Cosponsored Shareholder Resolutions 1970 to 1979 Over the Issue of Apartheid in the Republic of South Africa   *35*

2. Protestant Sponsored or Cosponsored Shareholder Resolutions 1970 to 1979 Over the Issue of Apartheid in Namibia   *41*

3. Protestant Sponsored or Cosponsored Shareholder Resolutions 1970 to 1979 Over the Issue of Apartheid in Rhodesia   *44*

4. Protestant Sponsored or Cosponsored Shareholder Resolutions 1970 to 1979 Over Colonialism in Angola, Guinea-Bissau and Mozambique   *47*

5. Protestant Sponsored or Cosponsored Shareholder Resolutions 1970 to 1979 Over the Issue of Human Rights in Chile   *48*

6. Protestant Sponsored or Cosponsored Shareholder Resolutions 1970 to 1979 Over the Issue of Human Rights in the Dominican Republic   *49*

7. Protestant Sponsored or Cosponsored Shareholder Resolutions 1970 to 1979 Over Questionable Labor Practices in Guatemala   *50*

8. Protestant Sponsored or Cosponsored Shareholder Resolutions 1970 to 1979 Over the Issue of Wages and Working Conditions in South Korea   *51*

9. Protestant Sponsored or Cosponsored Shareholder Resolutions 1970 to 1979 Over the Issue of Civil Liberties in the Philippines   *52*

x *List of Tables*

10. Protestant Sponsored or Cosponsored Shareholder Resolutions 1970 to 1979 Over the Issue of Labor Practices in Developing Countries   *53*

11. Protestant Sponsored or Cosponsored Shareholder Resolutions 1970 to 1979 Over the Issue of Foreign Military Sales   *55*

12. Protestant Sponsored or Cosponsored Shareholder Resolutions 1970 to 1979 Over the Issue of Distribution of Infant Formula in Third World Countries   *56*

13. Protestant Sponsored or Cosponsored Shareholder Resolutions 1970 to 1979 Over the Issue of Questionable Corporate Payments Overseas   *57*

14. Protestant Sponsored or Cosponsored Shareholder Resolutions 1970 to 1979 Over the Issue of Appropriate Farm Technology for Third World Societies   *59*

15. Protestant Sponsored or Cosponsored Shareholder Resolutions 1970 to 1979 Over the Issue of the Energy Crisis in the United States   *59*

16. Protestant Sponsored or Cosponsored Shareholder Resolutions 1970 to 1979 Over the Issue of Equal Employment Opportunities in the United States   *61*

17. Protestant Sponsored or Cosponsored Shareholder Resolutions 1970 to 1979 Over the Issue of Political Contributions in the United States   *63*

18. Protestant Sponsored or Cosponsored Shareholder Resolutions 1970 to 1979 Over the Issue of Redlining/Reinvestment by Banks in the United States   *64*

19. Protestant Sponsored or Cosponsored Shareholder Resolutions 1970 to 1979 Over the Issue of Strip Mining and Other Mining in the United States   *65*

20. Protestant Sponsored or Cosponsored Shareholder Resolutions 1970 to 1979 Over the Issue of the Nomination of a Woman to Board of Directors   *67*

21. Protestant Sponsored or Cosponsored Shareholder Resolutions 1970 to 1979 Over the Issue of the Influence of Television on Children's Nutrition *68*

22. Protestant Sponsored or Cosponsored Shareholder Resolutions 1970 to 1979 Over the Issue of the Stereotypical Images of Women in Advertising *69*

23. Protestant Sponsored or Cosponsored Shareholder Resolutions 1970 to 1979 Over the Issue of Sponsoring Television Programs Containing Violence *70*

24. Protestant Sponsored or Cosponsored Shareholder Resolutions 1970 to 1979 Over the Issue of Nuclear Weapons Production *70*

25. Protestant Sponsored or Cosponsored Shareholder Resolutions 1970 to 1979 (Social Issues Listed by Frequency) *72*

26. Protestant Shareholder Resolutions Filed 1970 to 1979 (Listed by Frequency by Year) *73*

27. Protestant Sponsored or Cosponsored Shareholder Resolutions 1970 to 1979 (Listed by Protestant Denomination and Frequency of Participation) *73*

28. American Corporations Involved with Protestant Sponsored or Cosponsored Shareholder Resolutions 1970 to 1979 (Listed Alphabetically) *74*

29. Protestant Sponsored or Cosponsored Shareholder Resolutions In the Year of 1971 *82*

30. Protestant Sponsored or Cosponsored Shareholder Resolutions In the Year of 1972 *84*

31. Protestant Sponsored or Cosponsored Shareholder Resolutions In the Year of 1973 *86*

32. Protestant Sponsored or Cosponsored Shareholder Resolutions In the Year of 1974 *88*

33. Protestant Sponsored or Cosponsored Shareholder Resolutions In the Year of 1975   *91*

34. Protestant Sponsored or Cosponsored Shareholder Resolutions In the Year of 1976   *93*

35. Protestant Sponsored or Cosponsored Shareholder Resolutions In the Year of 1977   *96*

36. Protestant Sponsored or Cosponsored Shareholder Resolutions In the Year of 1978   *99*

37. Protestant Sponsored or Cosponsored Shareholder Resolutions In the Year of 1979   *102*

1

Introduction

David I. Margolis, President of Colt Industries, is quoted in a 1979 *Business Week* article as saying that today's corporation is operating in an environment that is a "pressure cooker." "It is under siege from consumerists, environmentalists, women's liberation advocates, the civil rights movement, and other activity groups."[1] He declares further that "the activists are forcing changes in corporate operating policies that range from a halt to loans to South Africa to curtailment of infant milk formula sales in less developed countries."[2]

"Dissident Stockholders Begin to Get Somewhere at Last" headlines a *New York Times* article in May 1977. The subheading reads: "At Annual Meetings, Some of Their Proposals Are Now Taken Seriously."[3] Church and social service groups who have sought a greater role in shaping corporate standards and policies, the article points out, are seeing signs that "their success rate is improving and that they are being taken more seriously by corporate management."[4]

William E. Morley, special counsel at the Securities and Exchange Commission, in the same article, is quoted as saying:

> There seems to be an increasing willingness on the part of management to sit down with proponents and work out a proposal that the company is willing to put in [the proxy statement] or to voluntarily provide the kind of information requested so that the proposal will be withdrawn.[5]

The 1970s have been a significant decade in which corporations have met very serious challenges to their usual way of doing business. Never before has business been so vociferously criticized as to its responsibility to society. Society now is no longer satisfied with the production of goods and services only, but looks to corporations for participation in various societal concerns. The corporation, therefore, has become subject to increasing pressures by various segments of society, including the Protestant churches, to conduct its affairs more in terms of societal needs rather than purely for profits. In this regard, Cavanagh makes the terse observation that "if a firm is a sweatshop, makes a city or its surroundings dirtier, uglier, and more hectic, and more polluted, it can hardly be said to perform well, no matter what its profits or productivity."[6]

The change in American attitude caught business by surprise even though there were emerging signs that signalled a major upheaval. Decade upon decade business had been governed by the maxim that the "business of business is business." This maxim says that the business executive is to be concerned only with the accomplishment of the firm's primary task: the production of goods and services in a competent manner while at the same time generating income for the stockholders. This traditional position (that the business of business is business) is simply stated by the noted economist Milton Friedman in his remark that "the social responsibility of business is to increase its profits."[7]

Activist groups, including Protestant churches, reject the argument that profits should be the only goal for corporations. While this argument may have been valid in the past, activists argue, rules change in response to the needs of society and literal adherence to previous standards can no longer be valid for today. Political legitimacy of large business concerns depends on their ability to serve the needs of society and not the other way around.[8]

The Protestant churches possess millions of dollars of shareholder stock in major American corporations and their concern about the performance of any corporation in which they were part owners was not only a *financial* one but an *ethical* one as well. A stockholder benefits from the actions of a corporation and is at least in part responsible for those activities. This position is captured in this statement contained in *The Ethical Investor:* "We are . . . convinced that owning shares in a corporation does thrust upon the owner a responsibility for the social effects of corporate policy that he would not otherwise have."[9]

With this concern in mind, Protestant churches, as well as other religious and activist groups, have confronted corporations in the 1970s in a very direct manner, utilizing shareholder resolutions, public hearings, private meetings with management, letters to management, boycotts, attendance at shareholder meetings, and fact-finding trips, to press their causes. These tactics of direct contact with American corporations in behalf of social issues had not been utilized prior to the 1970s by Protestant churches, but their effectiveness was discovered by other activist groups in the late 1960s and they were then adopted by the Protestant churches.[10]

The Problem

During the ten-year period of 1970 to 1979, Protestant churches,[11] with the support of The National Council of Churches in Christ in the U.S.A. and coordinated with the help of the Interfaith Center on Corporate Responsibility, directly challenged corporations on issues of corporate social responsibility.

This book describes the specific issues presented as social concerns to corporations during 1970 to 1979 by Protestant churches, as well as discusses the manner in which these issues were brought to the attention of corporate management.

The book also describes the arguments presented by business in response to the specific social issues that were brought to the attention of management by Protestant churches by means of shareholder resolutions, boycotts, and other direct contacts.[12] Investigation is made as to whether some business practices were changed during the 1970s in connection with those social issues that were of concern to Protestant churches.

Research Questions

1. What were the specific social issues[13] that prompted the filing of shareholder resolutions, the initiating of boycotts, and other direct contacts with American corporations by Protestant churches[14] during the ten-year period of 1970 to 1979?

    a. What social issues dominated the attention of the Protestant churches during the 1970s?

    b. What corporations were involved with Protestant instigated shareholder resolutions and boycotts during this period?

    c. What Protestant denominations filed shareholder resolutions, engaged in boycotts, and made other direct contacts during this period?

2. What were the arguments presented by the targeted corporations[15] in answer to the challenges of the Protestant churches relative to the social issues that were presented by means of shareholder resolutions, boycotts, and other contacts during the ten-year period of 1970 to 1979?

3. What business practices were changed or modified during the 1970s in connection with those social issues which Protestant churches brought to the attention of corporate management during the period of 1970 to 1979?

Definitions

Corporate social responsibility. George Steiner, writing for *The Conference Board Record,* defines corporate social responsibility as follows:

4   *Introduction*

> Conceptually, social responsibility generally refers to actions which a company takes partially with a view to helping society achieve objectives which it sets for itself. They may also be classified into internal and external activities. Internally, they may refer to such matters as due process, justice, and equity in hiring, promoting or firing employees. Externally, they may concern a wide range of actions from improving consumer products to training and hiring hardcore unemployed. Finally, they may be considered in terms of profit. Some socially responsible actions may increase both short- and long-range profits. Others can reduce both.[16]

Shareholder resolution. A proposal regarding some aspect of the corporation's business submitted by a shareholder for consideration by all shareholders and to be voted upon at the next annual business meeting of the corporation.

Proxy statement. Booklet issued by the corporation which outlines all the business on the annual meeting agenda. Provision is made on the form for casting votes on matters contained in the agenda. The proxy statement must provide a place or a card for the shareowner to vote on shareowner proposals being considered at the forthcoming annual meeting.

Social issues or concerns. This term refers to issues or concerns which involve human rights issues as contrasted to concerns which involve economic issues only, with which American corporations have been primarily associated. The phrase "social issues that were of concern to Protestant churches in the 1970s" would refer to for example, particular human rights issues emphasized by the Protestant churches during the 1970s, such as apartheid in Namibia or South Africa, the harm to American Indians as a result of environmental destruction of strip mining in Appalachia, or lack of job opportunities for minorities and women. The full complement of these social concerns are described in this book.

National Council of Churches of Christ in the U.S.A. A cooperative agency with a membership of 30 Protestant and Orthodox denominations, composed of over 250 official representatives chosen by the churches. The Council was founded in 1950

> for the purpose of expressing . . . common faith and witness in cooperation with one another through various forums and programs. It was never intended to be a melting pot for convictions and traditions, but rather a mosaic where . . . differences could create a greater design.[17]

Interfaith Center on Corporate Responsibility. The Interfaith Center was established in 1974 and is affiliated with the National Council of Churches. Membership is composed of 14 Protestant denominations and 150 Roman

Catholic religious communities. The Center is a coalition and through the decisions of its Board and the services of a permanent staff, it acts as a clearinghouse and resource center for the independent actions of its member religious organizations. It functions primarily to assist its members, agencies, and instrumentalities to express social responsibility through investments.[18]

Delimitations of the Study

This book encompasses the time frame of 1970 to 1979 as it was during this time that major developments took place relevant to the Protestant churches' direct confrontations with American corporations.

The study is delimited to the United States of America. The word "American" is to be assumed whenever "corporation" or "Protestant churches" appear in the report.

The expression "Protestant churches" used throughout this book refers to the ten Protestant denominations enumerated earlier and their representatives, the National Council of Churches of Christ in the U.S.A., and sponsor-affiliate the Interfaith Center on Corporate Responsibility. The Interfaith Center acts as a coordinator of both Protestant and Roman Catholic efforts relative to the filing of shareholder resolutions and boycott actions.

Where specific Protestant denominations are shown as having filed shareholder resolutions, it is understood that a legal instrumentality of the particular denomination who were owners of the stock, did the actual filing of the shareholder resolutions.

Implications of the Problem

The Protestant churches have a long history of involvement with social concerns based on an underlying philosophy which declares that the gospel must be related to man's need in every situation.[19] This kind of message, known as the "social gospel," argues that there is more to being religious than simply repentance and salvation. And this "something more" is that salvation relates to society, its economic life, and the social institutions in society, as well as to individuals.[20]

John Bennett, in a commencement address to graduating seminarians, declared that "it is a distortion of the mission of the church to remain aloof from the struggles for justice and peace in society." He argued that the church is an agent for social change to bring "grace and truth" to the "secular world."[21]

In Old Testament times the prophets proclaimed a message of economic justice. Jesus and the Apostle Paul battled against racial bias. When the Roman Empire crumbled, the church assumed certain responsibilities in behalf of communal needs. In the Middle Ages, the church launched some programs which, in time, provided roots for hospitals, schools, and various kinds of welfare.

The Protestant churches continue today in programs that alleviate poverty, reduce racial strife, provide better housing, and generate world stability and peace. The churches view their ministry as a witness among the larger relations and structures of society. In addressing the corporate interests, the churches seek to perform their prophetic role of holding "powers" accountable.[22] The churches, therefore, participate with other groups who work for conditions that promote individual dignity, social justice, and civil peace.

The Protestant churches, in defining their social ministry as "holding powers accountable," have moved dynamically away from a placid role of issuing "social statements" to one of active involvement: shareholder resolutions, shareholder suits, boycotts, and the like. The Protestant churches have concerned themselves with such issues as agribusiness, community reinvestment and redlining, labor equality, energy, infant formula, militarism, and especially the concerns of apartheid in Southern Africa.

A study of the direct approach tactics by Protestant churches during the 1970s should be of interest to both business executives and denominational leaders who are caught up in this relatively new phenomenon. The Protestant churches' direct approach to corporations has been viewed by some in business as being anticorporate and anticapitalistic. In a recent article, *Fortune* labeled the Protestant churches as "Corporation Haters." The article was headed "The Corporation Haters" and bore a subtitle which read "The Spirit of the New Left Lives On In An Antibusiness Coalition—sponsored by none other than the National Council of Churches."[23] Author Herman Nickel comments that the "gap between the moderate-conservative mood of mainstream churchgoers and the militant zeal of the church functionaries on Riverside Drive is astonishing."[24] Nickel argues further that the "confluence of radical Christian and radical Marxist thinking has been under way for some time without arousing much opposition from individual congregations."[25]

Edgar Bundy, the head of a small ultraconservative Protestant group, labels the Protestant churches' approach to corporations as "an attempt by radical church groups . . . formed by avowed revolutionaries to bring American corporate policies into line with hardcore leftist dogma."[26]

The new breed of clergymen[27] may applaud the confrontations, but the older and more traditional members of the Protestant churches are not supportive of the confrontations. In fact, some openly oppose the tactics being employed by the activist Protestant churches. For example, I. J. Kirchoff, a conservative Presbyterian and President of Castle & Cooke (a company which, incidentally, has been subject to criticism by the activist Protestant churches) takes the position that

> the business community faces a conflict where the ammunition is ideas, values, and factual intelligence, and where political sophistry masquerades as theological opinion. . . . Marxist-Christian dialogue is a game designed to stabilize the Christian fabric which provides the foundation on which our system exists. It is incumbent upon each of us to become aware of the threat to our basic freedom and to examine carefully the methodology of our antagonists.[28]

Conservatives would also argue that the world community can be changed only if the heart is "regenerated and the entire personality changed by the Gospel."[29]

The Protestant churches' involvement with corporate social responsibility is a dilemma to business and to conservative Protestantism. Therefore, this study of the ten-year encounter of the Protestant churches with American corporations should provide data for decision making for business executives presently caught up with church-confrontation tactics as well as provide denominational executives with organized data which could prove helpful in formulating social actions plans for the 1980s.

In a recent issue of *Business International,* a weekly report to managers of worldwide business operations, business executives are cautioned:

> Companies have long underestimated the power of the critics who have taken them to task for alleged social injustices. New thrusts in the organization, objectives and tactics of these groups, however, require firms to pay closer attention to their activities.[30]

Business certainly does not want to find itself "fighting the church"— especially with relation to those issues where the public appears to be supportive. They recognize that arguing with, or even ignoring the churches' petitions, is poor public relations. The 1980s will certainly present similar challenges of direct approach by the churches and background data of the 1970s will prove useful.

In summary, this book is an account of social issues which engaged Protestant church activists in dialogue with American corporations during the period of 1970 to 1979. It clarifies the arguments that the churches offered in behalf of the social issues that precipitated the shareholder resolutions, boycotts, and other direct contacts. It reports the positions that corporations took relative to these social issues and the business philosophies adopted relative to corporate social responsibility. Both business executives and church leaders, as well as college and seminary teachers, should find the descriptive data of value for not only assessing the churches' impact upon the business community in the 1970s, but to provide guidance as well as to the handling of future interactions between the churches and American corporations.

Review of Related Literature

Literature is reviewed first as to the development and meaning of the term "corporate social responsibility" as understood today, and second, with relation to the rationale for the Protestant churches becoming involved in issues concerning corporate social responsibility.

The Emergence of the Concept of Corporate Social Responsibility

Codes governing business transactions emerged as early as the time of Hammurabi.[31] Early history also reveals that among the more advanced civilizations, such as the Greek and Roman Empires, a business occupation was not too highly regarded. Plato, for example, looked at commercial work as something to be avoided.[32] Aristotle derided the life of a tradesperson.[33] However, by the time of the Protestant Reformation, the businessman had become more highly regarded. Luther observed:

> Trade is permissible, provided that it is confined to the exchange of the necessaries and that the seller demands no more than will compensate him for his labor and risk. The unforgivable sins are idleness and covetousness, for they destroy the unity of the body of which Christians are members.[34]

Following the Protestant Reformation great emphasis was placed upon self-discipline and diligence. In fact, one's godliness could be measured by the amount of material success that was secured. There was material reward for hard work. This assured the wealthy that their wealth was justly earned—they worked hard for it and so had a right to it.[35] This spirit of hard work and diligence at one's occupation became known as the Protestant work ethic. John Calvin reinforced this view with his argument that frugality, industry, and wealth were considered earmarks of a man of God.[36]

When these persons who were espoused to the Protestant work ethic fled from Europe to America, they carried the same philosophy with them. These devout emigrés from Europe had considerable influence over American life and morals.[37] The prestigious private colleges of the eastern Establishment also taught the values of private property, free trade, and individualism. They taught conservative economic and business values along with their moral philosophy.[38]

Benjamin Franklin offered this advice in his "Advice to a Young Tradesman":

> Remember, that time is money . . .
> Remember, that credit is money . . .
> Remember, that money is of the prolific, generating nature.
> Money can beget money . . .
> Remember this saying, the good paymaster is lord of another man's purse . . .
> The most trifling actions that affect a man's credit are to be regarded.[39]

However, in time, in America, the Protestant work ethic became gradually emptied of its religious content causing John Wesley to argue: "I fear wherever riches have increased, the essence of religion has decreased in the same proportion. . . . So although the form of religion remains, the spirit is swiftly vanishing away."[40] Nonetheless, he did press that "we ought not to prevent people from being diligent and frugal; we must exhort all Christians to gain all they can, and to save all they can; that is, in effect, to grow rich."[41]

By the late 1800s small businesses began to give way to the larger enterprises. This was because there was a need for great concentrations of economic power to build a transcontinental railroad and to fund new iron, steel, and construction industries.

The larger enterprises became possible because a particular premise argued by John Locke was adopted: the importance of private property. Owning property was the natural right of man, Locke stressed, and the government should never be empowered to deny this right. This made it possible for a person or a business to own land, buildings, and equipment under the protection of the government. Without this guarantee, no corporation could be formed. Private property provided a theoretical and moral foundation upon which the giant corporations could build.[42]

In addition to keeping the privilege of owning private property sacrosanct, Adam Smith argued that the government had no right to get involved in business. Business should remain free at all times so that one business could compete against another and by this the law of supply and demand would dictate the price of goods and services. This was Adam Smith's very important concept of laissez-faire or the free enterprise system. Since all men under the free enterprise system are free to compete, they will do their very best when each promotes their own interests to the fullest.[43] Smith argued:

> Every individual is continually exerting himself to find the most advantageous employment for whatever capital he can command. It is his own advantage, indeed, and not that of the society which he has in view. But the study of his own advantage

> naturally, or rather necessarily, leads him to prefer that employment which is most advantageous to society. . . . He generally, indeed, neither intends to promote the public interest, nor knows how much he is promoting it. . . . He intends only his own gain, and he is in this . . . led by an invisible hand to promote an end which was not part of his intention. Nor is it always the worse for the society that was no part of it. By pursuing his own interest, he frequently promotes that of the society more effectually than when he really intends to promote it. I have never known much good done by those who affected to trade for the public good.[44]

What Adam Smith basically argued is that when a person works for his own personal gain, he is led by an "invisible hand" which ultimately benefits all society. A person working for his own benefit, however, must work in the context of a free enterprise system, where one competes with another. Every man and woman is free to choose what he or she wishes to buy and sell. As each individual's impact on the market would be quite small, no one person would control the market. Therefore the price at which a buyer would buy and a seller would sell, would be established in a free and open market. By this theory the market would find equilibrium.

The business social responsibility implications of the laissez-faire system were reflected in the following three principles: (a) observance of the principles of private property; (b) observance of contract; and (c) avoidance of deception and fraud.[45]

The free enterprise system as envisioned by Adam Smith did not operate in the way that it was supposed to. The spirit of free competition was extinguished in many cases where large enterprises crushed out the small. In some cases there were tendencies for businessmen to manipulate the distribution of merchandise, and there was a failure on the part of business to provide for the protection of life, limb, and health. There was also a frequent failure to recognize the human rights of workers.[46]

There were other problems too that violated a true laissez-faire economic system. Bowen summarizes these as,

> (1) growth of large scale enterprise and concentration of economic power; (2) fluctuating general business activity with recurrent periods of unemployment; (3) technological unemployment; (4) personal insecurity of people with reference to sickness, old age, and death; (5) disparities in the distribution of income; (6) disparities in the distribution of economic opportunity; (7) overly rapid and wasteful exploitation of natural resources; (8) materialistic, competitive, and invidious standards of consumption; and (9) frequent disregard for the social costs of economic activity and the social values that might be derived from economic activity.[47]

Business social responsibility became sullied because of the abuse of large concentrations of power. The government had to step in with legislation to protect the rights of the public, and this materially curtailed the undiluted concept of laissez-faire. These laws in a sense structured the ethics of corporations by compelling them to behave in certain ways. The first major act dealing with direct regulation of corporations was the Interstate Commerce Act of 1887. The act was aimed specifically at the railroads and it specified rates, fares and practices. The Sherman Antitrust Act of 1890 prohibited contracts which restrained trade. The Pure Food and Drugs Act of 1906 protected the public from injury which could result from adulterated or misbranded drugs. The Tilman Act of 1907 prohibited corporations from contributing to the campaigns of parties and candidates in federal elections. The Railway Labor Act of 1926 encouraged collective bargaining. In 1926, the Air Commerce Act imposed safety and navigation regulations on the air transport industry. In the 1930s more legislation was enacted restraining business in behalf of the benefit of society.[48]

The 1940s, 1950s, 1960s, and 1970s witnessed additional legislation controlling the behavior of American corporations and protecting the public. The Equal Pay Act of 1963, for example, prevented wage discrimination on the basis of sex. The Clean Air Act of 1963 provided grants to states to establish and maintain air pollution control agencies. The Civil Rights Act of 1964 eliminated job discrimination on the basis of race, color, religion, sex or national origin. There were more.[49]

Major legislation continued into the 1970s with the Water Quality Improvement Act of 1970 established to enhance the quality and value of the nation's water resources and to establish a national policy for the prevention, control and abatement of water pollution. The Job Safety and Health Act of 1970 established higher standards for safe and healthful working conditions. The Consumer Products Safety Act of 1972 protected consumers against unreasonable risks of injury by evaluating the safety of products.[50]

In 1978 Secretary of Commerce Juanita M. Kreps said that in the last 15 years Congress had enacted more than 150 major pieces of legislation regulating or restricting business activities that affect society. She stressed that "Federal Standards and regulation are an emphatic manifestation of public concern with business social performance."[51]

It was not only the force of law that edged corporations toward a larger consciousness of society and its needs but men in business also began to offer their commentary on business social responsibility. In 1923, John D. Rockefeller, Jr., observed: "In the light of the present, every thoughtful man must concede that the purpose of industry is quite as much the advancement of social well-being as the production of wealth."[52]

In 1933 Elton Mayo argued in his book *The Human Problems of an*

Industrial Civilization that the businessman should not be governed by profits alone but rather should devote some effort toward more responsible and socially acceptable goals. He felt that if this policy was followed, it would promote the welfare of the entire country.[53]

In 1949 *Fortune* magazine declared that the new generation of businessmen were prepared to accept the gospel of service.[54] In the same year, Bernard W. Dempsey, S.J., observed in *Business and Religion* that business had to consider the well-being of the individual as part of the goal of the business process.[55]

In 1953 Howard Bowen's significant book the *Social Responsibilities of the Businessman* was published.[56] This volume had been authorized by the National Council of Churches. While the National Council stressed that the book was not necessarily a statement or a pronouncement of the Council, the volume did express in many ways the concerns of the Protestant churches at the time. Bowen explored the already then much discussed concept of social responsibility as applied to businessmen. He observed that concern about the behavior of large corporations was heightened by the fact that several hundred of the largest business firms were vital centers of power and decision and therefore the "actions of these firms touch the lives of American people at many points."[57]

In 1964 The Conference Board published a report "Company Social Responsibility—Too Much or Not Enough?" and concluded generally that social responsibility was a kind of "good company citizenship."[58]

The 1960s were also witness to some very critical concerns, such as the ecological one, which ultimately were to put pressure on business in the 1970s. *Silent Spring* by Rachel Carson appeared in 1962.[59] While the book dealt primarily with the long-term effects of pesticides which were developed during World War II, it had a definite impact upon society and called attention to increasing air and water pollution. This tended to bring public pressures on business firms who were generating some of the damage to the environment to restrict their polluting activities and to remove industrial wastes that were adding to environmental deterioration.

In the 1960s another dynamic event occurred and that was the 1967 riots. These were ultimately to bring further pressure for a sense of societal responsibility on the part of corporations. Milton Moskowitz, a corporate social responsibility critic, declared that corporate social responsibility was born in the streets of Newark, Los Angeles and Chicago. Phillip T. Drotning, while director of urban affairs for Standard Oil Company (Indiana) in 1974, stated that "the flames of Detroit and Newark and Watts became the hot foot that stimulated increased corporate social concerns."[60]

Jules Cohn in his article "Is Business Meeting the Challenge of Urban Affairs?"[61] and William Kandel in "The Social Conscience in Hard Times"[62] both implicated the 1967 riots as pushing the social responsibility of corporations to the forefront of the public's mind.

By the 1970s responsible committees were being established to look at the entire issue of corporate social responsibility. In 1971 the Committee for Economic Development was assembled. This committee consisted of 200 leading businessmen and educators. As a result of their work, they issued a 66-page statement concerning the social responsibility of business corporations. They observed:

> Today it is clear that the terms of the contract between society and business are, in fact, changing in substantial and important ways. Business is being asked to assume broader responsibilities to society than ever before and to serve a wider range of human values. Business enterprises, in effect, are being asked to contribute more to the quality of American life than just supplying quantities of goods and services. Inasmuch as business exists to serve society, its future will depend on the quality of management's response to the changing expectations of the public.[63]

In 1971 President Nixon convened a White House Conference on "The Industrial World Ahead" which was attended by 1,500 leaders of American business, labor, government and academia. Arjay Miller, Dean of the Graduate School of Business at Stanford University, when at the conference, said:

> The central fact of business today is that we are in a new ball game. We cannot return to the old, familiar ground rules. It is really too bad, in a way, that Adam Smith and Milton Friedman are not right. Life would be so much simpler if our only tasks and our only responsibility was the narrow pursuits of profits. . . . As it happens, however, tremendous new demands are being made on this society and, these in turn are causing tremendous new demands on business.[64]

Another element for pressure on business for assuming more social responsibility was the fact that in the 1970s business suffered a rather severe sag in public opinion. Mayo Thompson, the Federal Trade Commissioner in 1973, displayed a survey that showed that 60 percent of those questioned held a low opinion of the business enterprise. In a comment to a graduating class, he said, "I'm sure I don't have to tell you that business is not well regarded by a majority of Americans in this year of 1973."[65]

According to Cavanagh the reasons for the decline in confidence in the business system was that business was pursuing its own rather narrowly construed ends and that in "pursuing narrowly construed goals, a self-righteousness results in indifference to consequences."[66] He argued that self-centered and success-oriented goals inevitably create conflicts, diseconomies, and injuries to society. One example, he said, is pollution. In some cases business generates the source of damage and then is not willing to pay the full cost for the removal of industrial wastes or other causes of environmental damage. Cavanagh states in dismay: "It is cheaper for the producers of pollution to push that part of the cost off onto someone else."[67] Cavanagh pursues his argument by saying that it is because the American people recognize corporations as wealthy and powerful institutions that they will not permit such powerful forces to follow only their own narrowly construed interests. Therefore a build-up of societal pressures for more corporate social responsibility.

Silk and Vogel in *Ethics & Profits* argued that the polls have left no room for doubt about the decline of the public's confidence in business and quote from a Harris poll that showed in 1966 that 55 percent of the American people had confidence in the heads of large corporations, but by 1973 the percentage had declined to 29 percent, and then in 1974 to 21 percent, and finally to 15 percent in 1975.[68]

This general discontent with business produced a whole host of activists in the 1970s. Probably the best known is Ralph Nader—but he was only one among many. In 1972 the Stanford Research Institute reported that there were sixteen major ecology activist groups, seventeen civil rights organizations, twelve public good or corporate pressure groups, six consumer protection groups, and three militant groups.[69]

In the 1970s one of the major activists seeking more social concern on the part of American corporations were the Protestant churches. The following describes the rationale of the Protestant churches for their involvement with American corporations on the issues of corporate social responsibility.

The Rationale of the Protestant Churches for Involvement with American Corporations on the Issues of Corporate Social Responsibility

More than seventy years ago, on December 4, 1908, "The Social Creed of the Churches" was adopted at the first meeting of the Federal Council of Churches in Philadelphia.[70] The Council at that time consisted of thirty-one Protestant denominations comprising some seventeen million members.[71] The "Creed" was devoted entirely to the field of industrial relations and is quoted in full below:

> The Federal Council of the Churches of Christ in America stands:
> For equal rights and complete justice for all men in all stations of life.
> For the abolition of child labor.
> For such regulation of the conditions of toil for women as shall safeguard the physical and moral health of the community.
> For the suppression of the "Sweating System."
> For the gradual and reasonable reduction of the hours of labor to the lowest practicable

point, and for that degree of leisure for all, which is the condition of the highest human life.

For a release from employment one day in seven.

For the right of all men to the opportunity for self-maintenance, a right ever to be wisely and strongly safeguarded against encroachments of every kind.

For the right of workers to some protection against the hardships often resulting from the swift crises of industrial change.

For a living wage as a minimum in every industry, and for the highest wage that each industry can afford.

For the protection of the worker from dangerous machinery, occupational disease, injuries, and mortality.

For suitable provision for the old age of the workers and for those incapacitated by injury.

For the principle of conciliation and arbitration in industrial dissensions.

For the abatement of poverty.

For the most equitable division of the products of industry that can ultimately be devised.[72]

Should the authors of this creed be alive today, they would indeed be pleased to note the great strides that have taken place in behalf of workers since 1908. It perhaps can also be argued that some of the concepts involving corporate social responsibility being presented by the Protestant churches today may appear to be far off, but given sufficient time and the changing mood of the American people, the "creeds" of the 1970s may evidence the same materialization as the creed of 1908.

Harry F. Ward, then the Associate Secretary of the Federal Council Commission on the Church and Social Service, in 1912, justly announced with pride that the adoption of industrial standards as reflected in the creed of 1908 by the Protestant denominations in the United States constituted a significant fact in the history of religion. He argued presciently that it marked the deliberate and conscious entrance of the church upon the field of social action—especially as it related to the world of business.[72a] Ward recognized at that time (an observation that remains true today) that the churches are "confronted with the task of applying these standards to life," and that the church must do whatever is necessary to bring about the realization of these high goals "by legislation, by State, or voluntary activity."[73]

Thus in 1908 a foundation was laid for the involvement of the Protestant churches with the business world by delineating specific industrial standards. These advocated standards were supported with these arguments:

We recognize the gravity of the social situation and the responsibility of the church collectively, and of its members severally, for bringing about better conditions, through the practical applications of the ethics of the New Testament. We hold it an imperative obligation that the church and all Christians interest themselves in such questions as those of the iniquitous exploitaton of child labor; the carelessness of life and limb too often shown in factory, in mine, and on railroads; the downward pressure sometime brought upon wages by the competitive system, the chronic phase of misunderstanding and industrial warfare between employers and employed; the regrettable breach caused by misconception on both sides of the spirit and purposes of each, which exists between a large number of artisans and the Church of Christ.[74]

The creed of 1908 and concomitant theological arguments were clear annunciations of the Protestant churches' willingness to involve themselves in the industrial situation in the cause of human rights. The gospel was being interpreted in terms of social needs as well as individual needs.[75] It marked "the emancipation of the Protestant denominations from the religious individualism that was the natural accompaniment of the pioneer period into a social consciousness that was required by an industrial society."[76] The emphasis of the churches prior to this time was on evangelism, personal salvation, and individual pietism and because the stress was only upon individual salvation, there could be no community gospel of social concern.

The movement toward more social involvement on the part of the churches became popularly known as the "social gospel." It was vigorously promoted by some of the Protestant denominations and equally opposed by others. Regardless of the opposition to the "social gospel," one positive contribution clearly emerged: it alerted many Protestant denominations to the fact that they had a responsibility to modify and reconstruct society.

Protestant denominations have continued to develop creeds covering many aspects of American society since 1908. These creeds have been adopted primarily in the form of "Social Statements" or "Policy Statements." A policy statement, as described by the National Council of Churches, "is an expression . . . outlining basic policy conviction or position with respect to Christian principles and their general application to today's society and world."[77] Policy statements, generally, are voted upon by the institution's governing body and strive to accomplish three purposes: (1) provide guidance for the program agencies within the denomination; (2) provide stimulating thought and instruction for members of the denomination; and (3) attempt to influence public opinion.

It was the influencing of public opinion that was its weakest link, for up until the 1970s these policy statements had little or no effect upon the business community. Business executives for the most part had never heard of these statements and if they had, paid no attention to them. Policy statements had no economic impact and therefore could be ignored.

There were also problems with "stimulating thought and instruction for members of the denomination" as the trickle down process to the local congregations was not a very secure process. Persons on the local congregational level many times were not aware of some of the social issues with which their own denominations were grappling. In some cases when the members were aware of some of the issues, they did not agree with the positions taken by their leaders.

One of the basic reasons for the differences in opinion between those who put together the social statements and the members of local congregations was the fact that the general membership did not understand some of the basic underlying dislocations of society. Further, the representation of annual conferences of the denominations consisted of at least half clergy persons and the other half of members selected from local churches. The lay persons, however, were highly selective in the sense that they were chosen on the basis that they had the time, money, and desire to make the trip, and probably were already far more knowledgeable with regard to the social issues than other members of local congregations.

The proponents and antagonists of the "social gospel" still wage war today. There are those in Protestantism who see a clear demarcation between that which is "spiritual" and that which could be considered "social awareness." In the minds of some Protestants both cannot be combined. Shoemaker observes that there are many Christians who would think of praying as "spiritual," but picketing in front of the Pentagon for some social cause as "humanistic endeavor."[78] Challenging a congressional committee to appropriate funds for the Food Stamp program is considered secular while singing hymns in church is spiritual."[79]

Protestant churches, such as those included in this study,[80] argue that there can be no splitting up of the Christian experience between "secular" and "spiritual." "One cannot exist without the other; spiritual renewal that is authentically rooted in the Word of God is the source of Christian social awareness."[81] This proposes that the church should not only attempt to shape policy of power structures implicit in government, but should also strive to "affect the decision making process of multinational corporations."[82]

This constitutes the Protestant churches' rationale for involvement with American corporations: corporations are "power structures" and are eminently in position to affect the lives of all people; therefore, the Protestant churches must involve themselves with this power structure in behalf of human rights and needs. Thomas Campbell noted in his article entitled "Capitalism and Christianity" that "religious ethics and religious living cannot be applied at certain times and places, only to be ignored at others."[83] He perceived that if such a religion does exist, it must be empty of content and meaning for it will be observed only when convenient. "A set of principles which are marked 'For Sunday Only' is no religion at all."[84]

Campbell discerns that there has been an effort on the part of businessmen "to divide God from Caesar" and by this argue that the two are irreconcilable. If this kind of argument is considered valid, Campbell contends that "we are driven to the assumption that one is good, and the other bad—that they are irreconcilable because they are out of harmony with each other, and that they are out of harmony because our economic system does not measure up to the standards and demands of our religion."[85] Campbell continues:

> So the argument inevitably runs, and it leads straight to many of the attacks on our enterprise system which businessmen so deplore. Unless they join hands with the theologian and face up to the issues involved, the religiously based criticisms of which they complain—and many of the political criticisms as well—will continue to flourish. In ducking the tough ones, by subscribing to the idea that "business and religion don't mix," by telling the church to "tend to its own affairs," they perpetuate the notion that religion and capitalism are in conflict.[86]

When consideration is made of the fact that the churches have hundreds of millions of dollars invested in American corporations, there is hardly a separation of church and corporation. The churches are concerned that money that is received as contributions, bequests and extraordinary gifts, is not channeled into businesses that are causing harm. The church not only has an obligation as to how it expends its money, but has a most serious obligation and responsibility as to how it generates funds, e.g., through interest, dividends, or capital gains. As one denomination stressed, while "the conventional expectation for church investments has been that they provide a sufficient profit to support programs and commitments designed to help people and witness to the gospel," this is not enough, for

> the church must be concerned to see that it does not by its investments, support uncritically, or without attempting to change them, institutions whose processes and products hurt more people than the church is able to help through programs supported by money earned from those investments.[86a]

This challenge to Christian investors was voiced quite clearly back in 1924 by Johnson and Holt who cautioned that how a Christian invests "bites into the social conscience."[87] The Christian is not to be satisfied with a company in which he owns stock if that company strives only to abide within the narrow limits of the law. The Christian must evaluate the social consequence of decisions made by the company and if he is disturbed about the social implications of any of the decisions made by the company in which he owns stock, he should direct his concern to corporate management. He may do this by addressing a letter to the management, attending an annual meeting, and making a public statement. In addition, he should solicit the help of fellow security holders with relation to the moral issues with which he is concerned.[88] If Christians maintained such concerns the writers ask, "What would happen if the Christian people of America for one week would take seriously their obligation as investors for industrial conditions in establishments which their money maintains? What would happen if they merely insisted on knowing the facts?"[89]

Johnson and Holt argue against the Christian just disposing of his securities.[90] What is the net result of this action, they ask. And they answer: "The securities have passed out of the hands of a conscientious holder into the hands of one less conscientious." What the investor then has done was "simply found an obliging individual who will do his sinning for him."[91]

Sixty-five years later a similar challenge was made to the churches that shareholder responsibilities cannot be neglected. Among those calling for a renewed sense of responsibility in investments was Horace Gale, who asked two rather pointed questions:

> If the church is indifferent to the responsibility of ownership with respect to its own securities, can church members be expected to take seriously their responsibility as stewards of their possessions?[92]
>
> How can the principles the church stands for—reverence for life, improvement of the human condition, etc.—be justified if its portfolio includes the stock of the top defense contractors; of companies which pollute the air and water and those whose products add to the imbalance of our ecology, of those companies which provide token or no opportunity for minority groups—through hiring practices, training programs, and recruitment; of companies which strip undeveloped countries of their resources without adequate payment and/or use the cheap labor for exploitation?[93]

Ten Protestant denominations in particular responded to this challenge[94] and in cooperation with the National Council of Churches and its affiliate, the Interfaith Center on Corporate Responsibility, developed programs relative to responsibility through investments. The United Presbyterian Church in the U.S.A., for example, took the following steps.[95] In 1971, the 183rd General Assembly of the United Presbyterian Church adopted a comprehensive policy on corporate responsibility describing how church members, presbyteries, synods, boards, agencies and other church-related institutions could use their investments to further the mission of the church. Called "Investment Policy Guidelines," it specifically directed boards, agencies, and church-related institutions under the authority of the General Assembly . . . to acquire and analyze information on both the economic and human aspects of investment . . . to exercise diligently the rights of the investor, including options such as inquiry, correspondence, visitation, participation in meetings, buying or selling, and when appropriate, litigation . . . to create an appropriate structure to deal with questions of social responsibility in investment . . . (and) to seek imaginative and innovative ways to make investments that promise high returns in terms of benefit to human need.[96]

Six themes were identified to help the church determine its course in corporate responsibility. These were: the pursuit of peace, racial justice, economic and social justice, environmental responsibility, women's concerns, and human rights.

In order to see that the directives of the General Assembly were put into effect, a committee was established for this purpose. It was known as the Committee on Social Responsibility in Investment. In 1973 it became a subcommittee of the General Assembly Mission Council with its primary objective to carry out the General Assembly policies that bear upon the behavior of corporations in which the church holds stock. Once particular positions are taken relative to specific social issues, the committee then analyzes the church's stock holdings in order to find out which corporations relate to pertinent issues. The committee then attempts where possible to discuss the social issues with the corporations involved and in this way tries to help corporate management become aware of its social responsibilities. When no apparent change is being effected, the church may resort to the use of shareholder resolutions, either to obtain needed information or to effect some change in corporate policy.

The foregoing was one denomination's response to the challenge for mission responsibility in investments. Other denominations underwent a similar process—each according to the customs of their own denominations. The theme, however, was recurrent. The American Baptist Churches: "Decisions corporations make effect the well-being of persons around the world and the kind of world in which we live."[97] The United Methodist Church: "If the Church is to play a redemptive role in modern society, then its people must become increasingly sensitive to what happens in the everyday business of the marketplace."[98] The United Church of Christ: "The church must enter into real dialogue with all elements of the culture: politics, religions, philosophies, arts, sciences, and technologies."[99] The Church of the Brethren: The church should "seek continuously to understand the church's goals and its relationship to other institutions in our present society in a fuller fashion: it is right to expect the General Board to know the heritage of faith and the nature of life sufficiently to apply Christian ethics to its participation in the economic life of today's world."[100] The Christian Church: "Whether through corporate entities or through individual reflection and action, the Church is called to make manifest the essential character of Christian witness in our contemporary world."[101] The Lutheran Church in America: "Integrity in the faith demands that Christians be in the forefront of the struggle to end exploitation of the poor and powerless, for such exploitation makes a mockery of the message of love and reconciliation in Christ."[102] The National Council of Churches of Christ: "The institutional church, recognizing its own imperfections and limitations has both the right and the obligation to challenge the policies and actions of other social institutions which in any way limit human freedom or cause social, political or economic injustice."[103]

Each of the Protestant denominations covered in this book developed guidelines for socially responsible investing. Generally the guidelines included actions which could be taken by the churches in order effectively to bring social issues to the attention of corporations. These could include (a) the writing of letters to the Chief Executive Officer of a corporation making query as to a particular social policy, (b) avoiding the purchase of stock in a corporation not acting in a socially responsible manner, (c) or just the opposite—disposing of the stock of an irresponsible corporation, (d) seeking out "socially responsible" firms and investing in these, (e) using the Proxy Option. In this connection, Frank White presciently said: "While more study and legal interpretations seems inevitable, the proxy option is today a viable strategy for use by church institutions that wish to act independently or in concert with other groups to make their views known and to influence corporate decisions,"[104] (f) filing stockholder class action suits: the stockholder sues the corporation for some violation of the law.[105]

Some of these options were exercised by the Protestant churches in the 1970s. These are described in the following chapters.

Methodology

Research Question 1

> What were the specific social issues that prompted the filing of shareholder resolutions, the initiating of boycotts, and other direct contacts with American corporations by the Protestant churches during the ten-year period of 1970 to 1979?[106]

With relation to those social issues that prompted the filing of shareholder resolutions, the following data were required:

a. A copy of every shareholder resolution that was filed between 1970 and 1979 by a Protestant denomination which showed the social issues involved, the corporation targeted, and the Protestant group filing the resolution.

b. Supplemental data, in addition to the shareholder resolution, which amplified the reasons for the Protestants' concern over the social issues precipitating the resolutions.

The sources of the data were:

a. The official records maintained by the Securities and Exchange Commission (SEC). The SEC maintains complete records of all corporate proxy statements of corporations listed in major stock exchanges.

b. The informal log maintained by the American Society of Corporate Secretaries, Inc., New York City, which contained a record of some of the shareholder resolutions that were prompted by social issues.

c. Particular reports published by the Investor Responsibility Research Center (IRRC) of Washington, D.C., which focused on shareholder resolutions prompted by social issues.

d. Special reports issued by the Interfaith Center on Corporate Responsibility which centered on shareholder resolutions initiated by religious organizations.

e. Newsletters issued by the Council on Economic Priorities which from time to time summarized certain shareholder resolutions initiated in behalf of social causes.

f. Annual reports, committee minutes, policy statements, newsletters, special-interest publications, of the ten Protestant denominations under study, as well as the National Council of Churches and the Interfaith Center on Corporate Responsibility which referred specifically to shareholder action taken by Protestant and other religious groups.

The data are presented as follows:

a. A comprehensive list has been made of all the social concerns that precipitated shareholder resolutions during the ten-year period of 1970 to 1979.

b. From the comprehensive list, a categorization was prepared breaking these data into concerns that are similar in nature, e.g., having to do with apartheid in South Africa, with labor relations, with community reinvestment and redlining, etc.

c. The social issues which have been listed were amplified to underscore the reasons which prompted the Protestant churches to get involved with American corporations on a direct basis.

d. Tables were prepared covering the social issues, the Protestant denominations involved, and the American corporations targeted (on a year-to-year basis and in a ten-year summary) to illustrate what social issues dominated in any one year, and in the ten-year period, as well as what Protestant denominations were most active and what corporations were primary targets.

With relation to the social issues that were the cause of boycotts and which precipitated other direct contacts, the following data were required:

a. A description of the boycotts in which Protestant churches participated during the period of 1970 to 1979.

b. Examples of "direct contacts" which could be located in public documents.[107]

The sources of the data were:

a. Annual reports, committee minutes, policy statements, newsletters, special interest publications, official statements and other data issued by the ten Protestant denominations under study, the National Council of Churches, and the Interfaith Center on Corporate Responsibility. These documents were published by the various Protestant church groups and contained references to boycott actions and provided write-ups of specific "direct contacts" with American corporate managements.

b. Business publications, such as the *Wall Street Journal, Forbes, Dun's Review, Fortune,* and *Business Week,* as well as other periodicals indexed in the *Business Periodicals Index.* These publications contained articles concerning church boycotts of business firms and reported other direct contacts with business on the part of the churches.

c. Visits to some headquarters of Protestant denominations under study, as well as the National Council of Churches and the Interfaith Center on Corporate Responsibility and engaging in informal conversations with Protestant church leaders who were able to provide some insight as to boycott actions and direct contacts with corporations by the Protestant churches. In several cases where the denomination headquarters were located some distance from New York City, contact was made by telephone and correspondence.

The data are presented as follows:

a. The several boycotts engaged in by Protestant churches during the 1970s were described delineating the social issues precipitating the boycotts, naming the corporations involved, and listing the Protestant denominations participating in the boycotts.

b. Examples of other direct contacts by Protestant churches with American corporations during the 1970s were also described, again delineating the social issues involved, naming the corporations contacted, and listing the Protestant denominations making the contacts.

Research Question 2

What were the arguments presented by the targeted corporations in answer to the challenges of the Protestant churches relative to social issues that were presented by means of shareholder resolutions, boycotts, and other direct contacts in the ten-year period of 1970 to 1979?

The following data were required:
The position of corporate management of the targeted corporations on each of the social issues that were presented by Protestant churches during the period of 1970 to 1979.

The sources of the data were:
a. The targeted corporations themselves: the position of corporate management was outlined in the proxy statement (in brief form). Management either recommended approval or disapproval of the resolution and presented their arguments for the position taken. It was rather rare that corporate management endorsed the shareholder resolutions when presented by dissatisfied shareholders. In some instances additional data was provided by the corporations in their annual reports or in other printed media amplifying their reasons for their recommendations to shareholders to vote "no" on the proposals being submitted by shareholders who disagreed with certain corporate policies.

b. *The Wall Street Journal, Forbes, Dun's Review, Fortune,* and *Business Week,* as well as the daily newspaper *The New York Times* (and other periodicals which are indexed in the *Business Periodical Index*). These carried stories from time to time relative to business reactions to activist shareholder resolutions, boycotts, and other direct contacts with corporations by activists.

c. Visits, telephone calls, or correspondence with the Chief Executive Officer or Corporate Social Responsibility Officer of the targeted corporations elicited some additional comments as to the corporations' stance on social issues presented by Protestant churches. Comments offered were pretty much in line with what had already been printed in the proxy statements. These contacts were made on an informal basis.

The data are presented as follows:
The material is presented in several segments.

a. The first segment provides an overview of business reaction to shareholder activism in general during the 1970s.

b. The second segment focuses on the specific responses, or arguments, which targeted corporations offered in response to the specific shareholder resolutions, boycotts, and other direct contacts initiated by Protestant churches during the 1970s. The summarization provides corporate responses to each of the specific social issues presented by the Protestant churches over the ten-year period of 1970 to 1979 delineating the positions of the targeted corporations and outlining their arguments for corporate recommendations to shareholders that they reject the proposals presented.

Research Question 3

> What business practices were changed or modified during the 1970s relative to those social issues which Protestant churches brought to the attention of corporate management during the period of 1970 to 1979?

The data required were:
Facts that substantiated some change in business practices relative to the social issues that were presented by Protestant churches to corporations during the period of 1970 to 1979.
The sources of these data were:
   a. The targeted corporations themselves. In some cases, corporations furnished some information as to some change in their practices in response to Protestant pressures.
   b. The *Wall Street Journal, Forbes, Dun's Review, Fortune,* and *Business Week,* as well as the daily newspaper, *The New York Times,* and other periodicals which are indexed in the *Business Periodicals Index.* These publications carried stories from time to time relative to changes in business practices related to social issues that were of concern to Protestant churches.
   c. Doctoral dissertations written during the 1970s on the subject of corporate social responsibility which contained some references to changes in business practices with relation to social issues.
   d. Reports, speeches, and publications of business associations, such as the U.S. Chamber of Commerce, National Association of Manufacturers, Machinery and Allied Products Institute, National Public Affairs Association, American Management Association, and The Conference Board, which provided some data relative to certain business modifications on social issues.
   e. Informal conversations with executives in corporations covered in this study and persons connected with the religious community provided some information as to changes in business practices involving social issues.
   f. Annual reports and other publications of targeted corporations provided additional insights as to business changes relative to social issues.
   The data are presented as follows:
The final segment of chapter 3 provides examples of some modifications in business practices in connection with social issues that were of concern to Protestant churches in the 1970s. The examples that are pro-

vided are illustrative of the types of modifications that were being made and are not intended to be comprehensive. It is recognized that in presenting certain business modifications that were made during the 1970s in behalf of social issues, such changes were effected not only by the efforts of the Protestant churches, but by other groups and organizations who, in many instances, also shared in the same thrust for changes. Further, it was discovered that corporations are reluctant to acknowledge that any change in business policies was in response to church pressures.

Organization of the Study

Chapter 1—Introduction. This chapter has presented the problem and the research questions. Definitions have been furnished as well as the delimitations of the study. Implications of the Problem have been outlined and the Methodology described. Relevant literature was reviewed as to the emergence of the concept of corporate social responsibility as well as the rationale for the Protestant churches involvement with American corporations on the issue of corporate social responsibility.

Chapter 2—Protestant Activism in the 1970s: Shareholder Resolutions, Boycotts, and Other Direct Contacts—The Social Issues Involved. This chapter deals with the direct involvements of Protestant churches with American corporations during the 1970s and covers the social issues that were the precipitating causes for the direct actions. The direct actions took the form of filing shareholder resolutions, the engagement in boycotts, and other direct contacts. The first section of the chapter provides basic background concerning the social issues involved so that the reasons for the initiation of these actions can be clearly understood. The second section details the actual shareholder resolutions and provides a series of tables that categorize the social issues and outline the frequency of their occurrences, both on a yearly basis and for the ten-year span of 1970 to 1979. These tables illustrate what social concerns dominated the thinking of the Protestant churches during the decade of the 1970s. They also enumerate the American corporations that were caught up in these challenges. The third segment of this chapter deals with boycotts and other direct contacts.

Chapter 3—Business Response to Protestant Activism in the 1970s. The response of business in this chapter is viewed in three perspectives. The first part of the chapter presents a general overview of the reactions of business to shareholder activism during the 1970s. The second section takes a more focused look at the specific responses, or arguments, which corporations offered in response to specific shareholder resolutions, boycotts, and other direct contacts initiated by the Protestant churches. The third section provides examples of some modifications in business practices in connection with social issues that were of concern to Protestant churches in the 1970s.

Chapter 4—Summary and Conclusions. This chapter summarizes the challenges to American corporations by Protestant churches on the issues of corporate social responsibility during the 1970s. A review is provided of the social issues presented by Protestant churches to American corporations during the 1970s together with the churches' arguments in behalf of these issues. A review is also provided of corporate responses to Protestant activism. Modifications of business practices in response to Protestant pressures during the 1970s are summarized. Conclusions and suggestions for further study are included in this chapter.

Chapter 5—Observations: The Transnational Corporations. This chapter discusses the transnational corporations and their potential benefit to mankind and suggests a concern that churches do not unwittingly discourage business from entering parts of the world where they may be most needed.

2

Protestant Activism in the 1970s: Shareholder Resolutions, Boycotts and Other Contacts—The Social Issues Involved

Introduction

During the ten-year period of 1970 to 1979, Protestant churches,[1] with the support of the National Council of Churches of Christ in the U.S.A. and coordinated with the help of the Interfaith Center on Corporate Responsibility, directly challenged corporations on the issues of corporate social responsibility.

This chapter describes the specific issues presented as social concerns to corporations during 1970 to 1979 by Protestant churches. These concerns were brought to the attention of management primarily through the use of shareholder resolutions. These were filed after face-to-face dialogues or written communications with the corporations involved failed to bring a satisfactory response to the churches' expressions of concern. Boycott action was also utilized. The Protestant churches also made other contacts with corporate management by appearing at shareholder meetings, arranging for conferences between business and church executives in symposiums, writing open letters, divesting stock, or as last resort, appealing to the Courts.

The first part of this chapter provides basic background concerning the specific social issues involved so that the rationale for the Protestant churches' involvement in these issues can be more clearly understood. These descriptions are presented on an issue-by-issue basis. Immediately following these descriptions are tables which provide statistics on the social issues. The last part of the chapter discusses the three boycotts in which certain Protestant denominations were involved, as well as providing examples of other contacts made by the churches in behalf of social concerns.

It is not surprising that it was 1970 before Protestant churches engaged in stockholder action, for, up to and including 1970 very few shareholders had exercised the option of filing shareholder resolutions. In 1970, for example, only 25 shareholders submitted 241 proposals to the Securities and Exchange Commission.[2] In view of the fact that there were over 25 million shareholders at the time, it is obvious that only a very small minority were interested in the process of utilizing shareholder resolutions to pressure corporations to change their policies. Of the 241 proposals submitted in 1970, more than half were initiated by the Gilbert brothers, and these concerned financial and economic matters, such as employee stock option plans, the amounts of directors' pensions, cumulative voting, and executive compensation.

However, immediately following the year of 1970 the number of shareholder resolutions filed with American corporations rapidly increased and the Protestant churches, as a group, became significant users of the shareholder resolution process during the 1970s.

The swing toward the use of shareholder resolutions was presciently noted in 1970 in a *Finance Magazine* article entitled "The Shareholder Comes to Life." Observation was made that "Shareholders clearly are not yet getting involved en masse . . . but change is evident. And out of this should come a healthy reassessment of the shareholder's role."[3]

The Protestant churches became involved with shareholder resolutions as a result of painful soul searching. The searching engendered increasing discomfort as they realized that some corporations in which they held stock were engaging in practices which the churches considered socially irresponsible. As part owners of these corporations, they were obligated to consider whether they were culpable for the acts of these corporations—and, if culpable, were they capable of effecting any changes in corporate policies. Bowman found no difficulty in answering the question of culpability and capability:

> Each stockholder is an owner of the corporation, benefits from the corporation's activities, and has invested in the corporation for those benefits; and many stockholders feel, at least in part, responsible for those activities.[4]

The authors of *The Ethical Investor* further supported and amplified this position. They were "convinced that owning shares in a corporation does thrust upon the owner a responsibility for the social effects of corporate policy that he would not otherwise have."[5] Once the shareholder is aware of a particular social injury, he has, in essence, received notice concerning the social injury and, therefore, has an obligation to do something about correcting the potential social harm. The obligation is implicit and cannot be ignored as the law defines the shareholder as an owner. The shareholder has the power to act and this squarely places the responsibility upon the shareholder to do something about the policies of the corporation he owns in part. The shareholder has a special responsibility, for example, which the noteholder does not. The shareholder has the power to intervene. Therefore, it makes "no difference that the power was received casually, that it was not the reason for purchasing the security, and that it was a by-product."[6]

The Protestant churches, influenced by this argument, agreed that as shareholders they were culpable and further, if culpable, they had an obligation to exercise what capabilities they had in their power as shareholders to effect changes in the policies of the corporations in which they were part owners. Therefore, commencing in 1971 they intensified their prerogatives as shareholders and began to vote stock, propose resolutions, and make their arguments known at corporate annual meetings. Throughout the decade of the 1970s they continued to prod for corporate change and to urge the companies to disclose information concerning their operations where human rights concerns were involved. The churches fully recognized that while their ownership of stock in any one corporation was miniscule when compared to the total number of outstanding shares, this was not a valid excuse for lack of action, for

> to argue that fractional power should not be exercised would radically undermine the principle of democratic voting, wherein the majority has power because of the simultaneous exercise of fractional power by many individuals, and the minority voice is understood to be significant simply because it has been heard.[7]

The minority voice of the Protestant churches was heard during the 1970s and the issues voiced are described in the following pages.

As can be seen in table 25, Protestant churches placed the heaviest emphasis on the apartheid issue in Southern Africa. More than half of the shareholder resolutions were filed in connection with this particular issue.

Other issues that captured the attention of the Protestant churches during the decade of the 1970s were: colonialism in Angola, Guinea-Bissau and Mozambique; human rights concerns in Chile, the Dominican Republic, Guatemala, Korea and Philippines.

Particular social concerns in developing countries gripped the Protestant churches and these focused on employment practices, foreign military sales, the distribution of infant formula, questionable corporate payments overseas, and the development of appropriate farm technology for small farms.

The social concerns involving issues within the United States included the energy crisis, equal employment opportunities for women and minorities, political contributions, redlining and reinvestment by banks, strip mining, the nomination of women to boards of directors, stereotypical images of women in advertising, impact of television advertising on children's nutrition, and nuclear weapons production.

The following pages describe these issues from the viewpoint of the Protestant churches. The responses of the corporations to these same issues are provided in chapter 3. With the exception of only a few cases, corporate management did not agree with the positions taken by the churches on these issues and stockholders were advised by business management to reject the proposals. The stockholders accepted managements' recommendations and overwhelmingly defeated the proposals in every instance. The churches were not dismayed at the statistical defeats for in the long term they felt their purposes had been served. They had brought the particular social concern to the attention of corporate management and had at the same time alerted the stockholders and the public, as well, concerning these matters. The churches felt that positive gains were realized even though the proposals received only a small percentage of the votes.

The Social Concerns

Apartheid in The Republic of South Africa

The Protestant churches, as well as other peoples and governments, protested the apartheid system in South Africa declaring that it was a gross violation of human rights. Some reasons for the churches' objections were:

>—apartheid deprives the black majority of the most basic of human rights. The African cannot vote, cannot collectively bargain, must live in racially segregated areas, cannot supervise white workers, and are paid grossly discriminatory wages.[8]
>
>—apartheid is maintained by a totalitarian force, reminiscent of Nazi Germany and is described by the International Commission of Jurists as "copying the worst features of Stalinism."[9]
>
>—apartheid perpetuates and deepens racial divisions in the body of Christ, thus violating the unity of the church.[10]
>
>—apartheid is gravely inimical to the present and future life, work and witness of the Christian church because its ruthless deeds are blasphemously perpetuated in the name of Christ.[11]

As early as 1960 the Presbyterian Church in the United States, for example, decried apartheid as sinful and expressed horror at the dangerous conditions in the Republic of South Africa and the inconsistencies and moral absurdities apartheid laws have brought. In 1965, the same denomination called the apartheid system one which dehumanized white and black South Africans, violated Biblical religion, and repudiated Christian ethics.

The domination of whites in South Africa can be traced back to 1652 when the Dutch left Europe in small groups to settle in South Africa in support of business activities of the Dutch East India Company. The Dutch Boers clustered in a location that is known today as Cape Town. These early settlers were soon followed by Germans and French. This grouping of Europeans eventually became known as the "Afrikaaners."

The early 1800s witnessed Europeans fighting among themselves. Eventually the Boers, resentful of British control of the Cape Colony, moved inland and established the Orange Free State and the Transvaal. In subsequent wars, the British prevailed and controlled most of the territory surrounding the Cape area. In 1910 the area surrounding the Cape became known as the Union of South Africa. By 1934 the Union had become an independent member of the British Commonwealth.

The strong South African economy, girded with economic strength from gold, diamonds, and supplies of platinum and maganese, unfortunately harbored an undisguised racist system which relegated the benefits of these natural resources into the hands of the whites only. The white population of the Republic of South Africa during the 1970s was about 4.5 million out of a total population of about 24 million. With complete political control in the hands of the whites, the bulk of the land remained under the iron hand of the whites with wide discrepancies in the standards of living between whites and blacks. The system of apartheid in the Republic of South Africa placed travel restrictions on the black population, deprived them of land ownership, limited labor organizing rights, provided deficient education, and in many other ways violated the human rights of the blacks. Further, harsh rules were enforced with a network of repressive laws and police power.

The Protestant churches, in sympathy with the blacks in South Africa, approached American corporations who were doing business in that part of Africa and contended that those corporations who were doing business in South Africa were in actuality buttressing a racist regime.

U.S. corporations have invested billions in the economy of South Africa and are in fact, the largest foreign investor in that country after Britain. Further, U.S. banks have bolstered the economy with billions of dollars in loans. The Protestant churches argue that it is these kinds of investments that have reinforced the grip of the government of the Republic of South Africa over its populace. In order to break the hold of the South African government over the blacks, the Protestant churches proposed numerous shareholder resolutions. In summary, these resolutions proposed that American corporations: close down their operations in South Africa or at least not expand their operations; put a stop to all direct or indirect sales that could possibly strengthen the military and police powers of that government; cut back on the flow of oil to South Africa which in turn was being funneled into Rhodesia in violation of economic sanctions imposed by the United Nations against Rhodesia; continue a policy of disclosure regarding employment policies covering black employees in American plants which would bring to the public's attention the conditions that exist in South Africa; move unilaterally to recognize black unions as collective bargaining representatives, even though this was not encouraged by the South African government; ban the importation of coal from South Africa, which supplied U.S. monies to the South African government; and halt all bank loans from U.S. banks that strengthen the apartheid regime.

The issue of apartheid in the Republic of South Africa has been debated in the United Nations for more than 25 years and continues to be emotional. Some of the events that deserve highlighting are:

> 1960: Following the "Sharpeville Massacre" in which 69 blacks were killed during a demonstration, the Security Council called on South Africa to bring about "racial harmony" and to "abandon its policies of apartheid."
>
> 1963: The Security Council recommended a voluntary embargo on shipments of arms and military vehicles to South Africa.
>
> 1970: The arms embargo was expanded to include spare parts, military licenses, patents, training, and technical assistance.
>
> 1974: Supported by a controversial procedural ruling by its President Abdelaziz Bouteflika of Algeria, the 29th General Assembly suspended South Africa from participation in the Assembly. South Africa has not returned since then but has participated in Security Council debates.
>
> 1976: Rioting over the use of the Afrikaans language in Bantu schools erupted in the Black township of Soweto outside Johannesburg. At least 176 people were killed. The Security Council unanimously condemned South Africa for its resort to deadly force and declared apartheid the real cause of the trouble.[12]

In filing the series of shareholder proposals with American corporations over the issue of apartheid in South Africa, the Protestant churches in effect supported the efforts of the United Nations as well as other groups in an attempt to ameliorate the apartheid grip in South Africa.

Table 1. Protestant Sponsored or Cosponsored Shareholder Resolutions 1970 to 1979 Over the Issue of Apartheid in the Republic of South Africa

Year	Corporation	Subject: South Africa	Denomination	% Vote
1971	GM	Cease activities	Episcopal	2.56%
1972	GM	Report: operations	Episcopal	2.34%
1972	Goodyear	Report: operations	Amer. Baptist	1.38%
1973	Caterpillar	Report: operations	United Methodist	8.6%
1973	Citicorp	Report: operations	Amer. Baptist	1.03%
1973	GE	Report: operations	Episcopal	2.3%
1973	IBM	Report: operations	Episcopal	2.6%
1973	Mobil	Equal employment	United Ch. Christ	1.8%
1973	Newmont	Equal employment	United Ch. Christ	0.3%
1974	Engelhard	Report: operations	Reformed Church	0.92%
1974	Foote Minerals	No add'l investments	United Ch. Christ	2.5%
1974	GE	Est. review committee	United Presby.	2.4%
1974	IBM	Report: operations	United Presby.	2.31%
1974	Newmont	Employment policies	United Ch. Christ	3.56%
1974	Union Carbide	Report: operations	United Presby.	2.78%
1975	IBM	No computer sales	Amer. Baptist, Christian Church, Episcopal, National Council, Reformed Church, United Ch. Christ, United Methodist*	1.64%
1975	Southern Co.	No importation of coal	United Ch. Christ	3.28%
1975	Union Carbide	Est. review committee	Christian Church*	2.67%
1976	Goodyear	Report: work'g conditions	United Methodist*	2.36%
1976	IBM	Report: computer sales	Christian Church, Episcopal, National Council, Reformed Church, United Methodist*	2.21%

Table 1 (continued)

Year	Corporation	Subject: South Africa	Denomination	% Vote
1976	Kennecott	No add'l investments	Christian Church, Episcopal*	3.62%
1976	Southern Co.	No importation of coal	United Ch. Christ	4.19%
1976	Standard Oil CA	No add'l investments	United Methodist	2.11%
1976	Texaco	No add'l investments	United Ch. Christ*	1.99%
1977	Citicorp	No further loans	Luth. Ch. Amer., Presbyterian U.S., United Methodist, United Presby.*	2.2%
1977	Ford	Withdraw operations	Amer. Baptist, Christian Church, United Presby.	1.81%
1977	GE	Withdraw operations	Reformed Church, United Methodist	1.8%
1977	Goodyear	Withdraw operations	United Methodist	1.95%
1977	Kennecott	No add'l investments	Episcopal*	4.83%
1977	Mfrs. Hanover	No further loans	Episcopal, United Ch. Christ*	3.3%
1977	J. P. Morgan	No further loans	Episcopal	2.81%
1977	Phelps Dodge	No add'l investments	Reformed Church*	2.6%
1977	Southern Co.	Report: import of coal	United Ch. Christ	5.9%
1977	Standard Oil CA	Withdraw operations	Christian Church, United Methodist	2.97%
1977	Texaco	Withdraw operations	Christian Church, Reformed Church, United Methodist*	3.67%
1977	Union Carbide	No add'l investments	Amer. Baptist*	3.35%
1978	Citicorp	Report: loans made	Luth. Ch. Amer., Presby. U.S., United Ch. Christ, United Methodist*	4.58%
1978	Continental Bank	Report: loans made	United Ch. Christ	8.2%
1978	Control Data	No sale of computers	United Presby.	4.58%

Table 1 (continued)

Year	Corporation	Subject: South Africa	Denomination	% Vote
1978	Kodak	No sales photo items	Amer. Baptist, Episcopal, United Methodist, United Presby.*	4.75%
1978	First Boston	No further loans	Luth. Ch. Amer. United Ch. Christ, United Methodist	8.17%
1978	IBM	No sale of computers	Christian Church, National Council, United Ch. Christ*	2.12%
1978	Mfrs. Hanover	No further loans	Episcopal, Reformed Church, United Ch. Christ*	5.51%
1978	3M	Withdraw operations	National Council*	1.9%
1978	Morgan	Report on loans	Episcopal*	4.38%
1978	Southern Co.	Report: coal import	Christian Church*	5.4%
1978	Texaco	Withdraw operations	Christian Church, United Methodist, United Presby.*	2.19%
1978	Union Carbide	No add'l investments	United Ch. Christ*	5.08%
1978	U.S. Steel	No add'l investments	Episcopal	5.69%
1979	Bank America	No add'l loans	United Ch. Christ*	8.4%
1979	Caterpillar	Est. review committee	Amer. Baptist, Christian Church, Episcopal*	3.5%
1979	Citicorp	Report on loans	Presby. U.S., United Ch. Christ*	4.4%
1979	Continental Bank	Report on loans	United Ch. Christ*	4.2%
1979	Control Data	No sales of computers	United Presby.	3.3%
1979	Kodak	No sales photo items	Amer. Baptist, Episcopal, United Ch. Christ*	3.1%
1979	Exxon	No further expansion	Christian Church, Episcopal*	4.9%
1979	First Chicago	Report on loans	Luth. Ch. Amer.*	2.2%

Table 1 (continued)

Year	Corporation	Subject: South Africa	Denomination	% Vote
1979	Ford	No sales of products	United Ch. Christ, United Presby.*	2.1%
1979	GM	No sales of products	Christian Church, United Ch. Christ, United Methodist, United Presby.*	2.98%
1979	Mfrs. Hanover	Report on loans	Episcopal, Reformed Church, United Ch. Christ	3.7%
1979	Morgan	Report on loans	Episcopal*	2.8%
1979	Phillips	Withdraw operations	Amer. Baptist, Episcopal, Reformed Church	5.6%
1979	Sperry Rand	No sales of computers	United Methodist*	3.3%
1979	Union Carbide	Withdraw operations	Church Brethren*	3.8%
1979	U.S. Steel	No further expansion	Episcopal	5.7%
1979	Wells Fargo	No new loans	United Methodist	7.3%
1972	IBM	Report on operations	Episcopal	Withdrawn
1972	Mobil	Report on operations	United Ch. Christ	Withdrawn
1973	Burroughs	Report on operations	United Presby.	Withdrawn
1973	Kodak	Report on operations	United Methodist	Withdrawn
1973	ITT	Report on operations	United Presby.	Withdrawn
1973	3M	Report on operations	National Council	Withdrawn
1973	Texaco	Report on operations	United Methodist	Withdrawn
1973	Xerox	Report on operations	Amer. Baptist	Withdrawn
1974	Burroughs	Report on operations	United Presby.	Withdrawn
1974	Chrysler	Report on operations	United Presby.	Withdrawn
1974	Colgate-Palm.	Report on operations	Reformed Church	Withdrawn
1974	Deere	Report on operations	United Methodist	Withdrawn
1974	Gillette	Report on operations	Episcopal	Withdrawn
1974	Int'l Harvester	Report on operations	National Council	Withdrawn
1974	Pfizer	Report on operations	Christian Church	Withdrawn

Table 1 (continued)

Year	Corporation	Subject: South Africa	Denomination	% Vote
1974	Weyerhaeuser	Report on operations	Amer. Baptist	Withdrawn
1975	ITT	Rev. of operations	United Presby.	Withdrawn
1976	ITT	Report on operations	Christian Church United Presby.*	Withdrawn
1977	G&W	Report on mining proj.	National Council	Withdrawn
1977	GM	Withdraw operations	Amer. Baptist, Christian Church, Reformed Church*	Withdrawn
1978	Crocker Bank	No further loans	Christian Church	Withdrawn
1978	Kennecott	Report on operations	Episcopal*	Withdrawn
1979	Borg-Warner	No further expansion	United Ch. Christ*	Withdrawn
1979	Burroughs	No sales of products	National Council*	Withdrawn
1979	First Boston	No further loans	Luth. Ch. Amer. United Ch. Christ, United Methodist*	Withdrawn
1979	3M	Report on operations	Amer. Baptist, National Council*	Withdrawn

Total Shareholder Resolutions: 92

As % of Total Shareholder Resolutions Filed 1970 to 1979: 41.6%

* and other religious groups

Apartheid in Namibia

Namibia, also known as South West Africa, has been a de facto province of the Republic of South Africa since 1920. In the year of 1920 it was given the status as a protectorate of South Africa, but in 1946 when the United Nations was established, the government of South Africa rejected the United Nations' effort to have it relinquish control, and to withdraw the protectorate status.

The Germans were the original settlers in Namibia and in the seventies about one third of the white population of that territory was German and the balance of 750,000 were black.

As was the case of the Republic of South Africa, executive power in Namibia remained in the hands of the white populace. The legislative power was in the hands of the whites, and the same restrictive policies that existed in South Africa in the seventies were replicated in Namibia.

The United Nations has struggled over the years with the restrictive conditions for blacks in Namibia and the highlights of United Nations' actions can be described as follows:

> 1946: The General Assembly refused a South African request to annex the territory and recommended that it be made a U.N. Trusteeship. South Africa did not press the issue and announced it would continue to abide by the "spirit of the mandate."
>
> 1950: In the advisory opinion requested by the Assembly, the International Court of Justice held that there was no legal obligation to bring South West Africa into the U.N. trusteeship's system.
>
> 1967: A special session of the General Assembly established The Council for South West Africa to establish U.N. authority there. (Its name was soon changed to The Council for Namibia.) South Africa has never permitted the Council to enter the territory.
>
> 1969: The Security Council endorsed the Assembly's termination of the mandate and called for South Africa's withdrawal.
>
> 1970: The Security Council asked all governments to cease all commercial, financial and political actions, which might imply recognition of South African authority over the territory.
>
> 1971: The International Court of Justice upheld all U.N. actions and recommendations.[13]

In 1973 the Protestant churches supported actions of the United Nations by requesting via shareholder resolutions that Phillips Petroleum, Continental Oil, Newmont Mining, and American Metal Climax withdraw from Namibia. The Protestant churches argued that if these corporations continued to remain in Namibia they would be acting counter to the judgments of the International Court of Justice, the United Nations Security Council resolutions, and stated U.S. foreign policy. By requesting that American corporations withdraw their presence in Namibia, they argued that this would avoid extracting scarce resources from Namibia at a time when the majority of the populace was not receiving an equitable return from those resources. Further, by U.S. corporations remaining in Namibia, they encouraged the current Namibian government by providing economic incentives and, in fact, implied that those corporations endorsed the employment practices and policies of that country.

Apartheid in Rhodesia

In the 1890s gold-seeking Europeans moved into Rhodesia and seized large expanses of territory from the indigenous tribes in Southern Africa.

Table 2. Protestant Sponsored or Cosponsored Shareholder Resolutions 1970 to 1979 Over the Issue of Apartheid in Namibia

Year	Corporation	Subject: Namibia	Denomination	% Vote
1972	Amer. Metal	Cease operations	Episcopal ECSA[§]	2.93%
1972	Newmont	Cease operations	Episcopal ECSA[§]	2.68%
1973	Amer. Metal	Cease operations	Episcopal ECSA[§]	2.1%
1973	Conoco	Cease operations	United Ch. Christ	5.4%
1973	Newmont	Cease operations	Episcopal ECSA[§]	1.4%
1973	Phillips	Cease operations	Episcopal	4.4%
1974	Conoco	Cease operations	United Ch. Christ	7.26%
1974	Getty	Cease operations	Amer. Baptist	1.36%
1974	Phillips	Cease operations	Episcopal	4.9%
1974	Standard Oil CA	Cease operations	United Methodist	4.3%
1975	Newmont	Equal employment	United Ch. Christ	3.11%
1977	Newmont	Report: Labor practices	United Ch. Christ	3.36%
1978	Newmont	Report: Labor practices	United Ch. Christ*	3.15%
1975	Getty	Cease operations	Amer. Baptist	Withdrawn
1975	Standard Oil CA	Cease operations	United Methodist	Withdrawn
1975	Newmont	Report: mine operations	United Ch. Christ	Withdrawn
1975	Phillips	Cease operations	Amer. Baptist, Episcopal, National Council, Reformed Church	Withdrawn
1977	Amer. Metal	Report: operations	Episcopal	Withdrawn

Total Shareholder Resolutions: 18

As % of Total Shareholder Resolutions Filed 1970 to 1979: 8.1%

[§] Episcopal Churchmen for South Africa
* and other religious groups

Although Rhodesia has never been directly under the control of the British government, neither has it enjoyed independence, having been primarily a protectorate of the British government.

In the 1960s there was movement by the British government to allow

Rhodesia to move toward independence. The British government made it clear to the white-dominated government of Rhodesia at that time that independence would be granted only if the black majority was given electoral rights. The whites refused to comply and, in 1965, the existing Rhodesian government unilaterally disaffiliated itself with Britain and issued a Unilateral Declaration of Independence. This in essence disengaged Rhodesia from Britain and placed the white-dominated Rhodesian government completely in control of the country. This insured that 220,000 whites held power over the seven million blacks.

The world community opposed the government of Rhodesia's action and various governments refused to grant formal diplomatic recognition to the new government. The United Nations in 1966 imposed mandatory economic sanctions against the rebel state primarily because of its intent to continue the practices of apartheid. The United Nations hoped by the imposition of sanctions that the government would be weakened due to the lack of shipment of arms and other materials into that country.

The Rhodesian government, however, survived the embargo and materials continued to flow into the country through various means. Rhodesia received, for instance, all the oil supplies that it required.

The Protestant churches, notably the United Church of Christ, expressed concern about the inflow of oil into Rhodesia and commenced an investigation into the reasons for this. The United Church of Christ in 1977 filed a shareholder resolution with Mobil Oil pointing out that

> it is illegal for U.S. corporations or U.S. personnel engaged in the management of business enterprises abroad to participate in transactions which, directly or indirectly, promote the sale or supply of any commodities or products to the illegal government of Rhodesia, or any business in that country.[13a]

The shareholder resolution further resolved that no Mobil products be supplied directly or indirectly to Rhodesia and that "no bulk-sales of products are made without verifiable guarantees by the purchasers that said products are not destined for resale or transfer to Rhodesia."[14]

In 1978 the United Church of Christ filed a shareholder resolution with Mobil Oil Company in which the following arguments were presented:

> —oil continues to be provided through South Africa to the internationally outlawed Rhodesian regime of Ian Smith, violating the twelve-year-old economic sanctions voted by the United Nations and backed by the United States;
>
> —South Africa hides the indirect sale of oil to Rhodesia through South African customers by the international oil companies that supply South Africa itself. Mobil being the largest of these and the number one U.S. corporate investor in South Africa;

—the government of Zambia and the British-Rhodesian pipeline company, Lonrho, instituted suits against Mobil and the other international oil companies since last year's shareholders meeting, charging they have for years circumvented sanctions through indirect sales to Genta, the official Rhodesian oil-procurement agency;

—it appears that oil sanctions can be effectively applied to Rhodesia only by materially reducing oil imports into South Africa, discouraging the South African government from continuing to serve as a conduit for Rhodesia;

—total Rhodesian oil imports during the past twelve years, calculated on the basis of Mobil figures submitted to the U.S. Senate, amounts to at least one-third of the current annual South African importation.[15]

The shareholder resolution then asked Mobil and its affiliate companies to ban indirect, as well as direct, sales to Rhodesia and in effect this would reduce the volume of Mobil Oil imports to South Africa and deflect any subsequent flow of oil into Rhodesia.

In 1979 a shareholder resolution was filed with the Standard Oil Company of California also with the intent of reducing the flow of oil through South Africa into Rhodesia.[16] The resolution asked that the company reduce the volume of imports into South Africa by at least one-third of the average annual volume of such imports during the ten years since the 1968 U.S. Presidential Executive Order made all indirect and direct sales to Rhodesia illegal.

The church supported its argument by stating that the proposal:

—does not ask the Corporation to make Rhodesia's foreign policy but rather to obey a policy we already have of no sales whose end destination is Rhodesia;

—does not call for an embargo of South Africa, but a refusal to sell South Africa more oil than it needs, thereby enabling it to supply Rhodesia;

—does not ask the Corporation to interfere in South Africa's domestic affairs, but to stop participating in South Africa's interference in Rhodesian affairs—to cease helping South Africa fuel an outlaw regime as its buffer-state to the north in which the white minority can go on holding the black majority down.[17]

Another step taken by a Protestant denomination, again the United Church of Christ, was to protest the importation of chrome ore from Rhodesia. This shareholder resolution, shown as Proposal No. 5, was filed with Union Carbide in 1976. The shareholder resolution proposed that Union Carbide would not directly, or through its affiliates, import any chrome ore from Rhodesia until such time as governmental power is transferred to the African majority and international economic sanctions against Rhodesia have been lifted.[18]

Table 3. Protestant Sponsored or Cosponsored Shareholder Resolutions 1970 to 1979 Over the Issue of Apartheid in Rhodesia

Year	Corporation	Subject: Rhodesia	Denomination	% Vote
1976	Union Carbide	No import chrome ore	United Ch. Christ	1.99%
1977	Mobil	No sales of oil	United Ch. Christ	1.75%
1978	Mobil	No sales of oil	United Ch. Christ*	3.25%
1978	Standard Oil CA	No sales of oil	Christian Church, United Ch. Christ, United Methodist	4.15%
1978	Texaco	Report: Caltex Oil sales	Christian Church, United Ch. Christ*	2.97%
1979	Mobil	Reduce oil to So. Africa so less flows to Rhodesia	United Ch. Christ	1.9%
1979	Standard Oil CA	Reduce oil to So. Africa so less flows to Rhodesia	Amer. Baptist, United Ch. Christ	1.95%
1979	Texaco	Reduce oil to So. Africa so less flows to Rhodesia	United Ch. Christ	2.7%

Total Shareholder Resolutions: 8

As % of Total Shareholder Resolutions Filed 1970 to 1979: 3.6%

* and other religious groups

Colonialism in Southern Africa

Three Southern African colonies were controlled by the Portuguese government during the 1970s; these were Angola, Guinea-Bissau and Mozambique. All three were struggling for independence from Portuguese domination and the Protestant churches provided support to the insurgents.

Angola. Angola is a large territory exceeding Texas and California combined. Its population at the time of Protestant involvement was approximately five million blacks who were controlled by some 400,000 Portuguese.

One of the Protestant churches' actions involving a shareholder resolution was over the Gulf Oil operation in Cabinda, a small enclave on the west coast of Angola. Prior to the shareholder resolution, church groups had already initiated a boycott campaign against Gulf because it was drilling for oil in Angola.

One reason the churches were interested in Angola was that they had long maintained missionaries there, who reported back to their home office tales of Portuguese cruelty as the colonial regime sought to suppress the Africans' struggle for independence. In addition, many like the United Church of Christ, had moved to the forefront of those fighting for equal rights for American blacks. The church considered the efforts of black African nations to become independent as part of the same struggle for equal rights.[19]

The Ohio Conference of the United Church of Christ urged members of its churches to boycott Gulf Oil products and to return their credit cards to the company because of Gulf's support for Portuguese domination over Angola and other Portuguese controlled colonies.[20]

Finally in the Spring of 1974, the United Church of Christ filed a shareholder resolution asking Gulf to disclose information about their Cabinda operation by listing reserves, shipments, contractual revisions, and the company's position regarding the Arab Oil embargo.

In summary, Gulf was being charged with aiding Portuguese colonialism by providing:

(1) tax and royalty payments totaling more than $175 million since 1975
(2) foreign exchange contributing toward financial stability and enabling war-related purchases
(3) a strategic resource that helps to ward off the effects of economic sanctions against Portugal
(4) a contractual relationship that indirectly influences U.S. policy toward support for Portugal's African wars
(5) a positive image of Portuguese colonialism in the U.S.[21]

Guinea-Bissau. Again, as the case of Angola, the Protestant churches argued that American corporations were assisting the Portuguese by providing that government with taxes and royalty payments that would tend to support colonialism in those territories.

The shareholder resolution filed with Exxon in 1974 asked that Exxon "not directly or through affiliates, conduct exploration, mining, oil drilling or oil production activities in the Republic of Guinea-Bissau. . . ."[22] It argued:

Guinea-Bissau nationalists have been fighting for independence from Portugal since 1963. Many governments, churches and private organizations support this resistance to foreign, colonial Portuguese occupation. The independence movement (the PAIGC) has liberated three-quarters of Guinea-Bissau. In September 1973 the National Assembly of Guinea-Bissau freely elected by Africans in the liberated areas, declared independence from Portugal. Over seventy nations have recognized this independent government as the rightful government of Guinea-Bissau. By a 93-7 vote, the United Nations General Assembly has recognized Guinea-Bissau's independence. Any royalty or tax payments made now by Exxon to Portugal helps Portugal at a particularly critical time.[23]

Mozambique. Again as the case of Portuguese-controlled Angola and Guinea-Bissau, the Protestant churches sought for independence for the Africans in Mozambique. The churches opposed investment by Bethlehem Steel in that area as they felt this provided the Portuguese government with taxes and royalty payments and aided foreign domination over that country. The resolution requested that Bethlehem "shall not directly, or through affiliates, conduct exploration or mining activities in Mozambique under concessions obtained from the Portuguese government and shall wind up any such operations currently underway in that country as expeditiously as possible."[24] The arguments presented in support of this resolution followed the same theme as those presented in behalf of Angola and Guinea-Bissau:

> In 1972 a consortium of which Bethlehem Steel is a member received from Portugal a concession to prospect for minerals in Mozambique. Nationalists have been fighting in Mozambique for independence since 1964 and reportedly now control one-fourth of the nation. The United Nations's General Assembly, Organization of African Unity, World Council of Churches and many governments, churches and private organizations support this resistance to foreign, colonial Portuguese occupation. Fighting is taking place in some parts of the concession territory, which could jeopardize company employees and investments. The press has recently reported a massacre of 400 villages by Portuguese soldiers. It is in the long range interest of American corporations to divorce themselves from the colonial regimes which may soon be overthrown, rather than to support them by the payment of taxes and royalties. The principal Mozambique movement for independence (FRELIMO) has stated that they oppose foreign investment in their nation at this time.[25]

Infringement of Human Rights in Chile

The Protestant churches argued that the military dictatorship in Chile systematically violated human rights. They pointed out that political power was seized in 1973 by the overthrow of an elected government and as a consequence the constitutional Republic that was founded in 1833 had been destroyed. The churches averred that the violation of human rights and repression in Chile has been well documented by

> the sources within and without Chile, including the Chilean Cardinals' Ecumenical Committee for Peace, World Council of Churches, Amnesty International, International Commission of Jurists, International Labor Organization, United Nations Human Rights, and the Commission and Organization of American States.[26]

As a statement against the practices of the Chilean government, three Protestant churches filed a shareholder resolution with General Motors in 1976 asking that "it adopt a policy that there should be no expansion of General Motors in Chile."[27] Dr. Howard Schomer, World Issues Sec-

Table 4. Protestant Sponsored or Cosponsored Shareholder Resolutions 1970 to 1979 Over Colonialism in Angola, Guinea-Bissau and Mozambique

Year	Corporation	Subject: Colonialism	Denomination	% Vote
1971	Gulf	Cease operations, Angola	United Presby.	2.2%
1972	Gulf	Report: operations, Angola	United Ch. Christ	2.93%
1974	Beth. Steel	Cease operations, Mozambique	United Methodist	0.005%
1974	Exxon	Cease operations in Guinea-Bissau	Amer. Baptist, Episcopal, National Council, United Ch. Christ, United Presby.	2.15%
1974	Gulf	Report operations, Angola	United Ch. Christ	1.6%

Total Shareholder Resolutions: 5

As % of Total Shareholder Resolutions Filed 1970 to 1979: 2.3%

retary of the United Church of Christ, when introducing this resolution at the 1976 stockholders meeting of General Motors said, "The churches do not ask General Motors to seek to redress the whole deplorable political situation of a society. . . . The proposal only asks General Motors to do that which it, as a progressive employer, should and can do in the defense of its own workers."[28]

In 1977 the United Christian Church asked ITT to disclose its activities in Chile for the period of 1969 to 1975.[29] In 1978 ITT was asked to disclose what political contributions it had made in Chile.[30] Finally, in 1979, Superior Oil was requested to make no further investments in that country. The basic argument underlying all these resolutions was that American business in Chile provided the Chilean regime with economic support.

Food shortages, Malnutrition, Low Wages in the Dominican Republic

In 1976 the National Council of Churches argued that large investments in export crops such as sugar in a country suffering shortages of food staples were bound to cause social problems. While it was true that sugar products had brought much needed foreign exchange into the country,

Table 5. Protestant Sponsored or Cosponsored Shareholder Resolutions 1970 to 1979 Over the Issue of Human Rights in Chile

Year	Corporation	Subject: Chile	Denomination	% Vote
1976	GM	No expansion of operations	Christian Church, United Ch. Christ, United Methodist	2.01%
1977	ITT	Report on activities from 1969 to 1975	Christian Church*	3.6%
1978	ITT	Report: political contributions	Christian Church*	3.7%
1979	Superior Oil	No expansion of operations	Amer. Baptist, Luth. Ch. Amer.	2.9%
- - -	- - -	- - -	- - -	- - -
1974	ITT	Report: on activities	Christian Church	Withdrawn
1977	GM	Labor practices	Christian Church United Methodist	Withdrawn

Total Shareholder Resolutions: 6

As % of Total Shareholder Resolutions Filed 1970 to 1979: 2.7%

* and other religious groups

the poor were receiving only a small portion of the income each year. Further, the National Council argued that malnutrition had become a severe problem and that wages were so low that it was difficult to support families directly. Therefore, the Council asked that Gulf & Western make available a special report on the role of G & W in the Dominican Republic.[31]

At the time of the filing of the shareholder resolution, Father Thomas E. Scheetz, had made a fact finding mission in the Dominican Republic and had commented that Gulf & Western

> seems to presume that it can deal with corrupt government officials without itself being corrupted, take out huge profits without a lasting effect in income distribution and create "company unions" without affecting labor rights. Although some of these ill effects can be ameliorated through well-run charitable programs, the central social issues cannot be resolved through charity.[32]

The Interfaith Center on Corporate Responsibility had conducted an inquiry in New York on September 14, 1975 on Gulf & Western's role in the Dominican Republic and had reached the following conclusion:

It is clear that the support by G & W and the U.S. government for Joaquin Balaguer has tended to strengthen a regime reportedly criticized for its violation of human rights. . . . While the country has registered a relatively high rate of growth over the past decade, it is growth measured only in terms of the value of increased production but definitely not in terms of general eradication of mass poverty, unemployment and inequality.[33]

Table 6. Protestant Sponsored or Cosponsored Shareholder Resolutions 1970 to 1979 Over the Issue of Human Rights in the Dominican Republic

Year	Corporation	Subject: Dominican Rep.	Denomination	% Vote
1975	G & W	Report on operations	National Council	4.5%
1976	G & W	Report on operations	National Council	6.01%
1979	G & W	Report on operations	National Council	3.3%
1977	G & W	Report on operations	National Council	Withdrawn

Total Shareholder Resolutions: 4

As % of Total Shareholder Resolutions Filed 1970 to 1979: 1.8%

Questionable Labor Practices in Guatemala

The United Presbyterian Church, concerned about questionable labor practices in Guatemala, requested that Coca-Cola make public a code of minimum labor standards required of its franchised bottlers as well as stipulate what procedures would be followed to enforce the code.[34]

The United Presbyterian Church argued that Coca-Cola is a well known and widely distributed product and has been associated with American goodwill and fairness for many years. The church averred that its success at being a profitable business can be linked to the fact that the company bears a good name. However, according to the church, Coca-Cola's reputation had been "sullied by some of the franchise bottlers." The church shareholders noted that Coca-Cola's franchised bottler *Embotelladora Guatemalteca* engaged in questionable labor practices that attracted public criticism and "cost the Company to lose a substantial share of the Guatemalan market."[35]

Resolutions had been initiated with Coca-Cola regarding the Guatemalan bottler in 1977 and 1978, but the resolutions were withdrawn in anticipation of some changes in labor practices. However, when these were not forthcoming the resolution was filed.

Table 7. Protestant Sponsored or Cosponsored Shareholder Resolutions 1970 to 1979 Over Questionable Labor Practices in Guatemala

Year	Corporation	Subject: Guatemala	Denomination	% Vote
1979	Coca-Cola	Establish labor policy	United Presby.*	1.7%
1977	Coca-Cola	Establish labor policy	United Presby.	Withdrawn
1978	Coca-Cola	Establish labor policy	United Presby.	Withdrawn

Total Shareholder Resolutions: 3

As % of Total Shareholder Resolutions Filed 1970 to 1979: 1.4%

* and other religious groups

Wages and Working Conditions in South Korea

The United Church of Christ and the Reformed Church, concerned over wages and working conditions in South Korea, filed a shareholder resolution in 1975 and 1976 with Motorola who operated a plant in that country. The resolution declared that "corporations must serve larger social interests than the immediate maximization of profits if they are to survive as viable institutions in our society."[36]

In view of this premise, these churches declared that "disclosures on wages, working conditions and relations with trade unions . . . will encourage our corporation to monitor practices in Korea more closely."[37] A report was then requested from Motorola which would include historical information about employees and working conditions as well as relations of Motorola with the Korean government. A statement in behalf of the resolution declared:

> As shareholders we believe our Corporation should not benefit unduly from a political situation in which human rights of a people are violated. At the very least, U.S. companies should follow laws which protect the Korean workers.[38]

The statement continued with the argument that the South Korean government had repeatedly violated the rights of workers in that while many labor laws were on the books in behalf of the rights of the workers, most companies did not follow them.

Table 8. Protestant Sponsored or Cosponsored Shareholder Resolutions 1970 to 1979 Over the Issue of Wages and Working Conditions in South Korea

Year	Corporation	Subject: South Korea	Denomination	% Vote
1975	Motorola	Report on labor practices	United Ch. Christ	3.87%
1976	Motorola	Report on labor practices	Reformed Church, United Ch. Christ	0.9%
1975	Control Data	Report on operations	United Ch. Christ	Withdrawn

Total Shareholder Resolutions: 3

As a % of Total Shareholder Resolutions Filed 1970 to 1979: 1.4%

Civil Liberties in the Philippines

Ferdinand E. Marcos was elected as President of the Philippines in 1965. He was reelected to a second term as President four years later. However, in 1972, before completing the four full years in the new term, he declared that the system was not working. He suspended the Congress and formulated a charter which established a Prime Minister as the head of the government and Marcos retained complete control by holding the office of President. Martial law was invoked to establish the new government. The military staff was more than doubled and officers were appointed who were loyal to Marcos. Loyalty was enhanced by conferring special privileges. In fact, military commanders assumed local political power and had much clout. Military tribunals arrested many for martial law infractions and all opposition was immediately crushed. President Marcos alone made and executed the law.

The United Church of Christ, together with the National Council of Churches, attempted to bring attention to the concern over the violation of human rights in the Philippines by filing a shareholder resolution with the Ford Motor Company in 1974. They argued that the "Filipino people are not at present free to express their own judgments on the conditions established by their governments to create an attractive investment environment" inasmuch as the Republic of the Philippines had been placed under martial law since September of 1972. Therefore, it was necessary for shareholders to know what those investment conditions were and be able to appraise them. The resolution requested that Ford provide a brief report on the history and current operations in the Philippines.[39] The two churches involved in the resolution stressed that there was a growing distrust of giant corporations and that it was important that Ford avoid "even the appearance of collusion with any government that overthrows or prevents majority rule."[40]

Table 9. Protestant Sponsored or Cosponsored Shareholder Resolutions 1970 to 1979 Over the Issue of Civil Liberties in the Philippines

Year	Corporation	Subject: Philippines	Denomination	% Vote
1974	Ford	Report on operations	National Council, United Ch. Christ	1.56%
	Total Shareholder Resolutions: 1			
	As % of Total Shareholder Resolutions Filed 1970 to 1979: 0.4%			

Employment Practices in Developing Countries

This social concern involved Castle & Cooke who had operations in various Third World countries. The Protestant churches who filed shareholder resolutions in 1977, 1978 and 1979 asked Castle & Cooke to develop a code of conduct covering labor practices. This was prompted by an observation that "the poverty of field and cannery workers, and complaints by workers that grievances go unheeded about transportation, shelter, safety, 12-hour cannery shifts, and mandatory Sunday work which prevents Sunday worship."[41]

The churches involved in the resolutions argued that a labor code would provide a very definite pattern for achieving human rights for the agricultural workers and, therefore, "a code of minimum standards" should be required for Castle & Cooke as it relates to labor operations worldwide. The churches were convinced that furnishing such information would give the churches, as well as "thoughtful shareholders," an opportunity to assess the company's relationship with their employees in Costa Rica, Ecuador, Honduras, Nicaragua, the Philippines, Thailand, and Hawaii. According to the resolution, disclosure of basic information would be the first step toward answering questions and improving performance.[42]

Dr. Howard Schomer, representing the United Church of Christ, attended the annual stockholders' meeting held in April 1977 in Honolulu and moved the adoption of the Shareholder Proposal his church was presenting. Some excerpts of his statement at that meeting follow:

> This Resolution is a request to the Board of Directors for information. It makes no criticism of the Corporation or Management. There is not a single judgmental word, there is no suggestion of an accusation in it.
>
> The three parts of the Resolution are all plainly focused on one practical question: how does the Corporation treat its employees? In a period of significant company expansion overseas, and of decreasing company employment in Hawaii, the Resolution calls for "sunlight"! It requests numbers and facts, not generalized statements of principle, policy, or intent.
>
> Contrary to Management's contention in its declared reasons for disfavoring our Resolution and the requested report, the publication of this hard data would serve several useful purposes related to the Company's business.[43]

Table 10. Protestant Sponsored or Cosponsored Shareholder Resolutions 1970 to 1979 Over the Issue of Labor Practices in Developing Countries

Year	Corporation	Subject: Castle & Cooke	Denomination	% Vote
1977	Castle & Cooke	Labor Practices	Christian Church, United Ch. Christ	3.24%
1978	Castle & Cooke	Labor Practices	Christian Church, United Ch. Christ*	2.89%
1979	Castle & Cooke	Labor Practices and payments to local officials	Christian Church, United Ch. Christ	Withdrawn

Total Shareholder Resolutions: 3

As % of Total Shareholder Resolutions Filed 1970 to 1979: 1.4%

* and other religious groups

Foreign Military Sales

The National Council of Churches, the United Church of Christ, and the United Methodist Churches, were Protestant elements involved with this issue with General Electric in 1977 and 1978. The churches expressed concern over the easy availability of military equipment which they claimed made the world a less secure place in which to live. In addition, the desire to secure military equipment, according to the churches, had caused developing countries to divert scarce resources from social development and to use these resources for the purchase of arms. The Protestant churches claimed that countries that purchased United States military equipment were those very nations who ironically had systematically violated the basic human rights of their own citizens.[44] The churches' arguments were supported with these affirmations:

> Concern with human rights around the globe is shared today not only by individuals and organizations such as Amnesty International, but also by the present Administration. One of the most disheartening aspects of this problem is the relationship between governments that violate human rights and U.S. military assistance and foreign military sales. The extent to which U.S. arms maintain unpopular and unjust regimes should be a concern not only of the U.S. government, but also of U.S. corporations. Indeed, we believe that, on such an important question, private corporations must make an independent evaluation and render an independent judgment before selling goods and services to a repressive government.[45]

In the resolutions filed with General Electric, the churches stressed that international trade in arms continued to escalate and the United States has been responsible for approximately one-half of the total sales of military equipment worldwide. Further, the military equipment being sold was being secured by governments known for their repressive policies, and the following countries were listed: Chile, Ethiopia, Iran, Malaysia, Peru and Taiwan.[46] Because of this concern for military equipment going into the hands of such governments, the following corporate policy was asked to be adopted:

> In its deliberations of foreign military sales/servicing agreements, the Corporate Policy Committee shall (1) evaluate the human rights situation in any country with which a contract is contemplated, reviewing available information from public and private sources; (2) establish criteria below which a country cannot fall and still remain a General Electric customer; (3) decline any sales to a country which does not meet these minimal standards; and (4) communicate to shareholders the criteria established and publish annually a list of the countries with which military sales/servicing agreements are in effect.[47]

The formulation of such a Corporate Policy Committee, according to the churches, would be an important first and would demonstrate to the public the seriousness with which management takes the arms sales question, especially when the Corporation has built in human rights as a sales criterion.

The 1977 shareholder resolution requested disclosure of military sales by General Electric, which disclosure was to include a description of the social, ethical and political criteria which the corporation would use to determine whether to accept or refuse specific requests for military equipment from foreign governments.

Table 11. Protestant Sponsored or Cosponsored Shareholder Resolutions 1970 to 1979 Over the Issue of Foreign Military Sales

Year	Corporation	Subject	Denomination	% Vote
1977	GE	Report on foreign military sales	United Ch. Christ United Methodist*	2.4%
1978	GE	Formulation of Policy Committee re sale of military equipment	United Ch. Christ	1.8%
		Total Shareholder Resolutions: 2		
		As % of Total Shareholder Resolutions Filed 1970 to 1979: 0.9%		

* and other religious groups

Infant Nutrition in Developing Countries

In the early 1970s public health specialists began to link malnutrition of infants in developing countries to the use of commercially prepared baby formula. The formula, manufactured by companies based in the United States as well as the largest producer Nestle, a Swiss-based company, was made up of vegetable fat, milk, sugar, vitamins, and minerals; while nutritious to some extent when properly used, it was not a comparable replacement for mother's milk. The problem was that Third World mothers were unwittingly mixing the powdered formula with contaminated water, or to save money, diluted it too much. Responsible medical researchers had demonstrated that any substitution of the commercial formula for breast milk, especially where poverty, illiteracy, impure water and inadequate sanitation prevail, resulted not only in infant malnutrition, but in illness, brain damage and even death.

The churches argued that the transnational corporations were compounding the problem by indiscriminate promotion of the infant formula products and cautioned that such tactics were questionable. The practice of promoting infant formula, according to Protestant reasoning, was that it encouraged women to abandon the natural resource of breastfeeding in favor of commercial preparations. The shareholder resolutions filed with

Bristol-Myers and American Home Products asked that these companies cease advertising its infant formula in areas where social, economic and environmental conditions are such that the formula was apt to damage the health and well-being of infants; remove "milk nurses" from hospitals and maternity clinics; discontinue free sample distribution to consumers; and terminate the giving of special incentives to doctors and other health professionals.

Table 12. Protestant Sponsored or Cosponsored Shareholder Resolutions 1970 to 1979 Over the Issue of Distribution of Infant Formula in Third World Countries

Year	Corporation	Subject: Infant Formula	Denomination	% Vote
1976	Bristol-Myers	Distribution practices	United Ch. Christ*	3.4%
1977	Amer. Home Prod.	Distribution practices	United Presby., Reformed Church, United Methodist*	2.92%
1978	Amer. Home Prod.	Establish Formula Review Committee	United Presby., United Methodist*	5.29%
1979	Amer. Home Prod.	Establish Formula Review Committee	Church Brethren, United Methodist, United Presby.*	3.2%
1979	Bristol-Myers	Distribution practices	United Ch. Christ*	3.9%
1976	Amer. Home	Distribution practices	United Methodist, United Presby.*	Withdrawn

Total Shareholder Resolutions: 6

As % of Total Shareholder Resolutions Filed 1970 to 1979: 2.7%

* and other religious groups

Questionable Corporate Payments Overseas

In a shareholder resolution filed with Tenneco in 1977, the United Church of Christ reported that public disclosures during the past two years had demonstrated that many U.S. corporations had made questionable payments overseas.[48] These payments were made to influence public policy.

> Although the people who have accepted such payments are as responsible for this unhealthy development as those who gave them, and while foreign competitors of U.S.

corporations have been involved in similar practices, it is imperative that U.S. corporations take the lead in establishing policies that prohibit such political payments with strict procedures for their enforcement.[49]

In the same resolution, which was representative of other resolutions filed by the churches on the same issue, the United Church of Christ emphasized that while there are corporate policies that prohibit the unlawful or improper use of company funds, the church was concerned also about legal political contributions utilized for influencing governmental decisions or procuring of favors. Therefore, the church asked that the corporation amend its "inadequate policy, joining more than 100 U.S. transnationals that prohibit all use of corporate assets for political purposes or at least restrict such contributions to modest amounts."[50]

Table 13. Protestant Sponsored or Cosponsored Shareholder Resolutions 1970 to 1979 Over the Issue of Questionable Corporate Payments Overseas

Year	Corporation	Subject: Contributions	Denomination	% Vote
1976	Exxon	Report on overseas political contributions	Christian Church*	2.97%
1976	Gulf	Ban on political contributions	United Ch. Christ*	2.36%
1976	ITT	Report on overseas political contributions	Christian Church*	6.92%
1976	Merck	Report on overseas political contributions	United Ch. Christ	1.74%
1976	Standard Oil CA	Report on overseas political contributions	United Ch. Christ	2.94%
1977	ITT	Report on overseas political contributions	Christian Church*	3.75%
1977	Tenneco	Ban on international political contributions	United Ch. Christ	5.22%
1978	Tenneco	Ban on international political contributions	United Ch. Christ, Christian Church	4.55%
1979	ITT	Terminate officers who make political contrib.	Christian Church	2.5%
1976	Amer. Home	Report on overseas political contributions	United Methodist. *Withdrawn	

Table 13 (continued)

Year	Corporation	Subject: Contributions	Denomination	% Vote
1976	Exxon	Report on overseas political contributions	Christian Church	Withdrawn
1976	Ford	Report on overseas political contributions	United Ch. Christ	Withdrawn
1976	Mobil	Report on overseas political contributions	United Ch. Christ	Withdrawn
1979	Castle & Cooke	Foreign political contrib.	United Ch. Christ	Withdrawn

Total Shareholder Resolutions: 14

As % of Total Shareholder Resolutions Filed 1970 to 1979: 6.3%

* and other religious groups

Appropriate Farm Technology for Developing Countries

This issue involved primarily Deere & Company in a shareholder resolution filed by the American Baptist Churches who expressed concern over the world food shortage and the pressing need for better production of agricultural commodities in developing nations. Farm goods productivity can only be increased in developing nations with the use of farm machinery specifically designed for rural labor. The denomination felt that Deere was admirably equipped to develop such farm machinery appropriate for the needs of a labor-intensive farm production. The church consequently asked Deere for a report "on the involvement of the Corporation in the creation of appropriate technologies for developing nations" that were suitable and appropriate for "the types of rural social organization and employable skills" in Third World societies.[51] The resolution was supported with this statement:

> Church groups are concerned that emphasis on large farm implements can have a detrimental effect on agricultural production in developing countries where the average size farm is often under ten acres. As stockholders, we petition the management to develop technologies appropriate to patterns of food-raising in which small farmers remain productive. Deere can best improve food availability if it is designed to perform in conjunction with small-scale farming methods and draft animals and to conserve vital energy supplies.[52]

The Energy Crisis in the United States

Exxon and Gulf Oil were both petitioned in 1974 by the American Baptist

Table 14. Protestant Sponsored or Cosponsored Shareholder Resolutions 1970 to 1979 Over the Issue of Appropriate Farm Technology for Third World Societies

Year	Corporation	Subject	Denomination	% Vote
1976	Deere	Report: need for appropriate farm equipment	Amer. Baptist	1.62%

Total Shareholder Resolutions: 1

As % of Total Shareholder Resolutions Filed 1970 to 1979: 0.4%

Churches and the United Church of Christ respectively over the issue of the energy crisis extant at that time. The resolutions were similar in nature and emphasized that the "energy crisis" was a matter of growing public concern and that oil companies were the key to the solution of the "crisis." These churches, therefore, asked for a report concerning the corporations' operations and their relation to the energy crisis.[53]

> The effects of the shortages of gasoline, diesel and jet fuel, and home heating oil are being felt by most citizens of the United States and many others around the world. Economic dislocation, cold homes, offices, schools and factories, pressures for elimination of environmental protection regulations, and a "hard sell" for nuclear power as a promising alternative, are some of the results of the current oil shortages.
> In recent months many have claimed that the crude oil shortage is a hoax and that oil companies are holding products in storage until prices rise and/or independent dealers are squeezed out of the market. The federal government seems unable or unwilling to provide any data that will prove or disprove this contention.[54]

In view of the lack of important data so deemed by the churches, Exxon and Gulf were asked to furnish what information they could concerning the matter.

Table 15. Protestant Sponsored or Cosponsored Shareholder Resolutions 1970 to 1979 Over the Issue of the Energy Crisis in the United States

Year	Corporation	Subject	Denomination	% Vote
1974	Exxon	Report: energy crisis	Amer. Baptist	2.62%
1974	Gulf Oil	Report: energy crisis	United Ch. Christ	2.2%

Total Shareholder Resolutions: 2

As % of Total Shareholder Resolutions Filed 1970 to 1979: 0.9%

Equal Employment Opportunities in the United States

Protestant churches participated in a special project entitled "Church Project on Equal Employment Opportunity." While there were laws on the books relative to nondiscrimination as it concerned women and minority groups, the churches were concerned over inequality in the recruitment, employment, training, and promotion of minorities and women. The policies pursued by corporations in these areas could materially affect the income and unemployment levels of these groups.

The Church Project on Equal Employment Opportunity filed similar resolutions with a number of companies. These are shown in table 16. The basic thrust of the resolutions were requests for reports concerning records being maintained as they related to equal employment. Churches determined that when corporations were required to report statistics concerning their employment practices, such actions would act as an incentive to improve performance and would give shareholders a basis for making assessment of corporate performances. A number of corporations, as shown in table 16, agreed to furnish the statistical data requested and the resolutions were consequently withdrawn. Support for the resolutions was couched in this language:

> We believe our Corporation's commitment to equal opportunity in employment regardless of race, color, religion, sex or national origins should be matched by public disclosure of information indicating progress in employment for women and minorities and concrete details of affirmative action programs. Elimination of discrimination in employment is a primary national priority. Public disclosure of this information would be an encouragement to our company to help meet this national priority. In addition, disclosure of such information is definitely in the best interests of shareholders. Several corporations have faced costly court challenges and settlements because of discriminatory employment practices. Shareholders need such information for a responsible assessment of our Corporation's profit picture.[55]

The shareholder resolutions filed with the J. P. Stevens Company were part of a larger plan which already involved boycotting and other activities. The purpose was to motivate that company to enter into collective bargaining arrangements with its employees. The matter of the J. P. Stevens Company labor problems are detailed in the boycott section of this study.[56]

The Xerox resolution filed in 1975 by the United Methodist Church sought to determine if there was any discrimination against women in hiring women for Xerox's sales staffs.

Table 16. Protestant Sponsored or Cosponsored Shareholder Resolutions 1970 to 1979 Over the Issue of Equal Employment Opportunities in the United States

Year	Corporation	Subject: Employment	Denomination	% Vote
1974	GE	Report on equal employment opportunities	Episcopal	2.3%
1974	IBM	Report on equal employment opportunities	National Council	2.26%
1975	Xerox	Report on equal employment opportunities	United Methodist	2.3%
1977	Stevens	Report on equal employment opportunities	United Methodist*	5.59%
1977	Stevens	Report on labor practices	United Methodist*	5.83%
1978	GE	Report on equal employment opportunities	Episcopal*	1.77%
1978	Stevens	Report on equal employment opportunities	United Methodist*	3.92%
1978	Stevens	Report on labor practices	United Methodist*	5.44%
1974	Kraft	Report on equal employment opportunities	United Presby.	Withdrawn
1974	GM	Report on equal employment opportunities	Amer. Baptist	Withdrawn
1974	Polaroid	Report on equal employment opportunities	Amer. Baptist	Withdrawn
1974	Sears, Roebuck	Report on equal employment opportunities	United Methodist	Withdrawn
1974	Xerox	Report on equal employment opportunities	United Methodist	Withdrawn
1975	Sears, Roebuck	Report on equal employment opportunities in Chicago	United Methodist	Withdrawn
1978	Mobil	Report on equal employment opportunities at Montgomery Ward	United Ch. Christ	Withdrawn
1979	CBS	Report on equal employment opportunities	United Methodist	Withdrawn

Total Shareholder Resolutions: 16
As % of Total Shareholder Resolutions Filed 1970 to 1979: 7.2%

* and other religious groups

Political Contributions in the United States

The Episcopal Church filed shareholder resolutions in 1974 and 1975 with the Phillips Petroleum Company over the donation of corporate funds to a Presidential Campaign Committee in violation of Federal criminal statutes. They also asked that the company implement internal procedures to assure that such illegal contributions could not be made again in the future. The argument was supported as follows:

> Since 1907 it has been illegal and a crime for any corporation to make any contribution in connection with any Federal election. Nevertheless in 1972 officers of our Corporation caused it to donate $100,000 to a presidential election committee in violation of the law. Our Corporation and its retired Chairman subsequently pled guilty to a charge brought with respect to this time. The Judge fined our Corporation $5,000. This donation and the subsequent conviction have caused very considerable adverse publicity to our Corporation. We believe that the shareholders should express disapproval of this illegal action. We also believe that the Corporation should take effective measures to guard against any possible repetition of this incident.[57]

In the 1975 resolution, the Episcopal Church strengthened its request by asking that corporation bylaws be amended so that any of the employees who fail to comply with federal and state laws relative to political contributions would be subject to disciplinary action, including termination.[58]

In one of the rare instances where management agreed with the proposal submitted by a church, the 3M Company agreed with the request that the Board of Directors implement procedures designed to assure that illegal contributions could not be made by the company or any of its officers. The 3M company sought to avoid a repetition of a similar occurrence. The resolution received a 97.7% favorable vote from the stockholders.

Redlining/Reinvestment by Banks in the United States

Redlining is a term which is affixed when there is a denial of credit to a particular geographic area. A real or imaginary "red line" is drawn around a particular location and no mortgage loans are issued to persons located in that area. These areas were frequently populated by minority groups. A slogan emerged which implied that when blacks move in, mortgage and home improvement monies move out.

In order to stop this practice, shareholder resolutions were filed by the United Methodist Church with Chemical New York and with the First National Bank of Boston. Requests were made of both these banks that

Table 17. Protestant Sponsored or Cosponsored Shareholder Resolutions 1970 to 1979 Over the Issue of Political Contributions in the United States

Year	Corporation	Subject	Denomination	% Vote
1974	3M	Implement procedures to avoid illegal contrib.	Episcopal	97.7%
1974	Phillips	Report on political contributions	Episcopal	7.0%
1975	Phillips	Report on political contributions	Episcopal	4.7%
1975	Phillips	Dismissal of those violating election laws	Episcopal	7.0%
1976	Phillips	Report on political contributions	Episcopal*	Withdrawn

Total Shareholder Resolutions: 5

As % of Total Shareholder Resolutions Filed 1970 to 1979: 2.3%

a Community Reinvestment Review Committee be established. The Committee would be made up of neighborhood representatives, as well as bank personnel, and would review and analyze information disclosed by the banks under the Home Mortgage Disclosure Act of 1975; specific attention would be given to the banks' lending patterns in certain neighborhoods. The Committee would devote its time to issues of redlining and community reinvestment and would recommend policies which hopefully could result in the increased availability of residential mortgages and creative programs for community reinvestment. The establishment of the Committee in essence would be an affirmative stance on the part of the bank that it not only does not redline but seeks new strategies for urban development.[59]

A similar practice of redlining began to emerge in the insurance field wherein insurance companies in many urban areas were avoiding writing insurance with minorities, or in some cases were refusing to renew existing policies. In response to this, the United Methodist Church filed a shareholder resolution with the Connecticut General Insurance Company seeking to affirm the availability of homeowner's insurance from that company for minorities. Evidently adequate information was provided or assurance received, and the Methodist Church withdrew the resolution.

Table 18. Protestant Sponsored or Cosponsored Shareholder Resolutions 1970 to 1979 Over the Issue of Redlining/Reinvestment by Banks in the United States

Year	Corporation	Subject	Denomination	% Vote
1978	Chemical NY	Establish Advisory Committee on reinvestment	United Methodist	2.08%
1979	Chemical NY	Report: mortgage and home improvement loans	United Methodist	5.3%
1979	First Boston	Establish Advisory Committee on reinvestment	United Methodist	5.4%
1978	First Boston	Community reinvestment	United Methodist	Withdrawn
1979	Connecticut General	Report on possible insurance redlining	United Methodist	Withdrawn

Total Shareholder Resolutions: 5

As % of Total Shareholder Resolutions Filed 1970 to 1979: 2.3%

Strip Mining and Effects of Other Mining Operations

One of the earliest shareholder resolutions filed by a Protestant denomination involved a concern over mining, smelting and refining operations in the United States. The Episcopal Church asked American Metal Climax (now known as AMAX) to "minimize in all feasible ways the ecological damage caused by such operations in compliance with all applicable ecological laws and regulations."[60] A similar proposal was made to the Kennecott Copper Corporation. The church asked that a report be furnished as to what steps had been taken to insure against ecological damage from such operations and supported this request with the following statement:

> Unless the Corporation demonstrates both its good faith in the area of ecology and the actual amelioration of past practices, the worldwide rise in ecological concern could pose a serious threat to the Corporation's future. Enlightened self-interest dictates that the Corporation not lag, but lead in dealing with ecological problems arising from mining ventures. This proposal would establish in the basic charter of the Corporation the policy that the Corporation shall use all feasible methods to minimize the ecological damage caused by its operations and that it will conduct all of its operations in compliance with applicable ecological laws.[61]

In 1974 concern on the part of Protestant churches embraced the potential damage by strip mining. The United Church of Christ in a resolution filed with American Metal Climax declared that "strip mining is the most environmentally destructive method of extracting coal" with the consequence that there was a deep concern about the social, economic and ecological effects of this type of mining. The churches, therefore, asked that noncompetitive information be provided about this portion of the corporation's business.[62]

As table 19 shows, there was a number of shareholder resolutions sponsored or cosponsored by Protestant churches on the subject of strip mining. The supporting theme was similar. Representative of the supporting statements was that included in the shareholder proposal filed with the Continental Oil Company (now known as Conoco) by the United Church of Christ with regard to the activities of the Consolidation Coal Company, a wholly-owned subsidiary of Continental Oil. This coal company is located and operates in the Northern Plains area of the United States. The supporting statement furnished by the church read:

> Mining in the Northern Plains area raises serious questions of corporate responsibility for shareholders to consider. A recent report issued by the National Academy of Sciences questions whether much of the Northern Plains might ever recover from the environmental damages caused by surface mining. Untold social disruption might accompany surface mining in the Northern Plains. In addition, surface minable reserves represent only 4% of the total coal reserves of this country. These facts raise serious questions about whether surface mining is a sound policy in the Northern Plains, ecologically, socially, or in the long run, financially.[63]

It should be noted in table 19 that with relation to strip mining, the church asked primarily for a report. The churches contended that in furnishing the report, the churches would be in a better position to assess the role of the corporation in strip mining.

Table 19. Protestant Sponsored or Cosponsored Shareholder Resolutions 1970 to 1979 Over the Issues of Strip Mining and Other Mining in the United States

Year	Corporation	Subject	Denomination	% Vote
1971	Kennecott	Ecological effects of smelting/mining	Episcopal	2.8%
1971	AMAX	Ecological effects of smelting/mining	Episcopal	3.3%
1972	AMAX	Ecological effects of smelting/mining	Episcopal	2.9%

Table 19 (continued)

Year	Corporation	Subject	Denomination	% Vote
1973	AMAX	Protecting Environment	Episcopal	2.9%
1974	AMAX	Report on strip mining in Northern Plains	United Ch. Christ	4.01%
1974	Conoco	Report on strip mining in Northern Plains	United Ch. Christ	4.09%
1974	Exxon	Report on strip mining in Northern Plains	United Ch. Christ	2.69%
1975	Amer. Electric	Report on strip mining in Appalachia	United Methodist*	4.59%
1976	Amer. Electric	Report on strip mining in Appalachia	United Presby.*	9.01%
1976	Conoco	Report on strip mining in Cheyenne Reservation	Amer. Baptist*	2.76%
1976	Pittston	Report on strip mining in Appalachia	Amer. Baptist*	6.51%
1976	Standard Oil CA	Report on strip mining in Cheyenne Reservation	United Ch. Christ	2.78%
1977	Exxon	Report on coal mining	United Presby.*	98.7%
1977	Pittston	Report on strip mining in Appalachia	Amer. Baptist*	Withdrawn

Total Shareholder Resolutions: 14

As % of Total Shareholder Resolutions Filed 1970 to 1979: 6.3%

* and other religous groups

Nomination of A Woman to Board of Directors

The Christian Church in a resolution filed in 1977 argued that the American Fletcher Corporation had consistently nominated only men to the Board of Directors and a woman director had never served on the Board. The church was convinced that there were women who were fully qualified to serve and that there were, in fact, women of exceptional qualifications right in Indianapolis itself (where the bank was located) that would bring competence and ability to the Board of Directors. The church argued that women are needed to help make decisions with respect to other women who are employees and officers of the bank. They would also be of value in being able to serve the wider interests and concerns of women who comprised a substantial part of depositors and customers of the bank. "As other large banks have discovered, women directors have brought a sensitivity and concern."[64]

Table 20. Protestant Sponsored or Cosponsored Shareholder Resolutions 1970 to 1979 Over the Issue of the Nomination of a Woman to Board of Directors

Year	Corporation	Subject	Denomination	% Vote
1977	Amer. Fletcher	Nomination of a woman to Board of Directors	Christian Church	9.6%
1978	Amer. Fletcher	Nomination of a woman to Board of Directors	Christian Church	Withdrawn

Total Shareholder Resolutions: 2
As % of Total Shareholder Resolutions Filed 1970 to 1979: 0.9%

Impact of Television Advertising on Children's Nutrition

The Church of the Brethren had filed a shareholder resolution with Pillsbury in 1979 over certain advertising of Burger King, a subsidiary. The resolution had asked that the company voluntarily adopt the guidelines on advertising to children as outlined by the Federal Trade Commission. The church withdrew the resolution when advised by Pillsbury that the company's advertising to children had been limited and was to be phased out altogether under their current advertising policy. A spokesperson for the Brethren said Pillsbury had been open and helpful and remained in continuing dialogue with the Church over the issue of Burger King advertising to children under 12.

The matter of television advertising to children has provoked concern as some of the advertising promoted highly sugared products which could lead to tooth decay, obesity, and malnutrition. Inasmuch as children viewing these advertisements could not evaluate the merits of the products promoted, the overall effect was the possibility of a change in diets of these children after many hours of such exposure to television advertising of these products. The subject has been controversial in that some assert that there is little scientific evidence to document allegations of damage to children's diets because of television advertising; further, they argued that it may not be the sugar content of the food product that should be called into question, but rather the frequency and nature of the consumption of the product. Manufacturers contend that the responsibility for a child's diet must rest with the parents.

Table 21. Protestant Sponsored or Cosponsored Shareholder Resolutions 1970 to 1979 Over the Issue of the Influence of Television on Children's Nutrition

Year	Corporation	Subject	Denomination	% Vote
1979	Pillsbury	Television advertising to children under 12 by Burger King	Church Brethren*	Withdrawn
		Total Shareholder Resolutions: 1		
		As % of Total Shareholder Resolutions Filed 1970 to 1979: 0.4%		

* and other religious groups

Stereotypical Images of Women in Advertising

This concern precipitated three shareholder resolutions on the part of Protestant churches. The rationale behind these resolutions followed this course: (a) mass communication media has a significant influence on the reinforcement of cultural attitudes; (b) advertising is a pervasive force; (c) women are presented in limited roles, such as housekeeper, mother, and sex object: therefore, the churches presenting the resolutions felt that a report of the content of current advertising would force the corporations involved to review their advertising as to how women are presented and if there are misrepresentations, then adjustments should be made. The churches argued that while women comprise some 38 percent of the workforce, they were being shown almost exclusively as housewives in commercials.[65]

Sponsoring TV Programs Containing Violence

All Protestant sponsored or cosponsored shareholder resolutions in connection with the sponsoring of television programs that contained violence were withdrawn when the companies agreed to avoid placing advertisements with broadcasting companies that permitted television programs to be aired that contained excessive and gratuitous violence.

Table 22. Protestant Sponsored or Cosponsored Shareholder Resolutions 1970 to 1979 Over the Issue of the Stereotypical Images of Women in Advertising

Year	Corporation	Subject	Denomination	% Vote
1975	P & G	Report: images of women in advertising	United Presby.	2.6%
1976	Colgate	Report: images of women in advertising	United Ch. Christ	2.08%
1977	CBS	Report: images of women in advertising	United Methodist*	Withdrawn

Total Shareholder Resolutions: 3

As a % of the Total Shareholder Resolutions Filed 1970 to 1979: 1.4%

* and other religious groups

The church had petitioned several corporations, as listed in table 23, to avoid placing advertising with those broadcasting companies that permitted programs on their stations that contained violence. It was the conviction of the churches that children do learn from violent acts and create in their minds unrealistic values. The churches did not dispute the fact that the American public evidently had a great appetite for action and adventure programming that contained a great deal of violence, but they did not want the companies in which they were part-owners to become associated with such programming.

Nuclear Weapons Production

There were three shareholder resolutions filed during 1979 on the issue of nuclear weapons production and all were subsequently withdrawn when information requested was furnished by the corporations involved. The resolutions were filed with General Electric, Monsanto, and Union Carbide and asked that a report be furnished as to the production of nuclear weapons.

These three proposals appeared in 1979, the last year covered by this study, but there is no question that the entire issue of nuclear power, in any form, will be in the forefront of the churches' concerns in the decade of the 1980s. It appears rather certain that antinuclear shareholder proposals will be filed by church groups with utilities, banks, and defense producers in the years to come.

Table 23. Protestant Sponsored or Cosponsored Shareholder Resolutions 1970 to 1979 Over the Issue of Sponsoring Television Programs Containing Violence

Year	Corporation	Subject	Denomination	% Vote
1977	McDonald's	Sponsoring programs with violence	Amer. Baptist	Withdrawn
1977	Pillsbury	Sponsoring programs with violence	Church Brethren	Withdrawn
1977	Procter & Gamble	Sponsoring programs with violence	Church Brethren	Withdrawn
1979	Sears, Roebuck	Sponsoring programs with violence	Presby. U.S.	Withdrawn

Total Shareholder Resolutions: 4

As % of Total Shareholder Resolutions Filed 1970 to 1979: 1.8%

Table 24. Protestant Sponsored or Cosponsored Shareholder Resolutions 1970 to 1979 Over the Issue of Nuclear Weapons Production

Year	Corporation	Subject	Denomination	% Vote
1979	GE	Nuclear weapons production	United Ch. Christ, United Methodist, United Presby.*	Withdrawn
1979	Monsanto	Nuclear weapons production	Church Brethren*	Withdrawn
1979	Union Carbide	Nuclear weapons production	Church Brethren, United Ch. Christ, United Presby.*	Withdrawn

Total Shareholder Resolutions: 3

As % of Total Shareholder Resolutions Filed 1970 to 1979: 1.4%

* and other religious groups

This completes the descriptions of the social concerns. The following series of tables summarize the issues involved, the denominations concerned, and the corporations targeted.

Statistical Summaries of the Issues

Table 25 lists the social issues by frequency for the ten-year period of 1970 to 1979. Protestant churches placed the heaviest emphasis on the apartheid issue in Southern Africa. More than half (53.4 percent) of these resolutions involved this issue. The next three issues, dropping precipitously from the 53.4 percent frequency for the apartheid issue, were concerns over equal employment opportunities for women and minorities (7.2 percent), the ecological effects of strip mining (6.3 percent), and questionable corporate payments overseas (6.3 percent). The balance of the issues had a frequency rating of 2.7 percent or less. Six or less shareholder resolutions out of a total of 221 filed pertained to any one issue.

Table 26 is a year-to-year listing covering the period of 1970 to 1979 and indicates an increased use of the shareholder resolutions during that period.

Table 27 lists the ten Protestant denominations, as well as the National Council of Churches, who were involved in the filing of shareholder resolutions during the years covered in this study. The listing is arranged in the order of frequency of sponsorship. The United Church of Christ was by far the most avid user of the shareholder resolution having participated in 69 resolutions. It should be recognized that the frequency of any one denomination in shareholder resolutions could be influenced by the type of investments held. A denomination obviously must currently be a beneficial owner of a corporation's stock in order to file a resolution with that company. In addition, some denominations show a lesser frequency because they waited later in the decade of the 1970s to commence more active participation. Finally, of course, particular denominations had their own reasons for deciding whether or not to participate in any one specific resolution.

Table 28 lists alphabetically the American corporations involved with Protestant-sponsored or cosponsored shareholder resolutions for the period of 1970 to 1979. The majority of the 71 corporations involved with Protestant shareholder resolutions had to cope with three resolutions or less in the ten-year span. As can be seen in the table, there was a maximum of nine shareholder resolutions filed with any one corporation. Of the total of 221 shareholder resolutions that were filed with these corporations, 66 were withdrawn after successful negotiation with the corporations concerned. This left a total of 155 which finally appeared in the proxy statements of the corporations involved.

Shareholder Resolution Activism: Year-by-Year, 1970 to 1979

The specific concerns of the Protestant churches for the period of 1970 to 1979 have been described in the previous segment on an issue-to-issue

Table 25. Protestant Sponsored or Cosponsored Shareholder Resolutions 1970 to 1979 (Social Issues Listed by Frequency)

Social Issue	In Proxy	Withdrawn	Total	%
Apartheid in Southern Africa (Republic of South Africa, Namibia and Rhodesia)	87	31	118	53.4%
Equal Employment Opportunities Labor Practices in U.S.	8	8	16	7.2%
Strip Mining/Land Reclamation	13	1	14	6.3%
Questionable Corporate Payments Overseas	9	5	14	6.3%
Infant Formula Distribution in Third World Societies	5	1	6	2.7%
Human Rights in Chile	4	2	6	2.7%
Colonialism in Southern Africa	5	0	5	2.3%
Political Contributions in the United States	4	1	5	2.3%
Redlining/Reinvestment by Banks	3	2	5	2.3%
Human Rights in the Dominican Republic	3	1	4	1.8%
Sponsorship of Television Programs Containing Violence	0	4	4	1.8%
Labor Practices in Third World Societies	2	1	3	1.4%
Employment Conditions in Korea	2	1	3	1.4%
Human Rights in Guatemala	1	2	3	1.4%
Stereotypical Images of Women in Advertising	2	1	3	1.4%
Nuclear Weapons Production	0	3	3	1.4%
Nomination of Woman to Board of Directors	1	1	2	0.9%
Foreign Military Sales	2	0	2	0.9%
Energy Crisis in the U.S.	2	0	2	0.9%
Human Rights in Philippines	1	0	1	0.4%

Table 25 (continued)

Social Issue	In Proxy	Withdrawn	Total	%
Appropriate Farm Technology for Developing Countries	1	0	1	0.4%
Impact of Television Advertising On Children's Nutrition	0	1	1	0.4%
	155	66	221	100.0%

Table 26. Protestant Shareholder Resolutions Filed 1970 to 1979, (Listed By Frequency By Year)

Year Filed	In Proxy	Withdrawn	Total	%
1970	0	0	0	0.0%
1971	4	0	4	1.8%
1972	6	2	8	3.6%
1973	11	6	17	7.7%
1974	23	14	37	16.7%
1975	10	7	17	7.7%
1976	23	7	30	13.6%
1977	24	11	35	15.8%
1978	26	6	32	14.5%
1979	28	13	41	18.6%
	155	66	221	100.0%

Table 27. Protestant Sponsored or Cosponsored Shareholder Resolutions 1970 to 1979 (Listed By Protestant Denomination With Frequency of Participation)

Protestant Denomination	In Proxy	Withdrawn	Total	%
United Church of Christ (United Ch. Christ)*	58	11	69	22.3%
United Methodist Church (United Methodist)	35	15	50	16.2%

Table 27 (continued)

Protestant Denomination	In Proxy	Withdrawn	Total	%
Episcopal Church (Episcopal)	37	6	43	13.9%
United Presbyterian Church in the U.S.A. (United Presby.)	22	13	35	11.3%
Christian Church (Christian Church)	26	8	34	11.0%
American Baptist Churches (Amer. Baptist)	17	11	28	9.2%
National Council of Churches (National Council)	11	7	18	5.8%
Reformed Church in America (Reformed Church)	11	3	14	4.5%
Church of the Brethren (Church Brethren)	2	6	8	2.6%
Lutheran Churches of America (Luth. Ch. Amer.)	4	1	5	1.6%
Presbyterian Church, U.S. (Presby. U.S.)	3	2	5	1.6%
	226	83	309	100.0%

*Denomination name shown in parenthesis is the abbreviated form used for convenience in the Tables in this study.

Table 28. American Corporations Involved with Protestant Sponsored or Cosponsored Shareholder Resolutions 1970 to 1979 (Listed Alphabetically)

American Corporation	In Proxy	Withdrawn	Total	%
American Electric Power Co.* (Amer. Electric)**	2	0	2	0.9%
American Fletcher Corp. (Amer. Fletcher)	1	1	2	0.9%
American Home Products Corp. (Amer. Home Prod.)	3	2	5	2.3%

Table 28 (continued)

American Corporation	In Proxy	Withdrawn	Total	%
AMAX, Inc. (AMAX)	6	1	7	3.2%
Bank of America National Trust & Savings Assn. (Bank America)	1	0	1	0.5%
Bethlehem Steel Corp. (Beth. Steel)	1	0	1	0.5%
Borg-Warner Corp. (Borg-Warner)	0	1	1	0.5%
Bristol-Myers Co. (Bristol-Myers)	2	0	2	0.9%
Burroughs Corporation (Burroughs)	0	3	3	1.4%
Castle & Cooke, Inc. (Castle & Cooke)	2	2	4	1.8%
Caterpillar Tractor Co. (Caterpillar)	2	0	2	0.9%
CBS Inc. (CBS)	0	2	2	0.9%
Chemical Bank (Chemical Bank)	2	0	2	0.9%
Chrysler Corp. (Chrysler)	0	1	1	0.5%
Citicorp (Citicorp)	4	0	4	1.8%
The Coca-Cola Company (Coca-Cola)	1	2	3	1.4%
Colgate-Palmolive Co. (Colgate-Palm.)	1	1	2	0.9%
Connecticut General Insurance Corp. (Conn. General)	0	1	1	0.5%
Continental Illinois National Bank & Trust Co. of Chicago (Continental Bank)	2	0	2	0.9%
Conoco, Inc. (Conoco)	4	0	4	1.8%

Table 28 (continued)

American Corporation	In Proxy	Withdrawn	Total	%
Control Data Corp. (Control Data)	2	1	3	1.4%
Crocker National Bank (Crocker Bank)	0	1	1	0.5%
Deere & Company (Deere)	1	1	2	0.9%
Eastman Kodak Co. (Kodak)	2	1	3	1.4%
Engelhard Minerals & Chemicals Corp. (Engelhard)	1	0	1	0.5%
Exxon Corporation (Exxon)	6	1	7	2.6%
First National Bank of Boston (First Boston)	2	2	4	1.8%
First National Bank of Chicago (First Chicago)	1	0	1	0.5%
Foote Mineral Company (Foote Mineral)	1	0	1	0.5%
Ford Motor Co. (Ford)	3	1	4	1.8%
General Electric Co. (GE)	7	1	8	3.7%
General Motors Corp. (GM)	4	3	7	3.2%
Getty Oil Co. (Getty)	1	1	2	0.9%
Gillette Co. (Gillette)	0	1	1	0.5%
Goodyear Tire & Rubber Company (Goodyear)	3	0	3	1.4%
Gulf Oil Corp. (Gulf)	5	0	5	2.3%
Gulf & Western Industries, Inc. (G&W)	3	2	5	2.3%
International Business Machines Corp. (IBM)	6	1	7	3.2%

Table 28 (continued)

American Corporation	In Proxy	Withdrawn	Total	%
International Harvester Co. (Int'l Harvester)	0	1	1	0.5%
International Telephone & Telegraph Corporation (ITT)	5	4	9	4.1%
Kennecott Corporation (Kennecott)	3	1	4	1.8%
Kraft Inc. (Kraft)	0	1	1	0.5%
Manufacturers Hanover Trust Co. (Mfrs. Hanover)	3	0	3	1.4%
McDonald's Corp. (McDonald's)	0	1	1	0.5%
Merck & Co., Inc. (Merck)	1	0	1	0.5%
Minnesota Mining & Mfg. Co. (3M)	2	2	4	1.8%
Mobil Oil Corp. (Mobil)	4	3	7	3.2%
Monsanto Company (Monsanto)	0	1	1	0.5%
Morgan Guaranty Trust Co. of New York (Morgan)	3	0	3	1.4%
Motorola, Inc. (Motorola)	2	0	2	0.9%
Newmont Mining Corp. (Newmont)	7	1	8	3.7%
Pfizer, Inc. (Pfizer)	0	1	1	0.5%
Phelps Dodge Corporation (Phelps Dodge)	1	0	1	0.5%
Phillips Petroleum Company (Phillips)	6	2	8	3.7%
Pillsbury Co. (Pillsbury)	0	2	2	0.9%

Table 28 (continued)

American Corporation	In Proxy	Withdrawn	Total	%
The Pittston Company (Pittston)	1	1	2	0.9%
Polaroid Corp. (Polaroid)	0	1	1	0.5%
Procter & Gamble Co. (P & G)	1	1	2	0.9%
Sears, Roebuck and Co. (Sears)	0	3	3	1.4%
Southern Co. (Southern)	4	0	4	1.8%
Sperry Corporation (Sperry)	1	0	1	0.5%
Standard Oil Co. of California (Standard Oil CA)	7	1	8	3.7%
J. P. Stevens & Co., Inc. (J. P. Stevens)	4	0	4	1.8%
The Superior Oil Company (Superior Oil)	1	0	1	0.5%
Tenneco Oil Co. (Tenneco)	2	0	2	0.9%
Texaco Inc. (Texaco)	5	1	6	2.8%
Union Carbide Corp. (Union Carbide)	6	1	7	3.2%
United States Steel Corp. (U.S. Steel)	2	0	2	0.9%
Wells Fargo & Co. (Wells Fargo)	1	0	1	0.5%
Weyerhaeuser Co. (Weyerhaeuser)	0	1	1	0.5%
Xerox Corp. (Xerox)	1	2	3	1.4%
	155	66	221	

   * Corporate names are the current official names of these companies as listed in Standard & Poor's Register of Corporations, 1981

  **Corporate name shown in parenthesis is the abbreviated form used for convenience in the tables in this study.

basis. In this segment, the concerns are outlined on a year-to-year basis. Shareholder resolutions were the most popular and effective tactic used by Protestant churches to reach corporate management. The resolutions provided high visibility for an issue that might not otherwise come before corporate management, the shareholders, and the general public. Furthermore, it was an inexpensive method in that it did not involve legal fees or long hours in filing affidavits in courts.

In filing these resolutions, the Protestant churches did anticipate defeat when the votes were taken. However, even in defeat the churches felt that the resolutions did put pressure on management to do what the resolutions sought. However, privately, many corporate executives regarded such shareholder resolutions as nuisances, especially in view of the fact that they had the potential of disrupting the annual meeting. In addition, the reports that were being requested were costly to compile. Publicly, however, the executives tended to temper their feelings.[66]

The Year 1970

The Protestant churches did not file any shareholder resolutions during the year of 1970. However, it was in 1970 that a firm foundation was laid for future shareholder social activism, especially by learning from the experiences of the "Campaign to Make GM Responsible."

Business Week reported in 1970 that the "siege of acerbic, precise, and persistent questions" from representatives of the "Campaign to Make GM Responsible" not only gave an unusual tone to the 62nd Annual Stockholders' Meeting of General Motors but "it could well have set a new style for shareholders' meetings, converting them into forums to debate questions of public policy."[67] Annual shareholders' meetings in the past were for the purpose of allowing shareholders the opportunity to question the corporations concerning company finances and business transactions, but the General Motors' meeting had little of that. According to *Business Week* "it seemed like an adversary proceeding with the Campaign GM speakers acting as prosecuting attorneys."[68]

This meeting, as well as shareholder meetings of the seventies, commenced a politicization of such meetings, converting them into forums for debating social policies. John T. Connor, Chairman of Allied Chemical Corporation and a GM board member at that time, noted the new departure and observed that up to "this time stockholders have always appreciated and observed the sanctity of the board room." He said he was "upset by the nature of the questions" and the "tone of the questions" as if the "board was a public body whose deliberations were a matter of public record."[69]

Campaign GM was a significant event, not only for the 1970 GM shareholders' meeting, but beyond, for it encouraged other activists such as the Protestant churches, to utilize the shareholder annual meetings as forums to air their views on matters concerning social issues. Campaign GM had accused GM of laxity in pollution control, car safety, and minority hiring. The Campaign had filed two shareholder resolutions: one proposal asked that three new directors be added to the GM board so that the interests of the public could be represented; the other proposal requested the formation of a public review committee that would be made up of persons from GM management, civic groups, and the United Auto Workers' Union.

Campaign GM's attempt to draw public attention to these issues was successful for more than 3,000 stockholders showed up at the annual meeting as contrasted to 724 the year before. In addition, 130 journalists were on the scene for first-hand reports.

The Protestant churches supported the efforts of Campaign GM. The United Presbyterian Church, for example, urged its members to support the resolutions and efforts were made to have representatives of the Presbyterian denomination at the stockholders' meeting to vote shares of the stock held by the church in favor of the resolutions.

When the tally of the votes were taken, only 2.7 percent of the votes were cast for the first resolution and 2.4 percent for the second resolution. However, the significance of the Campaign could not be measured by the vote count alone. *Business Week* noted that no one had expected that GM would change any of its policies because of the introduction of shareholder resolutions, but many would agree that they had an impact on GM to the extent that GM would make a "greater attempt to articulate corporation policy."[70] Chairman of the Board Roche made no jubilant claims of victory at the overwhelming vote in favor of management's position, but cautiously observed that: "We won a vote of confidence. We could lose it quickly if we do not respond to the shareholders' wishes."[71]

Campaign GM had its positive results as far as its proponents were concerned. The Campaign had (a) stimulated debate, (b) forced individuals and institutions to take a stand, (c) prompted many universities to hold campus-wide discussions, and (d) tended to reveal the very real and pervasive control of management when compared to that of the average stockholder who had very little to say about policy matters.

The Year of 1971

General Motors was asked in 1971 to "wind up all activities" in South Africa. *Business Week* reported that "this action is one example of how religious institutions are beginning to exert pressure on business through their investment portfolios."[72] The use of the annual stockholders' meeting of General Motors that year was a good example of the use of an annual meeting to discuss social issues. The Right Rev. Roger Blanchard, Executive Vice President of the Episcopal Church's Executive Council, read a letter from the Presiding Bishop of the Episcopal Church to General Motors' Chairman James Roche. The letter emphasized that the Episcopal Church was the owner of over $1 million worth of GM stock and thereby was concerned about its investment in an economy such as South Africa where the turmoil could have an adverse effect on GM's interests. Further, there was a serious moral issue in continuing to do business in South Africa. Because of the urgency of these concerns, it was felt that GM shareowners should vote on an amendment to the corporation's Certificate of Incorporation which would in effect demand that GM "wind up" activities in South Africa.

The United Presbyterian Church in the U.S.A. protested Gulf Oil's operations in the Cabinda Province of the Portuguese Colony of Angola. The effort was to publicize the colonial domination of Portugal over three South African countries, Angola, Guinea-Bissau, and Mozambique. Since February 1969, the Council for Christian Social Action of the United Church of Christ had passed social action resolutions within the denomination itself, successively stronger and more direct, condemning Portuguese colonialism; further, it spelled out the United Church's support for the liberation movement and urged members and congregations to protest Gulf's activities in Southern Africa. The Ohio Conference of the United Church of Christ did take active steps and urged members of its churches to boycott Gulf Oil products.

There were four proposals in the Gulf proxy. The proposals were to alert shareholders to Gulf's involvement in Southern Africa. Briefly the four proposals asked that Gulf: (1) set up a 14 to 20 member committee to study Gulf involvement in Southern Africa; (2) list charitable gifts to the Portuguese-run Mining Development Fund; (3) amend by-laws to enlarge the Board of Directors so that all interests were represented; and (4) no longer maintain any facilities in areas such as Mozambique and Angola.

The Episcopal Church in 1971 also filed two shareholder proposals over the issue of mining ventures. These were submitted to Kennecott Copper and American Metal Climax and concerned pollution caused in the air, water, and land by mining and smelting operations. The proposals in effect asked that these companies not enter into any new mining ventures unless provisions were made for proper rehabilitation of the land.

82 Protestant Activism in the 1970s

Further, it would be required of these companies to publish the details and costs of its pollution control efforts.

In 1971, Newsweek noted:

> Whatever the rationale, the impetus for change is real—and in the past year, it has undergone a transformation of its own. Where the corporate critics formerly concentrated on picketing, campus demonstrations, disruption of annual meetings and occasional acts of violence, they are now focusing on legal attempts to change corporate by-laws through the proxy system. . . . Apart from its publicity value, the proxy route to reform has a major advantage for the corporate dissidents: management can be forced to finance most of the battle with corporate funds.[73]

Table 29. Protestant Sponsored or Cosponsored Shareholder Resolutions In the Year of 1971

Corporation	Subject	Denomination	% Vote
GM	Cease activities in South Africa	Episcopal	2.6%
Gulf	Cease activities in Portuguese colonies in Southern Africa	United Presby.	2.2%
Kennecott	Concern over mining and smelting operations	Episcopal	2.8%
AMAX	Concern over mining and smelting operations	Episcopal	3.3%
	Total Shareholder Resolutions: 4		
	As a % of Total Shareholder Resolutions Filed 1970 to 1979: 1.8%		

The Year of 1972

The year of 1972 disclosed a trend toward more joint action on the part of Protestant churches in an attempt to influence corporate management relative to policies that impacted in some way on human rights. *Business Week,* noting this trend, declared:

> Until the late 1960s, church concern about corporate social responsibility was largely limited to vaguely worded policy statements. Some church groups refused to buy tobacco or liquor stocks. Others withheld proxies from Eastman Kodak Company, then under fire for its minority hiring policies. More recently, Presbyterian and United Church of Christ agencies launched proxy challenges against Gulf Oil Corporation and Episcopal groups against General Motors, Kennecott and Amax. The past half year has seen both sharply increased church activity and a growing trend toward joint action.[74]

The shareholder resolution filed in 1971 by the Episcopal Church with American Metal Climax had received more than 3 percent of the votes in the prior year and, therefore, was eligible to appear again in the 1972 proxy statement. In order for the same proposal to appear in 1973, it would have to receive more than 6 percent of the vote.

The issue of apartheid in Southern Africa came to the forefront as early as 1972 and remained the dominant issue for the Protestant churches throughout the 1970s. A Protestant coalition group, known as the Church Project on U.S. Investments in Southern Africa (CPOSA), was formulated in this year and was instrumental in a number of shareholder resolutions, not only in 1972, but subsequent years on the issue of apartheid in Southern Africa. The Church Project, after conducting some research on corporate investments of American corporations in Southern Africa, noted the following about business involvement in Southern Africa: (a) corporate officials have a general ignorance of the real conditions of non-whites in South Africa; (b) American companies are no more enlightened about employment practices in Southern Africa than companies from other countries; (c) as a consequence, most American companies did not give equal pay for equal work; and (d) there were no clear guidelines for American business relative to race relations in Southern Africa. While CPOSA guided efforts with regard to the filing of shareholder resolutions over the apartheid concern, it was the various agencies of the Protestant churches who were the beneficial owners of the stock that did the actual filing. As shown in table 30, shareholder resolutions filed with General Motors and Goodyear asked for a report of their operations in South Africa. The resolution filed with Gulf Oil asked for disclosure concerning operations in Angola. IBM and Mobil Oil, who had received similar proposals, agreed to publish most of the information called for and the resolutions were withdrawn.

The Episcopal Churchmen for South Africa (ECSA) submitted proposals to American Metal Climax and Newmont Mining over the Namibia apartheid concern. The resolutions requested that these companies: (a) suspend all operations in Namibia until negotiations were completed and the country placed under temporary United Nations control; (b) that the net profits from the Tsumeb mining operation be placed in an escrow account until a political settlement had been reached; and (c) that full disclosure be provided of corporate activity and native employment by these companies. The ECSA, while not an official agency of the Episcopal Church, was made up of 1,500 clergymen and lay people from that church. This group had purchased three shares of American Metal Climax and Newmont Mining stock and filed the shareholder resolutions when the group became concerned about apartheid in Namibia.

Business Week in 1972, recognizing the activism of the churches, commented:

> What is happening here? The groups involved would answer that they are finally practicing what they preach. Within the past few years, church groups of many denominations have begun consciously to apply their religious moral standards to a long list of issues affecting a multitude of companies. The companies are vulnerable not only because of the huge volume of church investments—an estimated $22 billion in securities held by the country's 360,000 Protestant churches alone—but because of the damaging publicity.[75]

Table 30. Protestant Sponsored or Cosponsored Shareholder Resolutions In the Year of 1972

Corporation	Subject	Denomination	% Vote
AMAX	Concern over mining and smelting operations	Episcopal	2.9%
AMAX	Cease operations in Namibia	Episcopal ECSA*	2.93%
GM	Report of operations in So. Africa	Episcopal	2.34%
Goodyear	Report of operations in So. Africa	Amer. Baptist	1.38%
Gulf	Report of operations in Angola	United Ch. Christ	2.93%
Newmont	Cease operations in Namibia	Episcopal ESCA*	1.40%
IBM	Report of operations in So. Africa	Episcopal	Withdrawn
Mobil	Report of operations in So. Africa	United Ch. Christ	Withdrawn

Total Shareholder Resolutions: 8

As % of Total Shareholder Resolutions Filed 1970 to 1979: 3.6%

* Episcopal Churchmen for South Africa

The Year of 1973

"Activists, better organized, plan even more activity at Annual Meetings," notes *Industry Week* in 1973.[76] *Business Week* echoed a similar view in an article entitled "Activists Step Up Their Annual Attacks" discerning that: "To challengers, winning isn't everything. Even though proxy proposals dealing with social responsibility draw only nominal support, the activists still consider them an effective tool to get their messages across."[77]

In 1973 a number of companies, via shareholder proposals, were asked to take specific action which the churches felt would weaken the economic base of Southern African governments and this, in turn, would work toward the alleviation of the oppressive apartheid practices. Specifically, corporations were asked to:

Corporation	Action
AMAX	Wind up operations in Namibia
Caterpillar	Disclose South African operations
Conoco	Wind up exploration operations in Namibia
Citicorp	Disclose South African operations
GE	Disclose South African operations
IBM	Disclose South African operations
Mobil	Establish equal opportunity as a general principle worldwide, with special reference to South Africa
Newmont	Wind up operations in Namibia, and establish equal opportunity as a general principle worldwide, with special reference to Namibia
Phillips	Wind up exploration operations in Namibia

As shown in table 31 almost all of the shareholder resolutions involved apartheid in Southern Africa. Disclosure resolutions filed with six corporations were withdrawn when the corporations agreed to furnish the information requested. Three of the proposals sent to shareholders for vote received more than 3 percent of the vote and, therefore, were eligible to be repeated in the 1974 proxy statements.

The Year of 1974

Business Week, in an article entitled "Proxy Statements Feel the Watergate Ripples," tells of increasing demands on corporations:

> Plenty of this year's issues have been raised before—demands that companies tell more about their operations in South Africa or their military business. But the hottest issues this spring are illegal political giving and equal employment opportunities as well as energy and the environment.[78]

The shareholder resolutions proposed by Protestant churches in 1974 concentrated heavily on the apartheid situation in Southern Africa. As can be seen in table 32 some ten resolutions were filed in connection with the

Table 31. Protestant Sponsored or Cosponsored Shareholder Resolutions In the Year of 1973

Corporation	Subject	Denomination	% Vote
AMAX	Wind up operations in Namibia	Episcopal ECSA*	2.1%
AMAX	Environmental Protection	Episcopal	2.9%
Caterpillar	Report on operations in South Africa	United Methodist	8.6%
Citicorp	Report on operations in South Africa	Amer. Baptist	1.03%
Conoco	Wind up operations in Namibia	United Ch. Christ	5.4%
GE	Report on operations in South Africa	United Presby.	2.3%
IBM	Report on operations in South Africa	Episcopal	2.6%
Mobil	Worldwide equal employment	United Ch. Christ	1.8%
Newmont	Wind up operations in Namibia	Episcopal ECSA*	1.4%
Newmont	Worldwide equal employment	United Ch. Christ	0.3%
Phillips	Wind up operations in Namibia	Episcopal	4.4%
Burroughs	Report on operations in South Africa	United Presby.	Withdrawn
Kodak	Report on operations in South Africa	United Methodist	Withdrawn
ITT	Report on operations in South Africa	United Presby.	Withdrawn
3M	Report on operations in South Africa	National Council	Withdrawn
Texaco	Report on operations in South Africa	United Methodist	Withdrawn
Xerox	Report on operations in South Africa	Amer. Baptist	Withdrawn

Total Shareholder Resolutions: 17

As % of Total Shareholder Resolutions Filed 1970 to 1979: 7.7%

* Episcopal Churchmen for South Africa

apartheid concern. The issue of colonialism in the Portuguese colonies of Angola, Guinea-Bissau, and Mozambique reappeared. New concerns emerged: strip mining, equal employment, political contributions, the energy crisis, and human rights concerns in the Philippines.

A church coalition called the Church Project on Equal Employment Opportunity was established and guided the filing of resolutions with a number of corporations over the issue of equal opportunities for women and minorities. Five corporations agreed to the request contained in the proposals and furnished information that was considered satisfactory to the churches and the proposals were withdrawn.

Resolutions were also sponsored or cosponsored over the issue of strip mining in the Northern Plains. Concern was expressed over the environmentally destructive effects of this mining method with the concomitant concern over the social, economic, and ecological effects of such mining processes.

Political contributions emerged as a concern. A proposal was filed with Phillips Petroleum asking that the company implement effective internal procedures to assure that illegal political contributions could not again be made in the future.

Ford Motor received a resolution in connection with its operations in the Philippines. The resolution was supported with this statement:

> In view of growing distrust of giant corporations, both in the United States and the Third World, it is important that the Company avoid even the appearance of collusion with any government that overthrows or prevents majority rule. Since the Philippines are often called a demonstration of the viability of American-style democracy in the Asian setting, U.S. corporations owe their shareholders and the public a full report on company relations with the Marcos' martial-law government, and company contributions to the economic and social welfare of the Filipino masses. Since the Filipino people are not at present free to express their own judgment on the conditions established by their government to create "an attractive investment environment," it is socially necessary for shareholders to know what those conditions are and to appraise them.[79]

The energy crisis of 1974 prompted a shareholder resolution which was filed with Gulf which requested that Gulf disclose data so that shareholders and the general public could get a better understanding of such a "crisis" as "in recent months many have claimed that the crude oil shortage is a hoax."[80]

In one of the few instances where management endorsed the churches' proposal, the 3M Company recommended that stockholders vote yes on the proposal for prohibitions on political contributions.

Table 32. Protestant Sponsored or Cosponsored Shareholder Resolutions In the Year of 1974

Corporation	Subject	Denomination	% Vote
AMAX	Strip mining in No. Plains	United Ch. Christ	4.01%
Beth. Steel	Withdraw from Mozambique	United Methodist	0.005%
Conoco	Strip mining in No. Plains	United Ch. Christ	4.09%
Conoco	Withdraw from Namibia	United Ch. Christ	7.26%
Engelhard	Report on operations So. Africa	Reformed Church	0.92%
Exxon	Report on energy crisis	Amer. Baptist	2.62%
Exxon	Withdraw from Guinea-Bissau	Amer. Baptist, Episcopal, National Council United Ch. Christ, United Presby.	2.15%
Exxon	Strip mining in No. Plains	United Ch. Christ	2.69%
Foote Minerals	Refrain investing in So. Africa	United Ch. Christ	2.5%
Ford	Report on operations Philippines	National Council, United Ch. Christ	1.56%
GE	Report on equal employment	Episcopal	2.3%
GE	Est. review committe So. Africa	United Presby.	2.4%
Getty	Withdraw from Namibia	Amer. Baptist	1.36%
Gulf	Report on energy crisis	United Ch. Christ	2.2%
Gulf	Report on operations in Angola	United Ch. Christ	1.6%
IBM	Report on equal employment	National Council	2.26%
IBM	Report on operations So. Africa	United Presby.	2.31%
3M	Report on political contributions	Episcopal	97.7%
Newmont	Report on employment policies in South Africa	United Ch. Christ	3.56%
Phillips	Withdraw from Namibia	Episcopal	4.9%
Phillips	Political contributions	Episcopal	7.0%
Standard Oil CA	Withdraw from Namibia	United Methodist	4.3%
Union Carbide	Report on operations So. Africa	United Presby.	2.78%
Burroughs	Report on operations So. Africa	United Presby.	Withdrawn

Table 32 (continued)

Corporation	Subject	Denomination	% Vote
Chrysler	Report on operations So. Africa	United Presby.	Withdrawn
Colgate-Palm.	Report on operations So. Africa	Reformed Church	Withdrawn
Deere	Report on operations So. Africa	United Methodist	Withdrawn
GM	Report on equal employment	Amer. Baptist	Withdrawn
Gillette	Report on operations So. Africa	Episcopal	Withdrawn
Int'l Harvester	Report on operations So. Africa	National Council	Withdrawn
ITT	Report on activities in Chile	Christian Church	Withdrawn
Kraft	Report on equal employment	United Presby.	Withdrawn
Pfizer	Report on operations So. Africa	Christian Church	Withdrawn
Polaroid	Report on equal employment	Amer. Baptist	Withdrawn
Sears, Roebuck	Report on equal employment	United Methodist	Withdrawn
Weyerhaeuser	Report on operations So. Africa	Amer. Baptist	Withdrawn
Xerox	Report on equal employment	United Methodist	Withdrawn

Total Shareholder Resolutions: 37

As % of Total Shareholder Resolutions Filed 1970 to 1979: 16.7%

The Year of 1975

Dun's Review recognized the presence of the church at annual shareholder meetings:

> The church groups, militant leaders of the army of dissent in the past two years, are still tightly organized and still active. Particularly at this time of the year, there is a buzz of activity at the Interfaith Center on Corporate Responsibility, the command post on Manhattan's Riverside Drive where the efforts of more than a dozen Protestant denominations and an increasing number of Catholic orders are coordinated. As one churchman puts it: "Certainly business knows that the church is there, looking over its massive international shoulders."[81]

The year of 1975 for Protestant churches revealed seven resolutions successfully negotiated as contrasted to the ten resolutions that could not be resolved and appeared in corporate proxy statements for shareholder vote. Table 33 shows that the issue of apartheid in Southern Africa continued as the number one effort of the Protestant churches. Other concerns continued, such as strip mining, political contributions, and equal employment opportunities for women and minorities. A new item was the concern over employment practices in Korea.

Another weapon was added to the arsenal of shareholder resolutions relative to the apartheid situation in Southern Africa. IBM was requested to cease furnishing its computers to the government of the Republic of South Africa. The rationale for this action was:

> Computers themselves are morally neutral and may be used for good or ill. In South Africa, the black majority is controlled and oppressed by a white minority. Unfortunately, computers have become part of the equipment of oppression. The United States Government has placed an embargo against arms shipments to South Africa. While not under the literal terms of the embargo, we believe computers sold to the South African Government ostensibly for peaceful purposes are of real assistance militarily and strategically. Thus, the spirit of this arms embargo is compromised. Furthermore, computers markedly increase that government's ability to control its citizens, infringe on their privacy, and implement its policy of white supremacy. For instance, computers are used to control where blacks can live and travel.[82]

The United Church of Christ sought to restrict the importation of coal from South Africa by the Southern Company.

The operations of Motorola in Korea became a Protestant concern when reports were received that certain labor practices were questionable. Motorola was asked to furnish a special report on working conditions in their plant in Korea.

Xerox was asked to take steps to increase the representation of women in sales jobs as it had done for minorities.

The Phillips resolution demanded that "any officer or employee of the company who fails to follow a standard of strict compliance with all federal and state political contribution laws shall be subject to appropriate disciplinary action, including discharge from employment."[83]

The issue of the images of women in advertising emerged for Protestant churches in 1975 with the United Presbyterian Church filing a shareholder resolution with Procter & Gamble. The resolution, however, was successfully negotiated and withdrawn. The resolution had asked for a summarization of the roles of both men and women who appeared in the company's 200 most frequently used television spots and 100 most frequently placed magazine advertisements.

The Year of 1976

The year 1976 showed a dramatic increase in shareholder resolutions filed by Protestant churches when contrasted with 1975. Of those resolutions

Table 33. Protestant Sponsored or Cosponsored Shareholder Resolutions In the Year of 1975

Corporation	Subject	Denomination	% Vote
Amer. Electric	Report on strip mining Appalachia	United Methodist*	4.5%
G & W	Report on operations in the Dominican Republic	National Council	4.5%
IBM	No computer sales to the South African Government	Amer. Baptist, Christian Church, Episcopal, National Council, Reformed Church, United Ch. Christ, United Methodist*	1.64%
Motorola	Report on employment practices in plant in Korea	United Ch. Christ	3.8%
P & G	Report on images of women in advertising	United Presby.	2.6%
Phillips	Report on past political contributions	Episcopal	4.7%
Phillips	Dismiss any employee violating Election Laws	Episcopal	7.0%
Southern Co.	Prohibit the importation of coal from South Africa	United Ch. Christ	3.28%
Union Carbide	Establish Review Committee on South African operations	Christian Church*	2.67%
Xerox	Report on equal employment opportunities in Sales Dept.	United Methodist	2.3%
Control Data	Report on operations in South Korea	United Ch. Christ	Withdrawn
Getty	Withdraw from Namibia	Amer. Baptist	Withdrawn
ITT	Report on operations in South Africa	United Presby.	Withdrawn
Newmont	Report on Namibia operations	United Ch. Christ	Withdrawn
Phillips	Review Committee for Namibia	Amer. Baptist, Episcopal, National Council, Reformed Church	Withdrawn

Table 33 (continued)

Corporation	Subject	Denomination	% Vote
Sears, Roebuck	Report on equal employment	United Methodist	Withdrawn
Standard Oil CA	Withdraw from Namibia	United Methodist	Withdrawn

Total Shareholder Resolutions: 17

As % of Total Shareholder Resolutions Filed 1970 to 1979: 7.7%

* and other religious groups

submitted to shareholders for vote, eight were filed in connection with the issue of apartheid in Southern Africa, four relative to strip mining in the Appalachian and Cheyenne Tribe areas, five relative to international political contributions and one each relating to infant formula distribution, images of women in advertising, appropriate farm technology, human rights in Chile, and employment practices in Korea. There were a number of resolutions successfully negotiated and withdrawn and these primarily had to do with foreign political contributions' reports.

Another approach to ameliorating the apartheid situation in Southern Africa was proposed to Union Carbide and this was a request that they no longer import chrome ore from Rhodesia "until such time as governmental power is transferred to the African majority and international economic sanctions against Rhodesia have been lifted."[84]

International political contributions were a major concern in 1976. Requests for disclosures on foreign political contributions were presented to a number of corporations. These disclosures asked for a "full written report concerning the political contributions, if any," that "were made with respect to nations outside of the United States, by or on behalf of the corporation."[85] This request was supported with the statement that "the image of our Corporation and the entire American business community has been harmed by these practices by several American corporations."[86]

Gulf & Western became a target in 1976 and was asked for a report of its operations in the Dominican Republic because of a concern over low wages and malnutrition in that area.

General Motors was asked to refrain from expansion in Chile because of that government's infringement on human rights. Dr. Howard Schomer, World Issues Secretary of the United Church of Christ, commented on the resolution: "The churches do not ask General Motors to seek to redress the whole deplorable political situation of a society. . . . The proposal only asks General Motors to do that which it, as a progressive employer, should and can do in defense of its own workers."[87]

Colgate-Palmolive was asked by the United Church of Christ to "publish a special report which will carefully examine the images of women in the Corporation's advertising."[88] It was felt that such a report would cause the company to review their advertising as it involved the portrayal of women and would cause them to seek ways to help portray women in a broader range of roles.

Infant formula and the manner of its distribution in Third World countries was the subject of the resolution filed with Bristol-Myers.[89]

A unique resolution was filed with Deere & Company asking that the company create farm implements and machinery appropriate for use on small farms in developing countries. This concern emerged from the determination that large farm implements "can have a detrimental effect on agricultural production in developing countries where the average size farm is often under ten acres."[90]

Table 34. Protestant Sponsored or Cosponsored Shareholder Resolutions In the Year of 1976

Corporation	Subject	Denomination	% Vote
Amer. Electric	Report on strip mining in Appalachia	United Presby.*	9.01%
Bristol-Myers	Report on distribution of infant formula Third World countries	United Ch. Christ*	3.4%
Colgate-Palm.	Report on the images of women in advertising	United Ch. Christ*	2.08%
Conoco	Report on strip mining in the Cheyenne Indian reservation	Amer. Baptist*	2.76%
Deere	Report on possibilities of farm implements for small farms	Amer. Baptist	1.62%
Exxon	Report and also request to establish policy of no political contributions overseas	Christian Church*	2.97%
GM	No expansion in Chile	Christian Church, United Ch. Christ, United Methodist	2.01%
G&W	Reports on operations in the Dominican Republic	National Council	6.01%
Goodyear	Report on working conditions in plant in South Africa	United Methodist*	2.36%

Table 34 (continued)

Corporation	Subject	Denomination	% Vote
Gulf	Report and also request to establish policy of no political contributions overseas	United Ch. Christ*	2.36%
IBM	Ban sales of computers to South Africa	Christian Church, Episcopal, National Council, Reformed Church, United Methodist*	2.21%
ITT	Report and also request to establish policy of no political contributions overseas	Christian Church*	6.92%
Kennecott	No further investments in South Africa	Christian Church, Episcopal*	3.62%
Merck	Report on and the establishing of policy of no overseas political contributions	United Ch. Christ	1.74%
Motorola	Report on employment practices in plant in Korea	Reformed Church, United Ch. Christ	0.9%
Pittston	Report on strip mining in Appalachia	Amer. Baptist*	6.51%
Southern Co.	No importing of coal from South Africa	United Ch. Christ	4.19%
Standard Oil CA	Report on strip mining in Cheyenne Indian Reservation	United Ch. Christ	2.78%
Standard Oil CA	No expansion of operations in South Africa	United Methodist	2.11%
Standard Oil CA	Report on and the establishing of policy of no overseas political contributions	United Ch. Christ	2.94%
Texaco	No expansion in South Africa	United Methodist*	2.28%
Union Carbide	No importing of chrome ore from Rhodesia	United Ch. Christ	1.99%
Amer. Home Prod.	Infant formula distribution	United Presby., United Methodist*	Withdrawn
Amer. Home Prod.	Report on and the establishing policy of no overseas political contributions	United Methodist	Withdrawn

Table 34 (continued)

Corporation	Subject	Denomination	% Vote
Exxon	Report on and the establishing policy of no overseas political contributions	Christian Church	Withdrawn
Ford	Report on and the establishing policy of no overseas political contributions	United Ch. Christ	Withdrawn
ITT	Report on sales to South Africa	Christian Church*	Withdrawn
Mobil	No overseas political contrib.	United Ch. Christ*	Withdrawn
Phillips	Political contributions in U.S.	Episcopal*	Withdrawn

Total Shareholder Resolutions: 30
As % of Total Shareholder Resolutions Filed 1970 to 1979: 13.6%

* and other religious groups

The Year of 1977

This was the first year that a Protestant denomination, namely the United Methodist Church, utilized shareholder resolutions in connection with labor practices of the J.P. Stevens Company. Stevens had over the years resisted unionization and was in violation of the law in many cases over its labor policies. The United Methodist resolution asserted: "We believe Stevens' labor practices violate mainstream American business ethics and the resulting isolation endangers the company."[91] The issue of J. P. Stevens's labor practices are covered in detail in the Boycott Section of this study.

For the first time for a Protestant denomination, the Christian Church petitioned a bank via a shareholder resolution to nominate a qualified woman to serve on the Board of Directors.

Concern was also expressed over foreign military sales. General Electric was asked to provide a full written report on military sales between 1970 to 1976. The Protestant churches involved in this shareholder resolution asserted that "the international arms trade is out of control. The easy availability of virtually any type of military equipment for the right price is making the world a less secure place in which to live."[92]

The resolution filed with Gulf & Western by the National Council of Churches over conditions in the Dominican Republic plant was withdrawn. After more than two years of dialogue, the National Council was able to prevail upon Gulf & Western to furnish a report on the wages and working conditions of the sugar cane cutters in that country. Table 35 shows that there were a number of other successful negotiations and the resolutions were withdrawn.

Table 35. Protestant Sponsored or Cosponsored Shareholder Resolutions In the Year of 1977

Corporation	Subject	Denomination	% Vote
Amer. Fletcher	Nomination of qualified woman	Christian Church	9.6%
Amer. Home	Infant formula distribution	Reformed Church, United Methodist, United Presby.*	2.92%
Castle & Cooke	Report on labor practices in Third World countries	Christian Church, United Ch. Christ	3.24%
Citicorp	No further loans to South Africa	Luth. Ch. Amer., Presbyterian U.S., United Methodist, United Presby.*	2.2%
Exxon	Report on coal mining	United Presby.*	98.7%
Ford	Withdraw from South Africa	Amer. Baptist, Christian Church, United Presby.	1.81%
GE	Report on foreign military sales	United Ch. Christ, United Methodist*	2.4%
GE	Withdraw from South Africa	Reformed Church, United Methodist	1.8%
Goodyear	Withdraw from South Africa	United Methodist	1.95%
ITT	Report on overseas political contributions	Christian Church*	3.75%
ITT	Report on activities in Chile	Christian Church*	3.6%
Kennecott	No expansion in South Africa	Episcopal*	4.83%
Mfrs. Hanover	No further loans to So. Africa	Episcopal, United Ch. Christ*	3.3%
Mobil	No sale of oil to Rhodesia	United Ch. Christ	1.75%
Morgan	No further loans to So. Africa	Episcopal	2.81%

Table 35 (continued)

Corporation	Subject	Denomination	% Vote
Newmont	Report on employment practices in South Africa	United Ch. Christ	3.36%
Phelps Dodge	No expansion in South Africa	Reformed Church*	2.6%
Southern Co.	No importation of coal from South Africa	United Ch. Christ	5.9%
Standard Oil CA	Withdraw from South Africa	Christian Church, United Methodist	2.97%
Stevens	Report on equal employment	United Methodist*	5.59%
Stevens	Report on labor policies	United Methodist*	5.83%
Tenneco	No international political contributions	United Ch. Christ	5.22%
Texaco	Withdraw from South Africa	Reformed Church, Christian Church, United Methodist*	3.67%
Union Carbide	No expansion in South Africa	Amer. Baptist*	3.35%
AMAX	Report on Namibia operations	Episcopal	Withdrawn
CBS	Report on images of women and minorities in television	United Methodist*	Withdrawn
Coca-Cola	Report on labor practices in Guatemala	United Presby.	Withdrawn
GM	Withdraw from South Africa	Amer. Baptist, Reformed Church, Christian Church*	Withdrawn
GM	Labor practices in Chile	Christian Church, United Methodist*	Withdrawn
G&W	Report on operations in the Dominican Republic	National Council	Withdrawn
G&W	Report on mining in South Africa	National Council	Withdrawn
McDonald	Sponsoring programs containing violence on television	Amer. Baptist*	Withdrawn
Pillsbury	Sponsoring programs containing violence on television	Church Brethren	Withdrawn
Pittston	Report on strip mining in Appalachia	Amer. Baptist*	Withdrawn

Table 35 (continued)

Corporation	Subject	Denomination	% Vote
Procter & Gamble	Sponsoring programs containing violence on television	Church Brethren	Withdrawn
Total Shareholder Resolutions: 35			
As % of Total Shareholder Resolutions Filed 1970 to 1979: 15.8%			

* and other religious groups

The Year of 1978

Familiar items again appeared in the year of 1978: infant formula distribution practices, labor policies in developing countries, banning of loans to South Africa, foreign military sales, no shipments of computers to governments using repressive force, political contributions and questionable payments.

Ten of the shareholder resolutions appearing in 1978 shown in table 36 were carried over and repeated from 1977. They were eligible for refiling because they had received more than 3 percent of the vote in 1977. The Securities and Exchange Commission allows the repetition of the same resolution on the following year if the shareholder vote is more than 3 percent of the proposal.

One new and interesting item was the attempt via shareholder resolutions to cause banks to become involved in revitalizing urban areas by setting up special committees for review of loan practices in blighted areas and for proposing ideas to rejuvenate those areas. Chemical New York was asked to commit itself, for example, "to the revitalization of New York neighborhoods by establishing a Community Reinvestment Review Committee."[93] The request was supported by this statement:

> New York's neighborhoods, like those of other major United States cities suffer severe housing deterioration. Lack of sufficient investment in existing neighborhoods is increasingly identified as a principal cause of decay. . . . We believe that Chemical has a responsibility to its city depositors and to all New York's citizens who bear the severe human and economic costs of disinvestment and should make a public commitment to the rehabilitation and preservation of existing housing and commercial facilities in mature neighborhoods.[94]

This concern, as expressed by the United Methodist Church, was undergirded by the feeling that it was not sufficient for a bank to state that it does not redline, but rather the bank should adopt an affirmative stance in "examining its own investment patterns and developing new strategies of urban development."[95]

With regard to defeating the apartheid system in South Africa, Kodak was asked not to make shipment of photographic equipment to that country. Mobil, Standard Oil, and Texaco were asked to reduce their allocations of oil so that it would not indirectly flow into Rhodesia.

Table 36. Protestant Sponsored or Cosponsored Shareholder Resolutions In the Year of 1978

Corporation	Subject	Denomination	% Vote
Amer. Home	Establish Infant Formula Review Committee	United Methodist, United Presby.*	5.29%
Castle & Cooke	Report on labor practices in developing countries	Christian Church, United Ch. Christ*	2.89%
Chemical Bank	Policy to revitalize New York neighborhoods	United Methodist	2.08%
Citicorp	Report on loans to South Africa	Luth. Ch. Amer., Presbyterian U.S., United Ch. Christ, United Methodist*	4.58%
Continental Bank	Report on loans to So. Africa	United Presby.	8.2%
Control Data	Report on sales to So. Africa	United Presby.	4.58%
Kodak	Policy of no sales of photographic equipment to the So. African government	Amer. Baptist, Episcopal, United Methodist, United Presby.*	4.75%
First Boston	No new loans to So. Africa	Luth. Ch. Amer., United Ch. Christ, United Methodist	8.17%
GE	Report on equal employment	Episcopal*	1.77%
GE	No sales of military equipment to countries that violate human rights	National Council, United Ch. Christ*	1.8%
IBM	No computer sales to governments that might use for repressive purposes	National Council, Christian Church, United Ch. Christ*	2.12%
ITT	Report on political contributions and questionable payments in Chile	Christian Church*	3.7%

Table 36 (continued)

Corporation	Subject	Denomination	% Vote
Mfrs. Hanover	No further loans to So. Africa	Episcopal, Reformed Church, United Ch. Christ*	5.51%
3 M	Withdraw from South Africa	National Council*	1.9%
Mobil	No direct or indirect sales of oil to Rhodesia	United Ch. Christ*	3.25%
Morgan	Report on loans to South Africa	Episcopal*	4.38%
Newmont	Report on labor practices in Namibia	United Ch. Christ*	3.15%
Southern Co.	No importation of coal from South Africa	Christian Church*	5.4%
Standard Oil CA	No direct or indirect sales of oil to Rhodesia	Christian Church, United Ch. Christ, United Methodist	4.15%
Stevens	Report on equal employment	United Methodist*	3.92%
Stevens	Report on labor policies	United Methodist*	5.44%
Tenneco	Report on foreign political contributions	Christian Church, United Ch. Christ	4.55%
Texaco	Report on Caltex's oil sales Rhodesia	Christian Church, United Ch. Christ*	2.97%
Texaco	Withdraw from South Africa	Christian Church, United Methodist, United Presby.*	2.19%
Union Carbide	No expansion in South Africa	United Ch. Christ*	5.08%
U.S. Steel	No expansion in South Africa	Episcopal	5.69%
Amer. Fletcher	Nomination of woman to the Board of Directors	Christian Church	Withdrawn
Coca-Cola	Report on labor practices in Guatemala	United Presby.	Withdrawn
Crocker Bank	No loans to South Africa	United Presby.	Withdrawn
First Boston	Community reinvestment	United Methodist	Withdrawn

Table 36 (continued)

Corporation	Subject	Denomination	% Vote
Kennecott	Report on operations in South Africa	Episcopal*	Withdrawn
Mobil	Report on equal employment at Montgomery Ward	United Ch. Christ*	Withdrawn
	Total Shareholder Resolutions: 32		
	As % of Total Shareholder Resolutions Filed 1970 to 1979: 14.5%		

* and other religious groups

The Year of 1979

South Africa, again in the year of 1979, was the subject of more shareholder resolutions than any other single concern. The resolutions dealt with the now already familiar theme of no new or renewed loans to South Africa, the establishment of a South African Review Committee relative to sales to South Africa, ban on computer and other product sales to the South African government, and withdrawal or no further expansion of operations in that country.

Eleven of the shareholder resolutions appearing in 1979 were repeats of those that appeared in the proxy statements in the year of 1978. They had received more than 3 percent of the shareholder votes and were eligible to appear in the 1979 proxies. Twelve shareholder resolutions were successfully negotiated and were withdrawn.

Two new items to appear in the shareholder resolution arena for Protestant churches were concerns over nuclear weapons production and the growing problem of insurance availability for homeowners in certain urban neighborhoods.

Three Protestant churches were involved with the filing of a shareholder resolution with General Electric over the issue of nuclear weapons production. The churches argued that a continued production of nuclear weapons would increase the likelihood of a global nuclear confrontation. There are also health hazards to those persons who might be located nearby the manufacturing plants. The resolution asked that a report be furnished concerning the nuclear weapons production so that General Electric shareholders might be alerted to the moral implications of such production. The resolution was successfully negotiated and the proposal withdrawn.

The Methodist Church had filed a resolution with Connecticut General Insurance Company which was directed primarily against its subsidiary the Aetna Insurance Company. There was concern over reports of cancellations and refusals to issue loans in certain urban neighborhoods whose population was primarily minorities. The church felt that this practice of insurance redlining was emerging from an industry-wide practice of underwriting which, though neutral on the surface, was in fact discriminatory against the old urban, minority-inhabited communities. The resolution was successfully negotiated and withdrawn.

Table 37. Protestant Sponsored or Cosponsored Shareholder Resolutions In the Year of 1979

Corporation	Subject	Denomination	% Vote
Amer. Home	Establish Infant Formula Review Commitee	Church Brethren, United Methodist, United Presby.*	3.2%
Bank America	No new or renewed loans to South Africa	United Ch. Christ*	8.4%
Bristol-Myers	Establish policy for distribution of infant formula in developing countries	United Ch. Christ*	3.9%
Caterpillar	Establish South African Review Committee re sales to South Africa	Amer. Baptist, Episcopal, Christian Church*	3.5%
Chemical Bank	Policy to revitalize New York neighborhoods	United Methodist	5.3%
Citicorp	Report on loans to South Africa	Presbyterian U.S., United Ch. Christ*	4.4%
Coca-Cola	Establish labor policy, with special reference to Guatemala	United Presby.*	1.7%
Continental Bank	Report on loans to South Africa	United Ch. Christ*	4.2%
Control Data	No sale of computers to South Africa	United Presby.	3.3%
Kodak	No sale of photographic products to So. African government	Amer. Baptist, Episcopal, United Ch. Christ*	3.1%
Exxon	No expansion in South Africa	Episcopal, Christian Church*	4.9%
First Boston	Establish Advisory Committee for community reinvestment	United Methodist	5.4%

Table 37 (continued)

Corporation	Subject	Denomination	% Vote
First Chicago	Report on loans to So. Africa	Luth. Ch. Amer.*	2.2%
Ford	No sales to South African government	United Ch. Christ, United Presby.*	2.1%
GM	No sales to South African government	Christian Church, United Ch. Christ, United Methodist, United Presby.	2.98%
G&W	Report on operations in the Dominican Republic	National Council	3.3%
ITT	Policy that Board of Directors' member be terminated if corporate funds used for political purposes	Christian Church	2.5%
Mfrs. Hanover	Report on loans to South Africa	Episcopal, Reformed Church, United Ch. Christ	3.7%
Mobil	No direct or indirect sales to Rhodesia	United Ch. Christ	1.9%
Morgan	Report on loans to So. Africa	Episcopal*	2.8%
Phillips	Withdraw from South Africa	Amer. Baptist, Episcopal, Reformed Church	5.6%
Sperry Rand	No sale of computers to South African government	United Methodist*	3.3%
Standard Oil CA	No direct or indirect sales to Rhodesia	Amer. Baptist, United Ch. Christ	1.9%
Superior Oil	No additional investments in Chile	Amer. Baptist Luth Ch. Amer.	2.9%
Texaco	No direct or indirect sales to Rhodesia	United Ch. Christ	2.7%
Union Carbide	Withdraw from South Africa	Church Brethren*	3.8%
U. S. Steel	No expansion in South Africa	Episcopal	5.7%
Wells Fargo	No loans to South Africa	United Methodist	7.3%
Borg-Warner	No expansion in South Africa	United Ch. Christ*	Withdrawn
Burroughs	No sales to South Africa	National Council*	Withdrawn

Table 37 (continued)

Corporation	Subject	Denomination	% Vote
Castle & Cooke	Establish labor code worldwide	Christian Church*	Withdrawn
Castle & Cooke	Report on payments to overseas governments	United Ch. Christ	Withdrawn
CBS	Report on images of women in advertising	United Methodist*	Withdrawn
Conn. General	Report on possible insurance redlining by Aetna	United Methodist	Withdrawn
First Boston	No loans to South Africa	Luth. Ch. Amer., Amer. Baptist, United Ch. Christ*	Withdrawn
GE	Report on nuclear weapons production	United Ch. Christ, United Methodist, United Presby.*	Withdrawn
Monsanto	Report on nuclear weapons	Church Brethren, Presbyterian U.S.*	Withdrawn
Pillsbury	Adopt guideline in television advertising of heavily sugared products to children	Church Brethren*	Withdrawn
3M	Report on operations in South Africa	Amer. Baptist, National Council*	Withdrawn
Union Carbide	Nuclear weapons production	Church Brethren, United Ch. Christ, United Presby.*	Withdrawn
Sears	Sponsoring TV programs containing violence	Church Brethren Presby. U.S.	Withdrawn

Total Shareholder Resolutions: 41

As % of Total Shareholder Resolutions Filed 1970 to 1979: 18.6%

* and other religious groups

Boycotts

The decision to engage in a consumer boycott or to recommend a boycott to agencies, judicatories and members of the United Presbyterian Church is a serious matter and always needs thoughtful consideration. Directing consumer activity *away from* a particular product, company, or establishment affects the livelihood of persons who produce, own, work in or are otherwise economically dependent on the activity. While it is true that most consumer boycotts result in directing the activity to another product, company or establishment so that the *overall* economic activity remains constant, Christians cannot ignore the *particular* hurt that may come to particular individuals."[96]

So said the United Presbyterian Church at its General Assembly in 1979. The General Assembly recognized that "given the potential dislocation inherent in boycott efforts . . . those instances will be reserved for rare occasions."[97] This is to say that all other means should be employed to resolve an issue before resorting to boycott action.

During the period of 1970 to 1979 some Protestant denominations engaged in boycotts. There were a total of three boycotts during this period. One involved the Gulf Oil Company because of that company's continuing operations in Angola—a nation at the time that was struggling for its independence from Portugal. The second boycott action involved the Nestle Company who was being accused of fostering malnutrition in Third World infants by virtue of its intensive zeal to sell infant formula which it manufactured. The third boycott action focused on J.P. Stevens, because of that company's failure to bargain in good faith with unions legally voted for by Stevens's employees. These three boycotts are described in this section.

A booklet entitled *Boycotts: Policy Analysis and Criteria* was issued by the United Presbyterian Church in 1979 and provides supportive arguments for churches' involvement in boycott actions. "Boycott" is defined in this booklet as an action which is performed in concert with others in a refusal to have dealings with persons, stores, or organizations in order to express disapproval or to force acceptance of certain conditions.[98] The booklet then describes certain activities of the Presbyterian churches in the past that would fit into the definition of boycott as given above. Members were urged to refrain from purchasing or using certain products or services, or from patronizing certain establishments in order to bring about some changes in policies or practices through economic pressures.

For example in 1910, the General Assembly of the United Presbyterian Church admonished its members to keep themselves "separate and apart" from the liquor traffic. The purpose was to "end this traffic" and that the people "be saved from its despoiling influence."[99]

In the same year, the church in a concern about keeping the Sabbath day holy, urged its members "not to buy anything on the Sabbath" and warned against the purchase of the Sunday newspaper, urging members "to refuse to subscribe to it or to read it or to advertise in it."[100]

In 1913, in a renewed protest against the use of liquor, Presbyterians were cautioned not to frequent any club or association that sold liquor. In 1917 they were advised to avoid establishments where liquor was served and to take space only at Temperance hotels.[101]

The rapidly growing popularity of moving pictures was a concern in 1922 and Presbyterians were asked to "refrain from attendance upon any theatre which permits upon its screen the presentation of pictures that are suggestive and unclean."[102]

Labor concerns emerged in 1937. The General Assembly advocated the adoption of legislation which forbade the shipment of goods which were manufactured by child labor.

In 1956 discrimination against minorities commanded the attention of the General Assembly and Presbyterians were encouraged to "give individual and corporate support to employers who have courageously employed Negroes on a nondiscriminatory basis."[103] Further, Presbyterians were urged to join the fight against racial discrimination by taking note of hotels, restaurants and other public accommodations that showed evidences of discrimination and "to communicate to the owners or managers their desire to see such discriminatory practices eliminated."[104] If there was then no evidence of changes in policy, Presbyterians were then to find other places of accommodation that served the public without discrimination.

In 1964, in a continuing protest against discrimination, the Board of National Missions was asked to "refrain from investing in the securities of any company that has an open, flagrant policy and/or practice of discriminatory hiring based on race or ethnic group."[105] In 1966 the United Presbyterian Foundation was asked to adopt "policies prohibiting the allocation of church funds where appropriate steps have not been taken toward racial integration."[106]

The common theme underlying all boycott actions on the part of church members was a practice of selective patronage. A Christian demonstrated his religion by where he made his purchases. This was an act of Christian stewardship and was the proper discharge of responsibility "as witness to and in service of the Lord of the Church and the world."[107]

The Gulf Oil Boycott

The Gulf Oil Company had conducted explorations for oil in Angola for years before realizing success in 1969. It was in the late 1960s that oil was finally located in the Cabinda province of Angola. It was also the same time that the people of Angola were struggling for independence from Portugal. As oil was extracted from Angolan ground, taxes and royalties were paid to the Portuguese in accordance with contractual arrangements with that government. These funds, according to the supporters of the liberation fighters, were being funneled back into Angola to strengthen military action against the insurgents. Thus the United Church of Christ and others involved in the issue over colonialism in Angola, argued that such payments of taxes and royalties were tantamount to supporting the suppression of the Angolans.

As an act of support for the liberation fighters and as an attempt to have the Gulf Oil Company withdraw from Angola, the Ohio Conference of the United Church of Christ urged its members to boycott Gulf. Members were exhorted to return their credit cards to Gulf as a visible demonstration of their displeasure of Gulf's continuing operations in Angola when that country was in a struggle for independence. Gulf reacted to the implications of the boycott action and threatened a lawsuit. The threat in actuality worked in the favor of the boycotters who now received national publicity and Gulf found itself somewhat embarrassed with the bad press it generated. The boycott action developed momentum with the appointment of a full-time organizer and the formation of a Gulf Boycott Coalition. Members of the coalition attended the 1973 Gulf shareholders' meeting and exhorted the company to cease operations in Angola until the country is granted self-determination. The Coalition also expended a great deal of effort in distributing bumper stickers, buttons, and various publicity devices.

Gulf, in order to defuse the boycott action, sought to placate members of the black community and offered to pay for trips for black clergy, civil rights leaders, and others to visit Angola. They also made a contribution of $50,000 to the Southern Christian Leadership Conference. They engaged a black public relations firm who was to advise them on how to reach the black community.

Basic to all of Gulf's defense for their operations in Angola was the contention that they were politically neutral and that their presence in that country benefitted the local populace. Gulf argued that they operated in 75 different nations and in all these countries they learned one thing and that is "when you are a guest in a foreign land you keep your nose out of their business. Since you are a guest, you must behave like one."[108] Further, they maintained that it was crucial that they "remain politically neutral" regardless of their own "personal feelings about what is going on."[109]

The churches and other supporters of the liberation movement continued to charge that Gulf was aiding Portuguese colonialism by providing Portugal with the following:

(1) tax and royalty payments totaling more than $175 million since 1954
(2) foreign exchange contributing toward financial stability and enabling war-related purchases
(3) a strategic resource that helps to ward off the effects of economic sanctions against Portugal

(4) a contractual relationship that indirectly influences U.S. policy toward support for Portugal's African wars
(5) a positive image of Portuguese colonialism in the United States[110]

The matter ultimately became resolved when the Salazar dictatorship in Portugal came to an end and Portugal's new government moved toward granting independence to its African colonies. The Gulf Oil Company, however, still found itself in a dilemma as to what faction in Angola was to receive the royalty checks and found itself on the opposite side of the United States government.[111]

The J. P. Stevens Boycott

The J. P. Stevens Company was held in civil contempt by the United States Court of Appeals Second Circuit on August 31, 1977. The Court found that Stevens had failed to comply with previous decrees of that Court and had failed to comply with various provisions of the National Labor Relations Act. The three Circuit Judges serving on the case concluded their judgment with these scathing remarks:

> The case, perhaps destined to be bleakly denominated as Stevens XVIII in a long list of Stevens litigation, has been a troublesome one . . . because it raises grave doubts about the ability of the courts to make the provisions of the federal labor law work in the face of persistent violations. It is now a decade since first we decided Stevens I and Stevens II. Since, then, the Company has twice been held in contempt of our prior orders, and a third NLRB petition charging contempt has been filed. It is true that the 71 discriminatory charges in Stevens I and the 18 similar charges in Stevens II constituted more blatant antiunion conduct then that now involved. But the conduct here was illegal nonetheless in direct violation of orders of this court, and occurred soon after our opinion in the prior contempt case. We do not take lightly the flouting of our orders not once, but twice. Nor can we view with equanimity the refusal of a large employer to abide by the law of the land and refrain from interfering with the rights of its employees. Should there be a repetition of the Company's contemptuous conduct in the future, we are quite prepared to consider more drastic sanctions both for the Company and for the individual respondents than those ordered here. In short, we are determined that respondents shall comply with the provisions of the National Labor Relations Act and that the decrees of this court ordering them to do so shall be obeyed. (U.S. Court of Appeals, Second Circuit, No. 671—September Term 1976. Decided August 31, 1977).[112]

These severe comments by the U.S. Court of Appeals Second Circuit clearly indicated that the J. P. Stevens's efforts over the years were devoted to stonewalling all efforts by their employees to gain collective bargaining. Efforts toward collective bargaining had started in 1963 and the company used various tactics to discourage unionization and was accused of intimidating employees, of selective enforcement of rules, of appeals to racial prejudices, and the illegal termination of those employees who demonstrated pro-union tendencies.

Even in view of the number of judgments won against the Stevens Company, legal efforts still did not bring fruitful results. In view of the continuing resistance on the part of Stevens, a boycott was initiated by the Amalgamated Clothing and Textile Workers Union. The boycott was subsequently supported by various Protestant denominations: The Methodist Church, The Christian Church (Disciples of Christ), the United Church of Christ, the United Presbyterian Church in the U.S.A., and the National Council of Churches. The churches felt that there was a real need to support the boycott action instituted by the union in view of the fact that the rights of Stevens's workers had been continually violated and that effective remedies through the legal system were not working. A report prepared by a Special Task Force of the United Presbyterian Church bemoaned the fact that the churches were not sufficiently sensitive to the deep fears and hurts of the people who had suffered from such a long dispute. The churches had been remiss in recognizing a need to witness to God's love and concern for all his people. The churches had not become sufficiently and actively involved so that they could act as "change agents" for the improvement in the relationships and conditions of the people involved in the dispute. Further, the report lamented, both clergy and lay leaders have been fearful of offending powerful secular forces which possibly could affect the health of their own church budgets. The report detailed a Biblical-Theological mandate for the churches' participation in the boycott action.[113]

The National Council of Churches, in joining the boycott, reiterated that it had long recognized the right of employees to organize for the purpose of collective bargaining. The position of the Council was that when they were convinced of the existence of exploitation, discrimination, or other forms of antisocial behavior, the Council would take action without regard for its own convenience or economic advantage. In the case of J.P. Stevens, the Council decried the fact that Stevens had: (a) repeatedly been found in violation of the National Labor Relations Act; (b) been found guilty by the U.S. District Court of violations of the Civil Rights Act of 1964; (c) been involved in racial and sexual discrimination at its plants in Roanoke Rapids and Stanley, N.C.; (d) been found guilty by the Fifth Circuit Court of Appeals in failing to bargain in good faith at its Statesboro, Ga. plant; (e) failed to bargain in good faith with the union at Roanoke Rapids; (f) flouted prior decrees of the Second Circuit Court of Appeals; (g) not shown any genuine attempt to correct previous errors, but used every legal means to delay final judgment; and (h) intimidated its own workers.[114] In view of these facts the National Council of

Churches recommended to its constituents that no goods be purchased from J. P. Stevens until such time as the boycott was lifted.

J. P. Stevens over the years opposed unionization and fought not only the unions, but the courts and the Labor Relations Board as well. However, toward the end of the 1970s Stevens began to revise its unimpressive record in litigation. Its labor policy was modified so that rather than take every union-related dispute to court, it strived to keep a lower profile and allow only sure cases to reach the National Labor Relations Board or the Appellate Courts. "It's sort of a system in advance of any problems," explained James R. Franklin, the company's director of corporate relations.[115] He detailed that the key element of the new Stevens's policy was the minimizing of labor relations flare-ups. Any potential source of conflict between supervisors and union-related matters was to be referred to top plant management for legally approved responses. Managers were instructed to attempt to resolve all unfair labor practice charges before they reached the courts. "The company simply does not want the court cases to mount up any more," cautiously noted Jerrold Mehlman, assistant general counsel for Stevens.[116] He added this caveat: "This doesn't mean we're any more inclined to accept unions as a benefit to our employees. We're still communicating our views to them."[117]

On October 19, 1980 a settlement was reached between organized labor and the J. P. Stevens Company that ended 17 years of open warfare. It was not necessarily a lopsided victory for the union. Nonetheless, it was a victory and in the long term could have significant impact for labor relations in the South. It did demonstrate quite conclusively that a highly aggressive union strategy that "combined legal, boycott and organizing pressures along with a new tactic, the use of financial leverage" could embarrass and weaken a corporation.[118]

In view of the settlement, churches lifted the boycott action. The United Presbyterian Church drew this conclusion at the end of the boycott action:

> We recognize that this is not a choice between a bad company and a good union or vice versa. The crux of the issue confronted in this situation is the right of employees to organize and select bargaining agents free from fear and intimidation as well as the responsibility of employers to bargain in good faith through such agents.[119]

The Nestle Boycott

In the opening of the decade of the 1970s, Dr. Derrick Jelliffer, a public health specialist, declared that malnutrition of infants in Third World societies could be linked to the use of baby formula. This formula was a product made up of vegetable fat, milk sugar, vitamins and minerals. The formula is nutritious when properly used. However, in some parts of the world unwitting mothers mixed the powdered formula with contaminated water, or to save money, diluted the product far too much. In view of the hazards of such practices, many segments of the world community became aroused and protested the widespread distribution of infant formula by large corporations in developing societies. In 1970 the Pan American Health Organization urged a restriction of advertising and promotion of commercial milk products and a discontinuance of the use of milk nurses, as well as a cessation of free milk samples. In 1973 the Food and Agriculture Organization of the United Nations issued a warning concerning the intensive promotion of the infant formula by transnational corporations. In 1974 the 27th World Health Assembly deplored all forms of publicity which inferred that the formula was superior to breastfeeding. As concern mounted over the use of the formula in developing countries, various groups launched protests against the manufacturers. In 1974 shareholder resolutions were introduced at the stockholders' meetings of American producers of the formula and a boycott was launched against Nestle. The shareholder resolution could not be utilized with Nestle as they are a Swiss-based firm.

By 1977 the boycott action became formalized with the organization of the Infant Formula Action Coalition (INFACT) who coordinated the activities of those who opposed the distribution of the formula and challenged the companies involved in the preparation of the commercially prepared milk for infants. In the same year the Interfaith Center on Corporate Responsibility joined the efforts of INFACT in challenging the method of distribution of the formula in Third World societies. In 1978 the World Health Assembly advocated that developing countries initiate educational programs relative to the superiority of breastfeeding as opposed to the use of the formula. In 1978 the National Council of Churches endorsed the boycott and joined Protestant churches already involved in the boycott action or soon to join the boycott. In addition to the National Council of Churches, the following Protestant denominations were participants in the Nestle boycott: American Lutheran Church, Presbyterian Church in the U.S., United Presbyterian Church in the U.S.A., United Methodist Church, and the Church of the Brethren.

The Church of the Brethren issued a brochure which very aptly sums up the contentions of the Protestant churches with Nestle as to the distribution of the infant formula: (a) breast milk is a natural food resource; it is ideal for infants; contains the correct balance of nutrients; provides antibodies capable of fighting off infections; (b) responsible medical research has demonstrated that any substitution of commercial formula for breast milk, especially where poverty, illiteracy, impure water and inadequate sanitation prevails, does result in infant malnutrition, illness, brain damage and death; (c) the practice of promoting infant formula does encourage women to abandon the natural resource of breastfeeding in favor of the commercial preparations; (d) the church is committed to work for justice, to identify with the oppressed and suffering; (e) the practice of multinational corporations should be redressed in those cases where illness and death of babies can be linked to the promotion of bottle feeding; and (f) since Nestle controls over one-third of the world's infant formula and is immune from shareholder action because its stock is not traded on the U.S. market, and since direct appeals to Nestle to change its sale promotion of infant formula in developing nations have been futile, the Church of the Brethren adopted the following action: it would call upon Nestle to (1) cease advertising its infant formula in areas where social, economic and environmental conditions are such that the use of the formula is apt to damage the health and well being of infants, (2) remove "milk nurses" from hospitals and maternity clinics, (3) discontinue free sample distribution to consumers, (4) put an end to giving some prize or bonus to doctors and other professionals to promote the formula. In addition, the Church of the Brethren urged its congregation to study matters of malnutrition, disease and death of infants in developing areas and to act in ways consistent with the mission of the church. It called on members of the denomination to cease purchasing Nestle products and to inform Nestle of their action.[120]

The business community was not in agreement with the boycott action, and *The Wall Street Journal* published an editorial on November 1, 1979 entitled "The Nestle Boycott Kills Babies." The editorial argued that it was not Nestle that caused infant mortality in poor countries but rather ignorance—ignorance of the principles of nutrition and sanitation. "The critics fail to mention that the same contaminated water that they fear gets mixed with formula was always mixed with traditional weaning foods."[121] Further, the editors determined that Nestle's advertising of the formula made a contribution toward overcoming lack of information as well as providing more nutritious products. "Now thanks to the efforts of certain suburbanites and church groups this public health resource has been cut off."[122]

Dr. Mark S. Haendel, Chief of the Department of Pediatrics, Kaiser Permanente Medical Center, West Los Angeles, Calif., protested the position of the *Wall Street Journal* editorial on the distribution of infant formula and wrote:

> Breastfeeding is the preferred nutrition for infants of all cultures—East, West and the Third World. The nutritional, psychological and immunologic benefits of mother's milk is well documented. Mothers in advanced countries do have the option of formula

feedings if desired or required. A safe sanitary water system, easy distribution and adequate refrigeration make formula feedings safe (although certainly not better).

There is no question that under certain conditions (severe maternal illness, mothers returning to work and unable to nurse) these formulas have provided replacement nutrition for the infant. The situation in the Third World countries is very different. Most of these nations have poor, often contaminated, water, no adequate refrigeration and poor distribution. This results in a prepared formula which is frequently contaminated and which cannot be stored properly. The expense of the product also causes mothers often to dilute the formula excessively. These practices often result in dehydration (sometimes fatal) and malnutrition.

Breastfed infants in developing countries are often the healthiest of the family until weaning moves the child into competition for the generally inadequate diet which is poor in protein and calories with the entire family. Nursing also provides a contraceptive effect for the mother. The glamorizing and advertising of infant formulas in undeveloped countries is certainly amazing to behold. All efforts are aimed at having the ignorant and poor mothers "modernized" by bottlefeeding the baby. It is also quite impressive to note that, however difficult it might be for medical supplies to find their way to remote villages, the Nestle truck is ubiquitous. All those interested in the welfare of children must keep this issue at the forefront and pressure those companies for more social responsibility.[123]

Nestle, of course, has protested the contentions of those who oppose the distribution practices of the company of its infant formula product. Nestle is a prime supplier of the formula in the Third World and in view of the mounting opposition to its method of formula distribution, Nestle commenced a program of modest adjustments which included better labeling on the formula itself which announced that breast feeding was best and provided simple instructions for the use of the formula. Further, it ended home visits by Nestle personnel and discontinued the uniforming in white of milk nurses.

David E. Guerrant, President of Nestle, in an undated letter that was mailed to the general public who inquired about the boycott, asserted that Nestle agreed that: (a) breastfeeding is best for infants, however most Third World infants need a supplement to mother's breast milk to sustain normal physical and mental growth; (b) the time when a mother must begin to supplement her baby's diet is dependent primarily on the quantity of milk she is producing; (c) infant mortality rates in developing countries have been decreasing during the past 30 years; and (4) the root causes of infant malnutrition and mortality in the Third World are poverty, lack of food, ignorance and poor sanitary conditions resulting in contaminated water.

In the same letter, President Guerrant furnished the following examples of how Nestle was educating mothers on the superiority of breast milk and in the proper use of formula products:

1. Every label of formula products contains the statement that breast milk is best. Detailed written instruction on preparing the formula is given and there are step-by-step illustrations showing proper use. The labels are printed in the official language of the country and in the main vernacular language.

2. Nestle employs qualified nurses or midwives to assist health professionals in holding clinics on such topics as the importance of breastfeeding, diet for mothers, general hygiene and proper use of formula products.

3. No advertising of formula products is done in developing countries.

4. Nestle gives no free samples of formula to mothers. Doctors, hospital staffs and government health services are given limited amounts of free samples. These health professionals, who are the best judge of the nutritional needs of mother and infant, are the proper intermediary between industry and infant formula users.

5. On occasion, Nestle is requested to provide formula products or medical equipment to missionaries, orphanages, doctors or hospitals. Nestle scrutinizes each request to insure that the requested item is intended to benefit the community as a whole. If there is community-wide benefit and if the request is reasonable, Nestle donates these items.[124]

Nestle officials deny that the boycott has injured sales, but the adverse publicity has damaged the multinational's corporate image.[125] The churches continue the boycott and will not be satisfied until Nestle discontinues (1) direct promotion to the consumer through the mass media, (2) distribution of free promotional samples through hospitals, clinics and to the homes of the newborn, (3) the use of "milk nurses" or similar promotional representatives, (4) promotion through health personnel and institutions by means of gift giving such as cases of formula products, medical equipment, and payment of conference expenses.[126]

In 1981 the World Health Organization voted for an international code which would restrict advertising and marketing of infant formula. It was a near consensus of opinion with 110 to 1 in favor of the code. The United States cast the only vote against the code. This action has raised a storm of protest among many groups in America who felt that the code was at least one step in the right direction. The code, eight pages in length, is a nonbinding document. It urges a global ban on the promotion and advertising of the formula, distribution of free samples, and gifts for promoting the use of the product. Inasmuch as the code is nonbinding, it is left to the individual governments to translate the code into their own laws.

Other Direct Contacts

This segment provides illustrations of contacts made by Protestant churches during the 1970s to gain corporate attention over particular social concerns. Most of these contacts involved preliminary conversations with corporate management prior to the filing of shareholder resolutions in the hope that a satisfactory solution could be attained which would avoid the instigation of a resolution.

The social issues for the most part for "other direct contacts" are the same as those that have already been enumerated in this study with regard to shareholder resolutions. Protestant churches focused on similar issues even though the confrontations took different forms. Dialogue, whether face-to-face or by correspondence, was a key method of contact. The United Church of Christ in its report on 1977–1979 Corporate Social Responsibility Actions specifically mentions dialogue as a key facet in corporate contact.

> Experience has demonstrated the importance of presenting to the corporation's top management a well-reasoned argument based on well-marshalled facts. In such a discussion the investor may learn at first hand about any errors in the facts or fallacies in its arguments, and about problems the corporation would have in carrying out the investor's proposal. It may be possible to modify the proposal so as to reduce the problems without reducing the basic thrust of the proposal. If the management is impressed by the investor's argument and appears sympathetic to the investor's concern, it may be possible to negotiate a solution that is satisfactory to all.[127]

The United Church of Christ during the 1970s participated in numerous exchanges with hundreds of U.S. corporations. In various dialogues this denomination was able to persuade fifty companies to make public statistics of their employment of women and minorities in the United States and more than twenty released employment figures in South Africa with indication of race, grade, and compensation levels.

In 1972 a meeting was held with IBM's Committee on Social Responsibility to discuss IBM's defense production and plans for economic conversion. In 1972 representatives of the Interfaith Center on Corporate Responsibility met with officials of the Northern Cheyenne Landowners Association to discuss the impact of proposed strip mining on the Cheyenne Reservation. In 1975 United Presbyterian Church officials met with the management of Procter & Gamble and asked for a report of the images of women in Procter & Gamble's television advertising. In 1976 representatives of the Interfaith Center on Corporate Responsibility met with bank officers of Chase Manhattan, Citibank, Manufacturers Hanover and Morgan Guaranty to discuss newly made loans to the South African government. In 1977 there were a series of dialogues between representatives of the United Methodist Church and RCA (NBC), ABC and CBS on issues of violence in television programming, as well as the stereotyping of women in advertising.[128]

The Lutheran Church in America reported in their minutes of a meeting on March 24, 1974 with IBM, which included Frank T. Carey, Chairman of the Board and two vice-presidents. In the two-hour discussion church representatives were able to present their position relative to a shareholder resolution which called upon IBM to cease furnishing computers and servicing of computers in South Africa. The minutes indicated that IBM management was candid and forthright in defending its position relative to its operations in South Africa. However, church representatives did note that IBM's management recognized the churches' deep concern for justice and the upholding of human rights in the face of South Africa's system of apartheid. There was disagreement, however, as to how changes should be effected.[129]

In another encounter regarding the apartheid situation in South Africa, representatives of the Lutheran Church in America, as well as representatives from the Presbyterian Church in the U.S.A., the United Church of Christ, the Episcopal Church, and members of the Interfaith Center met with Citibank over the issue of loans to the South African government. This meeting, held on November 15, 1978, had been called so that church representatives could hear Citibank's position relative to loans to South Africa and at the same time "to inform Citibank of the churches' strong objection to granting financial assistance to a regime which embodies apartheid."[130] While Citibank's management agreed with the churches' abhorrence of the South African government practice of apartheid, there was definite disagreement as to what was the best means of ameliorating the situation.

The First National Bank of Boston in 1978 was also a site for active dialogue with denominational executives. This meeting was called to discuss the bank's policy of granting loans to the government of South Africa. When no satisfactory conclusion could be reached, a shareholder resolution was filed, and Frank L. Jensen of the Lutheran Church in America made the following statement at the shareholders' meeting held on March 30th of that year:

> Mr. Chairman, my name is Frank L. Jensen. I serve as Consultant for Social Responsibility on the national staff of the Lutheran Church in America. I am here today representing a church which is beneficial owner of 3,700 shares and is one of the three co-sponsors of this shareholder proposal. The decision to co-sponsor this resolution was not taken lightly by the Lutheran Church in America. After considerable study and discussion, and authorized by the church's governing body, the Executive Council, we have joined in the call to banks to end loans to South Africa, particularly loans to the apartheid government itself. One reason for such action is the continuing concern we have for the large number of Lutherans among the black population of South Africa and Namibia who are being denied their human rights.[131]

During the year of 1978 representatives of the Presbyterian Church in the U.S.A. met with corporate managements of General Motors Corporation,

Ford Motor Company, Control Data Corporation, American Home Products, and U.S. Fidelity and Guaranty Insurance Company.[132] The United Church of Christ reported that during the period of 1977 to 1979 they had contact with officers of the following corporations: the Public Interest Committee of the Dow Chemical Board of Directors, the board chairmen of Bristol-Myers, Castle & Cooke, Control Data, First National Bank of Boston, General Motors, Mobil, Union Carbide, and other principal officers of Aetna Life and Casualty Union, Bank America, Borg-Warner, Connecticut General, Dow Corning, Ford Motor, General Electric, Manufacturers Hanover, Newmont Mining, Ralston-Purina, Standard Oil of California, Tenneco and Texaco.[133]

World Issues Secretary of the United Church of Christ, the Rev. Dr. Howard Schomer, was invited to Midland, Michigan in 1978 to meet with executives of the Dow Chemical Company who were interested in learning "whether church critics would care to make their case through consultation or are wedded to the tactics of confrontation."[134] The interesting aspect was that the United Church of Christ held no stock in Dow Chemical but the corporation was still interested in hearing Dr. Schomer's viewpoint. Dr. Schomer cooperated and attended the two-day conference and called the attention of the group to the fact that it was the United Church of Christ's standard policy to consult with management prior to filing any shareholder resolution, in the hope of securing a policy change. If that failed, then resort would be made to the use of the shareholder resolution. Dr. Schomer presented his views on the potential and the problems of transnational corporations. "These two days of shared ethical search spotlighted areas of agreement and of discord. They showed the need for continuing dialogue and a mutual desire to pursue it," concluded Dr. Schomer upon return from the conference.[134a]

Meetings were held subsequent to the filing of shareholder resolutions of stockholder proxy votes. For example, representatives of the United Methodist Church and the United Church of Christ met with officials of the Ralston-Purina company who voluntarily provided information concerning land formerly used for local agricultural production and now being converted to production of feed for animals rather than for people in Mexico, Brazil, Colombia, Venezuela and Peru. The churches' resolution had been defeated at the January 1978 stockholders' meeting, but church representatives were provided with the requested information.

The symposium was another method utilized by church representatives in meetings face-to-face with corporate management. As an example, one symposium was conducted in 1978 over the energy concern. The day-long symposium was arranged by the Presbyterian Church in Bartlesville,

Oklahoma and included management representatives from Kerr McGee Oil Company, Standard Oil of Indiana, the American Petroleum Institute, and the Department of Energy, as well as church representatives. The topics included Oil and Gas Resources for the Year 2000, Coal for Energy, Nuclear Energy, Alternate Energy Sources, U.S. Energy Policy and Sources and the Total Energy Overview. The purpose of the symposium was "to hear the industry point of view."[135]

A symposium was also held in Barrow, Alaska in June 1977 to allow the Inuit (Eskimo) people to express their concerns to corporate managements over the methodologies being used by the companies in the exploitation of oil and gas, especially those procedures which affected the physical and social environment of the Eskimo people. The meeting developed out of a conference with the Eskimos of Alaska, Northern Canada and Greenland, who had requested that the United Presbyterian Church "facilitate conversations between the oil companies and representatives of the conference."[136] Exxon Corporation was contacted by the Presbyterian denomination and agreed to bring together the representatives from the appropriate oil companies to discuss the concerns of the Inuit people.

Representatives of Protestant denominations have presented testimony from time to time to governmental agencies. For example, in 1975, the Episcopal Church, the United Methodist, American Baptists, United Church of Christ representatives testified before the Securities and Exchange Commission on the desirability of requiring companies to disclose socially significant matters. In 1976, the Interfaith Center testified before the Senate Sub-Committee on African Affairs regarding church concerns over the increase in loans from U.S. banks to the South African government.[137] The United Church of Christ in the Fall of 1977 presented a number of proposals to the Securities and Exchange Commission which that church deemed would be beneficial to shareholders. The church declared that this was "the first opportunity so offered since the adoption of the Securities and Exchange Act in 1934."[138]

Testimony was also offered before the United Nations. The National Council of Churches appeared before the United Nations committee on apartheid in South Africa in support of a halt to secret U.S. bank loans to the South African government.[139]

Contact by churches with corporate management was also accomplished through correspondence. For example, in October of 1977, church representatives wrote letters to fifty U.S. companies who had investments in South Africa. The letter stated the churches' objections to the continuance of these corporations in South Africa and asked that they terminate their stay in that country. Some of the major corporations receiving this letter were General Motors, Chrysler, IBM, International Harvester, Firestone, Ford, Mobil, 3M, Kodak, NCR, Masonite, General Electric, Burlington Industries, Carnation, Goodyear and Otis Elevator.[140]

On December 10, 1975 the United Church of Christ wrote letters to the chairmen of 281 of the largest U.S. corporations who were involved in international trade, making inquiry as to what written policies were in effect controlling the use of corporate assets that could possibly be used for "partisan political purposes or purchase of favorable treatment from governments."[141] The letter further sought to ascertain whether these corporations would be willing to make public their policies and any violations of these policies. Sixty-four replies were received and the answers ran the gamut from a strict prohibition of political payments or bribes to no policy at all.[142]

In the same year a study developed by the United Church of Christ called "The Role of Transnational Business in Mass Economic Development" was mailed to five thousand members of the boards of directors of U.S. transnational companies who were involved in U.S. exports and overseas operations. The same report appeared in the July 25, 1975 issue of the *Congressional Record* having been placed in the *Record* by the Chairman of the Senate Subcommittee on Multinational Corporations, Frank Church.

The United Church of Christ mailed a report of their survey on the political use of corporate assets to directors of major U.S. corporations. It was the intention of the mailing to help to interpret to business executives the position on this issue held by the General Synod of the United Church of Christ. In this connection, Dr. Howard Schomer cautioned: "It is our hope that corporate directors will exercise the authority vested in them by shareholders to adopt and enforce policies and procedures that effectively prohibit overseas political contributions and/or purchases of favored treatments."[143]

Other examples include a letter sent in 1974 by the National Council of Churches, the United Presbyterian Church, and the Christian Church (Disciples of Christ) to ITT repudiating ITT's interference in Chile's political processes. In 1975 members of the Northern California segment of the Interfaith Center on Corporate Responsibility wrote a letter to Chrysler, Ford and General Motors asking questions about proposed participation of these three auto makers in the reorganization of Chile's auto industry. In 1976, the National Council of Churches sent a letter to General Motors protesting advertisements by its South African subsidiary supporting military efforts of South Africa's apartheid government. In 1976 the Interfaith Center on Corporate Responsibility sent a letter of inquiry to Coca-Cola regarding efforts of that company's subsidiary to prevent unionization in Guatemala.[144]

The closing of a bank account as a protest act against policies of a bank has been used on occasion. For example, the National Council of Churches in 1978 closed its checking account with the Continental Illinois National Bank because of that bank's refusal to adopt a policy prohibiting loans to South Africa. The decision to close the account followed unsuccessful negotiations with bank officials.[145] On occasion stock has been divested as a notification to a corporation that the Protestant denomination stockholder was not in agreement with corporate policy. As an example, the American Baptist Churches in 1972 divested the stock of United Aircraft because of that company's substantial involvement in military arms production and its refusal to discuss conversion to nonmilitary products. However, it has been Protestant preference to retain stock and to exercise the prerogative as an owner to propose shareholder resolutions and in that way effect change.

Legal action has been employed from time to time. In 1974 the United Church of Christ participated with the Project on Corporate Responsibility in a lawsuit that demanded that Gulf Oil Company executives pay back company funds that were donated in political campaigns.[146] Also in 1974 five religious groups, the American Baptist Home Mission Society, the Atonement Friars, the National Council of Churches, the United Methodist Church and the United Presbyterian Church filed motions to intervene in two cases which had been brought by U.S. Steel and General Motors against the Department of Defense seeking to prevent the release of employment information concerning employees in specific locations. The Court directed all parties concerned to negotiate and mutually agree as to what information concerning employment data was disclosable and what was not.[147] In 1976 the American Baptists joined in litigation proceedings against the Securities and Exchange Commission and in behalf of environmentalists. The suit argued that companies should be required to disclose environmental and employment data.[148] In the same year the Episcopal Church, the United Methodist Church, and the United Presbyterian Church submitted legal commentary to the Security and Exchange Commission about the Commission's proposed changes in rules governing shareowner resolutions.[149]

Press releases have been utilized not only to inform the public concerning the Protestant churches' position on social issues but to influence corporate opinion as well. For example, in 1972 the World Council of Churches publicly called for the withdrawal of all investments in South Africa and issued a publication called "Time to Withdraw" explaining the churches' rationale for urging corporations to withdraw all investments in South Africa. In 1976 the United Church of Christ held a Press Conference at which time they released documents which implicated Mobil in a violation of international and U.S. sanctions against Rhodesia. In 1976 the Church of the Brethren announced a major investigation of the effects of television on viewers singling out violence in some television programming as well as the stereotyping of women in advertising.[150]

Two illustrations of the use of the press release are given below. One demonstrates how the Christian Church used the media with reference to its concern that a woman be nominated to the board of directors of the American Fletcher Corporation, a bank. The other, by the same church, expressed that denomination's concern over the proliferation of sales of military products to foreign governments.

> Press release. Indianapolis, Ind.—A resolution from the Christian Church (Disciples of Christ) asking an Indianapolis bank to nominate qualified women to its board of directors was defeated by stockholders the second year in a row here recently. Support for the issue is increasing, according to Dr. Wade D. Rubick, general counsel for the church who presented the resolution to stockholders of American Fletcher Corporation. Almost 10 percent of the stockholders favored nominating women to the board compared to 6.6 percent in 1976, he said. The vote was 337,459 favoring the resolution and 3,194,959 opposing. Although the bank has not had women on its board of directors, Frank E. McKinney, Jr., chairman, said "all qualified individuals are considered regardless of sex, race, color or creed. Mrs. Ben Blumberg, a stockholder from Terre Haute, Ind., questioned the bank's policy, saying the qualifications were "male oriented." The Disciples, who own 10,000 shares of stock through the United Christian Missionary Society, asked that steps be taken to nominate qualified women to the board and that management share detailed plans for nominating women to the board in 1978 within 90 days of the next meeting.[151]

> Press Release. Indianapolis, Ind.—Resolutions calling on General Electric to share information on minority employment and to decline sale of military equipment to countries based on their human rights situations were defeated by company stockholders here April 26. Representing the Christian Church (Disciples of Christ) which owns 1,000 shares worth roughly $52,000 were Dr. Wade D. Rubick, general counsel for the church, and Ian J. McCrae, director of economic justice and human values, department of church in society, both of Indianapolis. Although the resolutions brought by a number of religious organizations were defeated by more than 98 percent of the stockholders voting, Reginald H. Jones, chairman of the board, said the company does respond favorably to the stockholders' resolutions. Jones asked the Interfaith Center on Corporate Responsibility of the National Council of Churches for suggestions on policy related to the issue of military sales. Noting that the company is sensitive to human rights, Jones pointed out that the company does not sell military equipment to countries the U.S. government believes engaged in "gross violations of human rights," where the sale might be detrimental to the reputation of General Electric or harmful to its employees. Information on minority employment already is furnished on request, company officials said.[152]

One final comment should be made relative to the Protestant churches' use of "other" tactics to influence corporate policies involving social concerns of interest to the churches and that is the affirmative use of its money in behalf of social concerns. This could include providing loans to minority-owned small businesses, the issuing of home improvement and personal loans in special cases, depositing of funds in minority-owned banks, and similar. The United Presbyterian Church, for example, has a regular program of Creative Investment which was established by its 187th General Assembly in 1975. The goal of "creative investment" was to "invest funds on six continents for the promotion through investment of social concerns expressed by the General Assembly. (*Minutes,* 1975, Part I, p. 445)."[153] In 1978, as an example, a $40,000 deposit was made in the Franklin Community Federal Credit Union at Omaha, Nebraska. In addition, two former investments remained in place, one of $40,000 in the Pinon Federal Credit Union and a $20,000 certificate of deposit at the South Shore National Bank in Chicago. These deposits were made to assist the operation of these minority-owned banks. The total amount of funds available for Creative Investments in 1978 (including those already committed) was in the range of $1,200,000.[154]

Summary of "other" direct contacts. This segment of the study has provided examples of other direct contacts by Protestant churches with corporate management in efforts to influence corporate policy over concerns which were of interest to Protestant churches. Illustrations were provided of the extensive use of face-to-face contact with high level corporate officers, the use of group meetings and symposiums, the broad use of correspondence which took the form of open letters and letters of inquiry and mass mailing, the furnishing of testimony to governmental agencies, closing of bank accounts, divestment of stock, legal action, the use of press releases, and finally the affirmative use of church funds for social concerns.

3

Business Responses to Protestant Activism in the 1970s

In this chapter the responses of business to Protestant activism in the 1970s is viewed in three perspectives.

The first segment of this chapter presents a general overview of the reactions of business toward the concept of corporate social responsibility and shareholder activism in the 1970s.

The second segment takes a more focused look at the specific replies or arguments which the targeted corporations offered in response to the specific Protestant shareholder resolutions and boycotts initiated or participated in by Protestant churches during the 1970s.

The third segment provides some examples of modifications in business practices which were related to social issues that were of concern to Protestant churches.

Business Challenged in the 1970s Over Social Responsibility

Meeting challenges has never been new for business. Business has been challenged numerous times before and has succeeded in overcoming many difficulties.

The 1970s presented a very distinct challenge: a call for participation on the part of business in social concerns. Business was accused of having a lack of concern for social issues, such as damage to the environment, safety of manufactured products, minority employment, and the like. Of the social challenges in the 1970s the most difficult was the demand by Protestant churches that corporations use their vast economic power to ameliorate violations of human rights in Third World societies. This challenge proved puzzling to the business world. Basic social concerns, such as water and air pollution, were readily recognized by business as valid and business did respond in time.[1]

The slow response of business to environmental concerns in prior years can be partly attributable to the fact that the American public had accepted a certain amount of pollution which was part of the manufacturing process. The public had recognized that in order to produce low cost steel and paper, it was inevitable that some rivers would sustain a certain degree of pollution. Further, local communities, anxious for the retention of valued local employment, accepted the presence of industrial smoke stacks that daily spewed contaminants into the local atmosphere.

However, in an almost complete turnaround, society suddenly decided that it no longer wanted a continuation of water and air pollution resulting from industrial production and demanded that business take action to clean up the air and the water.

Business did respond to the environmental concern. A report prepared by the Resources and Environmental Quality Division of the Chamber of Commerce of the U.S.A., prepared in February 1980, revealed that private industry had made large investments in order to clean up the air and water. According to EPA sources, the industrial investment for the period of 1970 to 1977 for effluent controls was a cumulative $72.4 billion. In 1977 alone more than $14 billion had been expended. Other estimates placed industrial pollution control costs from $34.6 to $42.3 billion for the period of 1972–1976. Other estimates indicated that the total investment indeed was huge and there was every indication that such investments would continue at a high rate. As an example, operating costs for maintaining low emissions in just one industry, steel, is estimated at about $500 million per year. The report indicates that investments made toward cleaning up the air and water

> has resulted in a cleaner environment. Combined air quality data from 25 major metropolitan areas show that the number of unhealthful days declined by 15% between 1974 and 1977 while the number of very unhealthful days declined by 32%. Data from approximately 50 of the most polluted counties across the country show that violations of ambient air quality standards generally either stayed constant or decreased between 1974 and 1975, during a period of growing stricter enforcement.[2]

Dealing with cleaning up pollution caused by industrial wastes was a recognized business problem. It lent itself to a clear description as to the obvious steps to be taken to alleviate odious social conditions. However, the demands by the Protestant churches on American corporations to respond to adverse social conditions in developing countries, such as apartheid in Southern Africa, was another story. It was the contention of the churches that the very presence of American businesses in those countries with oppressive governments provided these governments with very vital economic support which has allowed the continuance of oppressive practices.

The demands by Protestant churches that American corporations cease operations in these Third World societies was steadfastly resisted by corporate managements throughout the 1970s, and this position was consistently supported by the stockholders. The managements of multinational corporations[3] made clear to activists that while they acknowledged that certain practices of oppressive governments were abhorrent to them, it was very basic that they had to abide by the laws and customs of the host countries. Further, even though the manufacturing plants were in locales dominated by oppressive governments, this did not imply that corporate managements endorsed policies such as apartheid. Management averred that only the Government of the United States can set foreign policy and that it is not within the province of the charter of American corporations to attempt to dictate foreign policy or force alterations in foreign political structures by the use of economic power. It is the United States government, empowered by persons voted into office by a free society, that should decide whether "Rhodesia should be recognized or how cities should be preserved."[4]

Increasing Criticisms of Business in the 1970s

Whether business wished to shrug off the pressures of society or no, several factors aided the intensification of such pressures. Lewis H. Young, editor-in-chief of *Business Week,* noted that pressures against corporations accelerated in the 1970s for several significant reasons. He observed that during the period of 1948 to 1968 business in America was considered as effectively doing its job. He notes:

> The economy grew on average 3.9% per year; the recovery from 1962 to 1968 was the longest in history, 28 million new jobs were created; corporate profits grew 102%, reached a peak of $43 billion in the fourth quarter in 1968; and the stock market soared with the Dow-Jones Industrial Average, rising from 181 on January 2, 1948 to a closing of 945 on the night of December 30, 1968."[5]

Consequently during the period of 1948 to 1968 there was little criticism voiced by the public and for the most part business management received little complaint, except from time to time some dissident shareholders complained that dividends should have been higher. Mr. Young observed that the primary object for most persons who purchased stock was to receive stock dividends and to appreciate the value of his stock. If a stockholder was not satisfied with the financial returns, he "could, and would, sell the stock, and with the proceeds seek out a better performer.

There was little concern and little interest in how management made decisions, unless the decisions were reflected in the price of the stock."[6]

In the 1970s, early in the decade, the value of stock plummeted. Investors blamed executives for incompetence and many times openly accused management of placing their own personal interests before that of the corporation. They were accused of augmenting their own compensation at the expense of the stockholders. More damaging were the abuses that began to surface and these increasingly upset the public; examples include, illegal campaign contributions, questionable transactions, bribes to foreign government officials, defects in products with potential danger to the public, and startling cases of pollution of the environment.[7]

To complicate the picture even further, activists of all stripes, including Protestant churches, were using "the corporate machinery to achieve certain social goals."[8]

The "Project for Corporate Responsibility" Provides a Model

One of the more effective uses of the "corporate machinery" in the early 1970s in behalf of social concerns was the effort known as the "Project for Corporate Responsibility." Incorporated as part of the Project was a campaign known as "Campaign GM." Campaign GM made significant use of the corporate proxy statement of General Motors to bring social issues to the attention of corporate management and at the same time to the public in general. Campaign GM set up a model that others were soon to copy.

Campaign GM accused General Motors of laxity in pollution control, carelessness in car safety, and shortsightedness in minority hiring. Two shareholder resolutions were filed by the Campaign in 1970. One resolution proposed that three new directors be added to the General Motors' Board of Directors so that the interests of the public could be broadly represented. The second proposal requested the formation of a Public Review Committee, which committee would look out for the interests of the public. The Committee, it was recommended, should be made up of persons from General Motors' management, civic groups, and the United Auto Workers' Union.

A bitter battle ensued and while General Motors attempted to minimize the efforts of the Campaign, it did have its effect. General Motors did amend its corporate position and sought to achieve better emission controls and to improve the safety of automobiles in the event of a collision. General Motors hired environmental and personnel experts and elected a well-known black, Dr. Leon Sullivan, to its Board of Directors.

Campaign GM's tactics and partial success, as indicated, were noted by others. The effective use of shareholder resolutions was particularly recognized as a potent method of bringing social concerns to the attention of corporate management. Further, it also acted as an effective vehicle for informing the public. Campaign GM, as a very minimum, demonstrated that a mammoth corporation could be approached and that there were possibilities of effecting changes.

With reference to Campaign GM, Donald Schwartz in an essay entitled "Reforming the Corporation from Within" observed:

> Campaign GM never expected its view to prevail among the shareholders, most of whom regard their stock strictly in terms of interest and dividends. Still the Campaign was not tilting at windmills, for it was skeptical as to whether the machinery of corporate democracy transmitted the views of shareholders effectively. Campaign GM thus intended to use the machinery of corporate democracy to marshall public opinion in its support. It knew that the actual shareholder resolutions it submitted . . . would be defeated, but the fate of the resolution was secondary and could be dismissed as either irrelevant or essentially predetermined by the system.[9]

Campaign GM established a model—a model that demonstrated that the use of shareholder resolutions can influence corporate policy. Further, it converted the annual corporate meeting into a public forum where social concerns could be aired not only before shareholders but the public as well.

The business world responded to Protestant activism in the 1970s in various ways, from being openly critical of the tactics of church activists to a more moderate and considerate view. These are described below.

Business Response: Openly Critical of the Tactics of Church Activists

While officials of corporate entities maintained a dignified aloofness and refrained from openly criticizing activists lest they themselves or their corporations come under attack, the business media reflected what some businessmen were thinking but feared to say out loud.

An example of this view appeared in *Fortune* magazine in early 1980. The article, written by Herman Nickel, and entitled "The Corporation Haters," accused activist Protestant denominations and the National Council of Churches of being anticapitalistic and anticorporation. According to Nickel, church activists viewed business quite negatively. In fact, Nickel says, activists claim that

> U.S. corporations thrive on racist suppression in South Africa and profit from starvation wages in the Caribbean and parts of Asia. Hand in glove with corrupt and repressive governments in Central America, giants of U.S. agribusiness like Castle & Cooke and United Brands try to perpetuate the pattern of dependent plantation

economies, blocking the emergence of self-reliant, truly independent nations. At home and abroad, huge conglomerates variously rape and poison Mother Earth, whether through strip-mining, herbicides, or pollution. Once their old mills and factories start losing money, runaway employers leave behind dying communities, like so much industrial waste. Life itself is threatened by the reckless construction and operation of nuclear plants. Even innocent children are not safe from the greedy corporate reach. Seductive TV commercials lure them to nutritionally worthless junk foods. Worse yet, by pushing infant formula on Third World mothers who can neither afford it in sufficient amounts nor prepare it in sufficient amounts, the companies are responsible for disastrous consequences of a significant fall-off in breast-feeding.[10]

Nickel claims that Protestant activists demonstrate a "generalized sympathy toward the economic plight of the Third World" which took a very specific antibusiness direction. This antibusiness emphasis originated in the World Council of Churches' five-year-old campaign against multinationals. The work of the churches "sounds like a replay of the New Left of the protesting Sixties."[11] The student radicals of the 1970s then joined groups such as the Interfaith Center on Corporate Responsibility and in time occupied key positions. Once in a key position they coordinated and orchestrated shareholder resolutions. "To generalize, the resolutions seemed designed less to uplift the world's less fortunate people than to indict the business establishment."[12]

Nickel contended:

> Much of the data on which the church actvists rely are supplied by radical research organizations. For South African issues, the Institute for Policy Studies and the American Committee on Africa provide properly revolutionary analyses. Another important resource is the unabashedly pro-Castro North American Congress on Latin America in New York.[13]

Nickel accused the church groups of affiliating with "radicals" who use the church as a tax exemption shield and for "respectability and legitimacy" as well as providing a "large organizational network." "What better way to challenge the existing system than to brand it as an offense to the will of God?"[14] Nickel faults the church activists for presenting "business related issues as morally clear-cut and simple—when in fact they are usually complex, morally ambiguous and involve difficult policy trade-offs."[15]

John C. Boland in the financial weekly *Barron's* reported that "Management has welcomed the critics as warmly as it would a Leninist brigade mounting the ramparts."[16] He accused the director of the Interfaith Center on Corporate Responsibility, the Rev. Mr. Timothy Smith, of managing the Center's program to such an extent that it reflects his own personal interests in the priority of social concerns, especially Southern Africa.

The article perceives that while Mr. Smith claims that the various member denominations set the goals for the Center through administrative machinery,

> yet over the years there has been a persistent selectivity in the aims of the churches' resolutions that seem to fit comfortably with Tim Smith's interests. A transplanted Canadian, Smith took a divinity degree at Union Theological Seminary and launched into an intensive study of Africa that appears to have brought him into more than casual contact with supporters of Marxist guerilla movements.[17]

Michael Jensen and William Meckling of the Center for Research in Government Policy and Business, the Graduate School of Management, University of Rochester, also put into words the feelings and thoughts of some business people, especially when they say that corporations are being coerced "to serve as vehicles for effecting almost any social concern which happens to take someone's fancy."[18] Imposition of corporate social responsibility, whether by law or coercive activity, is a "brilliant fallacy" for a moment's thought

> will convince almost anyone that since the corporation is not human (in fact, it is only a legal fiction which serves as a nexus for a very complex set of contracts between individuals) . . . and to speak of imposing costs or benefits on it is just as sensible as speaking about imposing costs or benefits on a rock or a machine.[19]

The authors argue that what really happens is that in the name of corporate social responsibility money is transferred from the owners of the corporation to certain beneficiaries, usually those designated by the special interest groups. A corporation cannot operate in this manner for when this procedure is followed it becomes abundantly clear that this sort of behavior is

> abrogating the rights of the owners; the value of corporate ownership will fall, and corporations will be unable to raise new capital, or will be able to raise it only at very high costs. The costs imposed on the owners of corporations through the implementation of the notion of corporate responsibility (often accomplished through procedures which are only thinly disguised blackmail) is generally equivalent to the imposition of special taxes on these owners.[20]

Deane Carson writing in the *New York Times* (with an appropriate title for a Christmas day article, "Companies as Heroes? Bah! Hambug!") states that advocates of modern corporate social responsibility have created an illusion. This illusion develops from the view that the corporation is an appropriate institution for the achievement of socio-economic reform.[21] Carson argues that the corporation is "notoriously ill-suited" to take on responsibilities for social reform, primarily because corporations are owned by particular stockholders who do not necessarily represent the population at large. Further, under the present corporate structure, there is no way that a private company can be held publicly accountable for social decisions.

> The political illusion that corporations are equipped to measure and implement public interest is more than matched by the economic illusions of the new view. The most outrageous of these is that the corporation and its stockholders bear the cost of its forays into the field of nonmarket social responsibility.[22]

"Non-market social responsibility" is highly objectionable, according to Carson, as it demands that profits be used to pay for social adventures. This, in turn, forces companies to charge higher prices for their products which then ultimately means the consumer becomes an unwilling accomplice to these social ventures. "In this sense, the corporation acts as Robin Hood, with the significant difference that while Robin Hood robbed only the rich to distribute to the poor, the corporate Robin Hood robs rich and poor indiscriminately."[23]

Some conservative Protestant churchmen also voiced strong objections to Protestant churches' involvement in business activities. In June 1978 the Church League of America, a small conservative Protestant group, labeled corporate responsibility as no more than an attack on American industry and subversion by Proxy.[24] The activity of Protestant churches with relation to corporations was no more than "an attempt by radical church groups in collaboration with an organization formed by avowed revolutionaries" with only one purpose and that was to bring "American corporate policies into line with hard-core leftist dogma."[25] The Church League warned that work by Protestant churches in the arena of corporate social responsibility is "not a reform movement."[26] Further,

> the corporate responsibility movement is not a popularized version of the venerable and almost forgotten Better Business Bureau that for years has arbitrated customer complaints about the quality of goods and services received from private companies. The Better Business Bureau has primarily served the local community and has always strived to do what its name implied; that is, to make business better. The corporate responsibility movement, on the other hand, is not concerned with the quality of local retail service, nor with customer complaints, not even with "truth in advertising." Rather than trying to make business better, the movement is trying to replace business with an "alternative system."[27]

The "alternative system" the Church League claims is that of socialism. The article was followed up with a *Special Report* in 1979 that blazoned "American Businessmen Must Understand the Soviet Propaganda Attack on Corporations." The article, written by Sidney Jaffe, President of Great Minibooks, Inc., warned: "If you are a corporation with overseas branches, your name may be on a hit list at the Interfaith Center on Corporate Responsibility."[28] Jaffe argued that the destruction of confidence in American industry is the "Kremlin method" and it is the use of this method that would diminish the power of the United States to stand in the way of the Soviets for world conquest. Jaffe claimed that the so-called "public interest" coalitions capture naive supporters and stage media events and utilize "distorted language" to heap insult upon injury on corporations hiding behind the term "corporation responsibility." "It sounds pure, it is readily embraced by men of genuine good will who are naive and wish to satisfy the public."[29] Jaffe continues:

> But the enemy repeats relentlessly its same absurdities, typical of hundreds of similar campaigns, launched against corporations, adding up to the present hostile atmosphere. Good deeds do not assuage them, nor sound economic reasoning.[30]

The Church League argued that the church activists' "war-on-business" was prompted only by a desire to weaken the American corporation and thereby destroy the public's confidence in the free enterprise system. This ultimately will play into the hands of the Soviets. "Incredibly," Jaffe asserts, "propaganda attacks have been mainly channeled through tax-free, noble-sounding organizations, with church leaders and church institutions in the forefront initiating the attack."[31]

Business Response: Reaffirmation of the Classical or Traditional Position

The classical or traditional position of business as it relates to the concept of corporate social responsibility is succinctly described in the words of Nobel Laureate economist Milton Friedman:

> There is one and only one social responsibility of business—to use its resources and engage in activities designed to increase its profits so long as it stays within the rules of the game, which is to say, engages in open and free competiton without deception or fraud. . . . Few trends could so thoroughly undermine the very foundations of our free society as the acceptance by corporate officials of a social responsibility other than to make as much money for their shareholders as possible.[32]

This view essentially states that managers cannot give away what is not theirs to give. Managers are employed by shareholders and, therefore, can only utilize corporate assets for money making purposes. The classic view sees social responsibility as a form of charity which in turn reduces corporate efficiency. In the extreme perspective, social responsibility is outright theft.[33] According to Friedman, engaging in any form of social responsibility is nonprofit maximizing behavior which has been undertaken to benefit persons who are not shareholders.

The classical view of corporate social responsibility is an outgrowth of the original argument for laissez faire in the conduct of business originally voiced by Adam Smith in early American business life. Smith argued that as each man pursued economic gain for his own purposes, he would be led by an invisible hand which would work for the benefit of all of society. A laissez faire kind of environment assures a beneficial allocation of resources through the marketplace. It is in the marketplace that a seller will sell only what a buyer is willing to buy and where an employee will work only where an employer will provide an adequate wage. "And the market does this impersonally and without centralized authority."[34]

While the government should use its power to protect the businessman, it is up to the businessman alone to decide how business capital should be invested. The power of the government is never to be used as a coercive force as these kinds of pressures are not conducive to a free economy.

According to Friedman, the concept of corporate social responsibility is not consistent with the character and nature of a free economy.

> The discussions of "social responsibilities of business" are notable for their analytical looseness and lack of rigor. What does it mean to say that "business" has responsibilities? A corporation is an artificial person and in this sense may have artificial responsibilities, but "business" as a whole cannot be said to have responsibilities, even in this vague sense.[35]

Further, how is the executive to determine in what measure he is to participate in those so-called social responsibilities. "What is his appropriate share and what is the appropriate share of others? And whether he wants to or not, can he get away with spending his stockholders', customers' or employees' money?"[36] Business has limited resources. It is not a bottomless pit of funds to be utilized in various ways at the whim of those who control corporate funds. It is not right for society to demand of business that goods and services be produced in an efficient manner and at the same time to also demand that other problems also be shouldered which are not related to direct business functions. Friedman declared that social responsibility was a "subversive doctrine" as it saps the profit intentions of business managers.[37]

Theodore Levitt, in an article in the *Harvard Business Review* entitled "The Dangers of Social Responsibility," declared that there are always certain narrow interest groups who are in the midst of endeavors to influence and dominate the private lives of citizens. Each are out to promote their own ideas and each wants to "do what it honestly believes is best for society" and "there is nothing more corrupting than self-righteousness and nothing more intolerant than an ardent man who is convinced he is on the side of the angels."[38] According to Levitt, society benefits when business succeeds—and business succeeds only when it does so economically. Corporations are not in the business of welfare and the only "function of business is to produce sustained high-level profits."[39] If corporations attempt to involve themselves deeply in any form of "corporate social responsibility" they will be assuming the role of government, as only the government should be involved in the welfare of society. Imagine, he cautioned, if the government and the corporation should team up with one view towards the welfare of society; the corporation could then

> eventually invest itself with all-embracing duties, obligations, and finally power—ministering to the whole man and molding him and society into the image of the corporation's narrow ambitions and its essentially unsocial needs.[40]

There is danger, warns Levitt, of moving toward a monolithic society as the more corporations are involved in social affairs, the more the institutional, social, cultural and political aspects of society would be influenced by corporate dictates. There is only one way to avoid this, states Levitt, and that is to pursue "the rule of capitalism"—something is good only if it pays, as "sentiment or idealism ought not be let in by the door. Sentiment is a corrupting and a debilitating influence in business. It fosters leniency, inefficiency, sluggishness, extravagance, and hardens the innovative arteries."[41]

Hacker was another advocate and interpreter of the so-called classical position of business with relation to corporate social responsibility. He declared forthrightly: "For all the self-congratulatory handouts depicting the large firms as 'good citizens,' the fact remains that a business enterprise exists purely and simply to make more profits."[42] Businessmen cannot be "philosopher-kings" and, therefore, it should come as no surprise to note that no American corporation has fostered large scale civil rights programs. Corporations have tremendous economic power and should they become involved in societal affairs in a large way, it could result in a mixed blessing. "For then the rest of us would have to let corporate management define just what constitutes 'good citizenship' and we would have to accept such benefactions without an excuse or comment or criticism."[43]

Business Response: Moderate View of Business Toward Corporate Social Responsibility

In a book published by the American Management Association, John Humble advises:

> Clearly it is a myth that business concerned basically with profit is free to treat social responsibilities as an "optional extra." Whether it likes it or not, business has always been obliged to adapt itself to changing expectations of the community in order to survive.[44]

This sentiment is echoed by a company chief executive officer:

> Today's business executive is engaging more fully in community and national affairs because it is natural and inevitable that he should, and because he cannot survive outside pressures if he does not. The executive sees that social action is not an option.[45]

Kastenholz noted in the *Financial Executive* that "social responsibility is a basic principle of business operation in today's climate. It is an investment in long-range goodwill and in freedom from government intervention."[46]

The Conference Board noted in 1979 that "most sophisticated businessmen" recognize their obligations to society and therefore express a "willingness to undertake charitable and citizenlike activities" which in fact are "far beyond what they would accept as their legal duty." "In so doing they are helping to soften and civilize the attitudinal problems inevitably associated with corporate size and influence."[47]

Davis, writing in the *Academy of Management Journal,* suggested the following reasons for business wanting to assume responsibility for social concerns: enlightened self-interest, public image, viability of business, avoidance of government regulations, socio-cultural norms, stockholders' interest, and profitability.[48]

Bowman and Haire advocated a positive response because corporate social involvement is a "signal of good, sensitive, informed, balanced, modern, negotiating, co-opting management."[49]

Jerry Kinard in his doctoral dissertation "A Survey of Industrial Corporate Executives' Attitudes Toward Social Responsibility" concluded that industrial corporate executives' attitudes toward social responsibility have become substantially positive.[50]

Peter Drucker, a well-known business authority, in endorsing a moderate view of corporate social responsibility, suggested upper and lower limits as parameters for corporate involvement in social responsibility.[51] He argued that the primary duty of the corporation is to provide society with products and services of the quality it wants and at a price it is willing to pay. In order to accomplish these objectives, the corporation must be managed profitably. Engagement in activities which diminish the effectiveness of the corporation in performing its primary economic duties is socially irresponsible. There is no benefit to a local community when a plant shuts down because of inefficiency. Closing a plant is neither an act of a good neighbor or a good employer. The upper limits, then, provide a boundary beyond which a corporation should not traverse—that is, expending its economic resources for social concerns which tend to impair the corporation's economic effectiveness. Business must remain in those areas where it can retain its competency and economic strength; to plunge into social activities that are beyond its own basic charter is in actuality taxation without representation on the part of shareholders. There are, however, lower limits which corporations also should be cautious about violating. There is an absolute minimum which no responsible corporation should fall below. Simply, no industry should inflict upon society harmful by-products issuing out of the production of company products. Further, not only should business take definite steps to curb harmful by-products, they should also offer assistance in its own industry in the formulation of legislation to regulate the industry so as to minimize the effects of harmful by-products.

In 1975 the American Management Association conducted a survey—perhaps one of the largest ever conducted on the subject of corporate social responsibility. Questionnaires were mailed to some 4,820 corporate presidents. The mailing resulted in some 644 usable replies, or about 13 percent of the recipients. Replies were received from heads of large and small companies and represented companies in various manufacturing and service industries. More than 68 percent of the respondents agreed with this statement:

> We have reason to be concerned whether the corporation as we know it . . . will survive into the next century. . . . The corporation itself must change, consciously evolving into an institution adapted to the new environment.[52]

Further, the study showed the respondents as affirming that business must "do more than the law demands" as far as social concerns were involved. Eighty-six percent of the respondents said that the companies they represented had already instituted voluntary programs, as well as some mandated programs, in behalf of social concerns. These executives asserted that they do feel a need to serve society in a better way, but they are under constraints because of the nature of the corporate charters which demand that profits must come first. Further, these same executives advise that they become puzzled as to whose "demands" they are to respond to, as demands emanate from a host of special interest groups who are concerned only with their own specific interests. As a consequence it becomes difficult to identify "social problems" or appropriate targets. In addition, executives express concern as to how far they can go in committing corporate funds and resources to any one specific target.[53]

Definitions of the term corporate social responsibility emerging in the 1970s are also indicative of a shift on the part of at least a segment of business toward a more moderate view. George A. Steiner, writing in The *Conference Board Record* provided the following definition which reflects a concern for society as well as recognizing the profit impact on corporations:

> Conceptually, social responsibility generally refers to actions which a company takes partially with a view of helping society achieve objectives which it sets for itself. They may also be classified into internal and external activities. Internally, they may refer to such matters as due process, justice and equity in hiring, promoting or firing employees. Externally, they may concern a wide range of actions from improving consumer products to training and hiring hardcore unemployed. Finally, they may be considered in terms of profit. Some socially responsible actions may increase both short- and long-range profits. Others can reduce both.[54]

Steiner's comments regarding profits should be noted. Some definitions of corporate social responsibility place emphasis on profits . . . or the lack of . . . when corporations take on socially-oriented endeavors. Charles Clark, in his Ph.D. dissertation, defines social responsibility as "any function of the corporation internal or external which is not connected with or tends to militate against the immediate maximization of profits."[55] Steven Dilley concurs with this in *CA Magazine* when he describes socially relevant activities as those performed by private enterprise without the expectation of direct economic gain or loss.[56] Manne, writing for the American Enterprise Institute for Policy Research, sees corporations earning less when taking on socially-related commitments as contrasted to more profitable returns had the same money been invested in business enterprises.[57]

While some definitions reflect on the possibility of some decrease in profits when corporations involve themselves in social responsibility, a positive view is maintained. Dan Fenn, in his book *Business Responsibility in Action,* sees corporate social involvement as a "modern amalgam of corporate good citizenship, personal ethics, and rational management."[58] Prof. Gray of the Business School of Louisiana concurs and argues that in a minimum sense, social responsibility involves an expanded awareness on the part of the businessman of the social environment in which his firm operates and a commitment to help in the solution of social problems.[59]

The Chamber of Commerce in the U.S.A. provides an excellent definition exemplifying the moderate view of business toward corporate social responsibility. They describe it on four levels: (1) meeting legal requirements; (2) meeting the standards of performance that the public expects; (3) anticipating new demands from society and making advance preparation to meet them; and (4) acting as a leader in setting new performance standards.[60]

Joseph Monsen observed in *Business and the Changing Environment* that a socially responsible firm is "one that anticipates what the public will expect from it and attempts to meet these demands before the public focuses its criticisms upon it."[61]

In a book prepared as a guide to universities relative to ethical investing, the authors find that while there is disagreement as to the precise definition of social responsibility, there is a "moral minimum" for which persons, and including corporations, should abide by and that is the avoidance and correction of social injury for which they may be responsible.[62] The authors caution that they do not mean to distinguish "between negative injunctions and affirmative duties" but rather

> we call it a "moral minimum" implying that however one may choose to limit the concept of social responsibility, one cannot exclude this negative injunction. Although reasons may exist why certain persons or institutions cannot or should not be required to pursue moral or social good in all situations, there are many fewer reasons why one should be excused from the injunction against injuring others.[63]

This observation was also reflected in Alden G. Lank's Ph.D. dissertation when he noted that any definition of social responsibility must include a key element: corporations must always be conscious of their role as efficient producers of goods and services and they "must of necessity be conscious of the non-economic, detrimental effects of their activities."[64]

Corporate Philanthropy. It would not be appropriate to conclude the segment on the moderate view of business toward social responsibility without commenting on business efforts in the realm of philanthropy and other social endeavors. These very clearly indicate a movement away from a rigid traditional concept of corporate social responsibility and recognize a need for a certain amount of social involvement.

Corporate philanthropy did not emerge in the 1970s from pressures of society; rather, it developed out of necessity in the mid-1880s. Railroads sought housing for their employees, especially as tracks began to traverse great stretches of land throughout the United States. In order to provide living quarters at various division points and localities, the railroads teamed up with the Young Men's Christian Association to provide housing. The railroads contributed about 60 percent to the cost of the buildings and the employees paid the balance.

World War I created new needs. The Red Cross undertook some of the more urgent needs and received a substantial amount of their support from American corporations. Corporations also contributed to the United War Work Campaign which funded a number of charitable organizations.

Following World War I, corporations continued to contribute to united funds as well as educational and cultural efforts. The Conference Board reported that corporations gave $2.07 billion in 1978. This represents actual dollars and does not take into consideration the time, talent and administrative costs involved with the collection of the money for various fund drives.

Contributions by corporations to charitable causes, including educational institutions, have not been without challenge on the part of stockholders. There are stockholders who take strong exception to corporations using corporate funds in efforts other than business ventures which produce profits. In a landmark case involving a corporate donation to Princeton University *(A. P. Smith* v. *Barlow,* 1956), legal precedents were set for the continued involvement of American business in philanthropy. The New Jersey Supreme Court ruled in favor of corporate contributions and commented that "contributions here in question are toward a cause which is ultimately tied into the preservation of American business and the American way of life. In the Court's view, charitable giving amounts to a solemn duty."[65] Based on this court decision the legality of a contribution to Princeton University was confirmed as appropriate and the American tradition of corporate contributions upheld.

Following this landmark case, contributions to educational institutions by corporations have continued unabated. A Harris Poll, sponsored by the Council for Financial Aid to Education, indicated that colleges and universities have a growing dependence on the business community.[66]

Activities in Corporate Social Responsibility. In addition to philanthropic efforts, corporations were involved in a wide range of social efforts during the 1970s; again indicating a more moderate view of corporate social responsibility. Below are listed some typical examples of these activities.

Finding jobs and training opportunities in collaboration with the National Alliance of Businessmen.

Supporting basic and applied research to enhance the quality of life and to encourage economic growth.
Carrying on drug abuse educational programs for employees.
Providing free drugs for indigent patients.
Hiring Vietnam veterans.
Hiring ex-convicts.
Sponsoring sports events for local causes.
On loan personnel to business-government teamwork.
Working to improve business management and education in local schools.
Conducting regional planning studies.
Participating in local fund raising efforts to provide day-to-day care for persons qualifying under approved institutions, and spearheading fund raising programs for new buildings, privately operated and managed, for organizations such as the YMCA, YWCA, Salvation Army, and others serving the indigent, the physically handicapped, and the mentally retarded.
Participating in financial campaigns for new hospitals or extensions of existing hospital facilities.
Providing management assistance to urban school systems.
Involvement in rehabilitation of physically handicapped.
Sponsoring engineering education for minorities.
Making capital grants for community hospitals.
Providing business to minority-owned vendors.
Building a variety of retailing facilities within the inner cities.
Training high school students and adults in sound personal money management.
Matching gifts program for employees.
Financing low- and middle-income housing.
Maintaining plants and sales offices in the ghettos.
Supporting the development of black-managed banks.
Promoting the developing of housing, services, and activities for aged persons.
Supporting ecological projects.
Assisting with various community development projects.
Supporting youth-work programs.
Providing opportunities for continuing education.[67]

This segment has provided descriptions of three responses of business toward corporate social responsibility: (1) the more radical, outspoken, critical opponents of church activism; (2) the reaffirmation on the part of business of the classical or traditional view of corporate social responsibility; and (3) the more moderate view of corporate social responsibility which appears to be filtering throughout the business community.

The following section presents specific responses of various corporations to specific shareholder resolutions that were filed by Protestant churches in behalf of particular social concerns.

Specific Responses by Business to Protestant Shareholder Resolutions

The particular issues involved have been described in chapter 2 and were presented from the viewpoint of the proponents. This segment provides the viewpoints of the targeted corporations involved. The responses on the part of corporate management are provided on an issue-to-issue basis and follow the same sequence as given in chapter 2.

Apartheid in the Republic of South Africa.

It was reasoned by the Protestant churches that the continued presence of American corporations in South Africa buttressed the oppressive governing regime. The purpose of Protestant churches filing shareholder resolutions with American corporations (who had operations in South Africa) was to influence these corporations to use their vast economic power to influence South Africa's government to ameliorate their attitude toward apartheid. While corporate managements appreciated the social concern of the churches over the oppressive practices of apartheid in South Africa, business leaders concluded that to withdraw would be a failure to live up to the obligations they owed to the populace in South Africa and to work for constructive change. Further, closing down plants in that country would only impede South Africa's economic development and this would not contribute to a solution of South Africa's racial problem.[68] Withdrawal of international financing to South Africa would lead to a constriction of that country's economy and probably would have a disproportionate adverse effect upon the black community.[69] In fact, adoption of Protestant shareholder resolutions for withdrawal of American companies from South Africa would run counter to the frequently expressed desire of some nonwhite leaders in South Africa who have urged an increase in foreign investment there to provide jobs and raise the living standards of nonwhites.[70] Further, management argued that doing business in South Africa did not constitute a general endorsement of that country's laws or economic policy.[71] However, business leaders would hasten to say that it was imperative that they comply with the regulations of the host government. There were also business worries that a failure to expand investments in South Africa could jeopardize a corporation's ability to maintain a competitive position as many foreign companies were also operating in South Africa. Outright withdrawal of operations from that nation could result in substantial losses which would impact adversely on stockholders.[72] As far as the sale of specific products, such as computers and photographic equipment, were concerned, management argued that U.S. laws do not prohibit the shipment of such items; further, corporations cannot control the actions of their customers and it would be futile and misleading to adopt criteria for their use.[73] Finally, business argued that United States foreign policy should be conducted by the U.S. government and not by corporations. If Protestant shareholder resolutions were adopted it would subordinate business decisions to foreign goals of particular shareholders.[74]

Apartheid in Namibia

The white populace, holding complete legislative power, maintained the same restrictive policies of apartheid that existed in the Republic of South Africa. Protestant churches sought to support the actions of the United Nations and appealed to the American corporations for their help in an amelioration of the strictures of apartheid. Shareholder resolutions were filed with a number of corporations asking that they withdraw their operations from Namibia. Churches argued that by the U.S. corporations remaining in Namibia, they were encouraging the current Namibian government by providing economic incentives. While corporate management agreed that the apartheid system was "abhorrent" they did feel, contrary to the churches' view, that the black Namibian was being benefitted by American business presence.[75] The oil companies who were exploring for new sources of oil opined that it was necessary for them to explore wherever possible because of the energy shortage.[76] Management contended that American business presence did not imply an endorsement of Namibian governmental policies.[77] They were guests in a host country and "to attempt directly or indirectly, to influence the political views of any nation or its people or to terminate its profitable operations where those views may be distasteful to the Company's management or some of its stockholders" is poor judgment.[78] Finally, the presence or absence of an American plant will not in the long run affect the social structure of that country. When an American company withdraws, another company of non-U.S. origin will move in to take its place.[79]

Apartheid in Rhodesia

In 1965 the existing Rhodesian government unilaterally disaffiliated itself with Britain and issued a Unilateral Declaration of Independence. This in essence disengaged Rhodesia from Britain and placed the white-dominated Rhodesian government completely in control of the country. The world community opposed this action by the Rhodesian government and through the United Nations sanctions were sought against Rhodesia. The Protestant churches sought to support the effectiveness of these sanctions by filing shareholder resolutions with various corporations to ban direct or indirect oil sales to Rhodesia. A shareholder resolution was filed with Union Carbide asking that corporation not to purchase chrome ore from Rhodesia. With regard to the importation of chrome ore, Union Carbide argued that ferrochrome (which requires the chrome ore) was of vital importance to United States' security and economic well-being, that it had been importing chrome from Rhodesia for many years and, further, in 1972 it was authorized by law to continue importation.[80] The oil companies with whom shareholder resolutions were filed relative to preventing the direct or indirect flow of oil into Rhodesia, argued that the Protestant churches were attempting to preempt the foreign policy making function of the United States government by asking the companies to impose a partial trade embargo. Mobil argued that it was inappropriate for a multinational commercial enterprise to meddle in delicate diplomatic matters. Mobil further stated that church groups were suggesting "nothing more or less than organized economic sanctions against South Africa" and "sanctions can be properly instituted, if at all, only by governments and not by private companies."[81] "Indeed for private companies to undertake any such activities in concert with each other or with private individuals would, in many instances, constitute a violation of various laws prohibiting combinations and conspiracies in restraint of trade."[82]

Colonialism in the Portuguese Territories of Angola, Guinea-Bissau and Mozambique

In the early 1970s these three countries were under the control of the Portuguese government. All three were struggling for independence and the Protestant churches sought to support this struggle by filing shareholder resolutions with three American companies asking that they withdraw their operations from these countries. The Protestants argued that Portuguese colonialism was being aided by taxes and royalty payments from American business. In response to the Protestant questions concerning colonialism in Angola, Gulf Oil through its spokesman Mr. Connolly, advised that (1) as a guest, they must behave like one, (2) activists were attempting to use Gulf as a political tool, and (3) the issue is not one of racism but political intervention.[83] Connolly states:

> At our first meeting with these five church people back in early March of 1970, it was soon evident that even they did not believe it was racism and that the real issue was their decision to furnish active support to forces attempting to seize control of Angola from the Portuguese.[84]

Connolly contended that no matter how Gulf may feel about political changes in Angola, Gulf was in a good position to contribute to the social progress of that country by helping to raise the standard of living through revenues that flow directly into the local economy.

The situation involving Guinea-Bissau was similar to that of Angola. Guinea-Bissau also sought independence from Portugal. Exxon was involved in oil exploration in that country when a shareholder resolution was filed asking that they close down their operations there. Exxon disputed this contention and asserted that: (1) they had entered into a contract with a legally constituted government which was recognized by the United States government; (2) Exxon's activities in Guinea-Bissau was part of a continuing worldwide exploration program to find new sources of oil; and (3) management must be mindful of the corporation's basic responsibility, and indeed its basic principal for being, and that was to find and bring to market energy required to meet mankind's needs.[85]

The Mozambique scenario was the same as Angola and Guinea-Bissau but in this case it was Bethlehem Steel Corporation that was involved. The shareholder resolutions had been filed too late for inclusion in the proxy statement and therefore was brought up at the annual meeting from the floor. Bethlehem's position was that the concession in Mozambique was essentially inactive and which had been the case since 1969. Further, there was no reason to give up the concession as it was possible that at a future date, when the political and military situation in Mozambique was stabilized, Bethlehem may want to continue operations there.

Human Rights in Chile

Protestant churches, concerned about the military dictatorship in Chile, which they claimed systematically violated human rights, filed shareholder resolutions with General Motors, ITT, and Superior Oil in the latter half of the 1970s. GM was asked not to expand its operations in that country. GM refuted the churches' arguments and declared that they had been doing business in Chile since 1908 and it was their firm belief that their presence in that country was of material advantage to the Chilean people. Further, GM affirmed that it has abided by all the laws of Chile; has treated its employees fairly and equitably; and will continue to exert every reasonable effort to improve the social and economic conditions of its Chilean employees.[86] ITT was petitioned relative to political contributions it had made in Chile in the past. ITT affirmed that it had made adequate disclosure as to its activities in Chile. In fact, many reports had been furnished to the media so that any further disclosure would only be redundant.[87] Superior Oil was requested not to make any further investments in Chile. The Management of Superior chose not to make any response to the Protestant demands.[88]

Malnutrition, Low Wages and Food Shortages in the Dominican Republic

The National Council of Churches filed a shareholder resolution which contended that Gulf & Western's large investments in export crops such as sugar in a country suffering shortages of food staples were bound to cause problems. The poor received only a small portion of the income; malnutrition stalked the country; wages were low and the family was difficult to support. Gulf & Western, the only corporation targeted on this issue by a Protestant group, responded by stating that they were more saddened than upset by the allegations. G&W felt that although the resolution patently asked for information about G&W's operations in the Dominican Republic, the wording of the resolution created an erroneous impression as to G&W's role in that country.[89] The Chairman of the Board of Gulf & Western, in response to a question asked by one of the analysts at the New York Society of Security Analysts meeting held on June 10, 1974, asserted that "Gulf & Western has done more in the last eight years for the development of the economy and culture of the Dominican Republic than any United States company has ever done in the history of Latin America."[90] Further, he argued, "We are not exploiters of people or resources. We are not stripping the Dominican Republic of its natural assets. We believe G&W is setting an example as a socially responsible American private enterprise."[91] In 1979, when another shareholder resolution was filed with G&W, the corporation judged that the statements furnished in support of the proposed resolution were "either false, misleading, or overly simplistic."[92] In view of the extensive dialogue with proponents of the resolution over a three-year period, G&W concluded that "there comes a point when continued discussion with the proponents of the resolution covering the same ground over and over again becomes an end unto itself and a pointless waste of management time."[93] G&W therefore questioned if any useful purpose was served by engaging in continued dialogue with the church groups.

Questionable Labor Practices in Guatemala

The United Presbyterian Church in the U.S.A. concerned about questionable labor practices in Guatemala requested that Coca-Cola make public a code of minimum labor standards that would be required of its franchised bottlers. The denomination felt that Coca-Cola's reputation, whose shares they held, had become sullied by some franchise bottlers—specifically the bottler in Guatemala. The Coca-Cola Company responded to the Presbyterian allegations by stating that it would be an improper and unnecessary intrusion by the company into the affairs of the local bottlers to adopt such a code. "The laws of many countries protect the rights of workers to organize and collectively bargain. Thus, in many situations, such a clause would serve no purpose."[94] Further, the company affirmed, the adoption of such a proposal could make Coca-Cola a party to industrial controversies between independent bottlers and their employees and could make the company liable for acts or omissions of the independent bottlers. Coca-Cola concluded that they "do not believe that the proxy statement is a proper forum in which to discuss labor relations of a particular independent bottler and its employees."[95]

Wages and Working Conditions in South Korea

The United Church of Christ and the Reformed Church, concerned over wages and working conditions in South Korea, filed shareholder resolutions with Motorola, who operated a plant in that country. The resolutions, filed in 1975 and 1976, asked for disclosure relative to wages, working conditions and relations with trade unions. Motorola responded by observing that such a report singling out characteristics of one Motorola facility could lead to attempted union organization of employees in South Korea or elsewhere, which could result in excessive demands. Ultimately, the time and attention of management would be dissipated to the detriment of Motorola's stockholders and employees. Motorola affirmed that they had already provided what information the proponents of the resolution had requested. Further, they argued that employment and working conditions of their Korean employees were among the best in the area and were properly respectful of the dignity and needs of each employee.[96]

Human Rights in the Philippines

The National Council of Churches and the United Church of Christ concerned about restrictions on human rights in the Philippines, filed a shareholder resolution with the Ford Motor Company in 1974. They asked that Ford provide a report of its history and current operations in the Philippines. Ford responded by declaring that regular or special reports should not be determined by vote of the stockholders. The issuing of such reports must remain the basic responsibility of management and could be considered part of the ordinary business of the corporation. "Moreover, management in this instance, believes that, although the proposal is in the form of the reporting of information, the tenor of it suggests the desirability of a particular change in the Philippines' social and political structure."[97] Ford concluded then that it could not interfere in the internal affairs of the Philippine people and must always operate in accordance with the laws of the host nation.

Employment Practices in Developing Countries

The Christian Church and the United Church of Christ filed resolutions in the latter half of the 1970s requesting a report of Castle & Cooke's labor practices in Costa Rica, Ecuador, Honduras, Nicaragua, Philippines, and Thailand. Castle & Cooke responded by saying that such information would be of use to competitors who would be able to gain valuable proprietary cost information by studying the report. Further, the compilation of the information would be difficult and expensive and inasmuch as it is comprehensive, it would necessitate a voluminous study which, in the long run, would be of interest to only a few shareholders. The company argued that the churches' only apparent purpose was to press the company to attempt social and cultural change beyond the company's ability and resources to achieve. They deplored the churches' effort to malign the corporation through "innuendo, distortion, and outright misstatements."[98] Finally, Castle & Cooke affirmed that it was their conviction that

> the way that the Company can make society more equal and just both at home and in the foreign countries in which it is a guest is to conduct an efficient and prosperous operation, which offers meaningful employment to local citizens and produces goods and services that can be consumed or exported from those countries, thus contributing to their increasing standard of living.[99]

Foreign Military Sales

Three Protestant denominations, concerned over the easy availability of military equipment which they claimed made the world a less secure place in which to live, filed shareholder resolutions with General Electric in 1977 and 1978 and asked for the formation of a Corporate Policy Committee that could evaluate human rights situations in those countries where military equipment was destined. Criteria would be established by the Committee and when those countries who requested military equipment fell below the standards as established, they would not be sold the materials they requested. General Electric responded to the proposals by reminding the churches that only the United States government could set foreign policy for only in this manner would such policies be consistent with U.S. international goals and strategic interests. "Substituting corporate for governmental judgment on these matters seem to us to be presumptuous in a democracy."[100] Further, all military sales to foreign governments continue to be subject to close scrutiny by the Departments of State and Defense and must be approved by the United States government before any sales can be made, GE management argued. Finally, General Electric affirmed that it already had in place adequate procedures which would guarantee that "such transactions" were in harmony with United States policies, as well as insuring that "the Company's reputation, personnel and other interests are fully considered."[101]

Infant Malnutrition Attributable to Infant Formula Use

Nutrition experts affirmed that the improper use of infant formula utilized in place of breast feeding in developing countries, was a cause of malnutrition. Protestant churches joined other groups in an effort to have American corporations, as well as foreign-based Nestle Corporation, cease promotional efforts of the formula. The churches argued that the promotion of the formula undermined Third World governments' breast feeding campaigns and nutrition programs. (Inasmuch as Nestle is not an American corporation, no shareholder resolutions could be filed and instead a boycott was instituted. The matter of the Nestle boycott is discussed in the "Boycott Section" of this study.) Shareholder resolutions were filed with Bristol-Myers and American Home Products by Protestants. Management of these corporations responded to the allegations by asserting that many infants in all parts of the world need a high quality nutritional milk supply when their mothers are unable or unwilling to breast feed them.[102] Decisions as to the availability of infant formulas are prerogatives of foreign governments and their respective health authorities. The use of medical personnel, distribution through medical personnel, and dispersal through medical institutions are appropriate methods as these persons and institutions are in the best position to decide on the proper use of infant formula products. The promotional literature that is furnished by these firms, management affirms, adheres to sound medical practices and is subject to local laws and regulations. American Home Products affirmed that the promotion of their products is subject to international codes of ethics and that the codes do provide for: (1) product information and labeling recognizing breast milk as the feeding of choice; (2) not making product claims that imply its superiority over breast milk; and (3) supplying the user with explicitly worded instructions for use of the product. While agreeing that the milk of the healthy mother was nutritionally superior and ideal, nevertheless, a prepared formula should be available for those occasions when, through sickness, lack of lactation, nipple problems, etc., such formula is essential for the survival of the baby; for supplemental feeding in cases of inadequate lactation; after weaning has commenced; and while working or traveling; and for those mothers who choose not to breast feed. Such a prepared formula should, like your Corporation's products, be based on modern nutritional research, and should approximate the composition of breast milk as nearly as possible.[103]

American Home Products, therefore, was convinced that there was a need for infant formula products throughout the world, including undeveloped countries.

Questionable Corporate Payments Overseas

The churches were alarmed at the disclosures of corporate payments overseas to secure favors for business operations and to influence local governments where American plants were located overseas. Shareholder resolutions were filed asking that a policy be established to prohibit the use of corporate assets that would influence foreign governments in their favor or would allow the securing of favorable contracts by use of bribes. Corporations responded by affirming that they already had firm policies in place that prohibit illegal and improper payments for political purposes.[104] Business leaders also advised that corporate political contributions are legal in certain countries. "With respect to public disclosure of such contributions, the Directors feel that the requirements of host countries should not be superseded by those of the United States and that the contributions should not be disclosed unless such disclosure is required by the host country."[105] In all cases corporations urged stockholders to reject the resolutions while at the same time asserting that "the Directors are neither concealing nor condoning illegal or improper payments or contributions."[106]

Need for Appropriate Farm Technology for Use in Developing Countries

The American Baptist Churches focused on Deere & Company and asked for a report on the involvement of that corporation in the creation of appropriate farm technologies for developing nations that were suitable in cost, scale and energy use for the types of rural social organizations and employable skills located there. Deere responded to the request for small farm equipment manufacture and opined that the wording of the resolution clearly demonstrated that the proponents were seeking shareholder support for certain views which they held about the needs of developing countries and the kinds of farm equipment that would be useful there. "The main purpose of this material is to test the Company's acceptance of the proponent's view."[107] Deere took the position that the agricultural needs of developing countries are varied and the policies and objectives of different governments greatly affect what can be done in foreign countries. Therefore, it was the judgment of Deere that

> a major commitment of resources to the development and production of equipment specifically tailored to very small scale farming is not justified either commercially or as a contribution to the real needs of these countries as we understand them. Moreover, our studies show that appropriate equipment is already available from others, notably Japanese manufacturers.[108]

The Energy Crisis in the United States

Exxon and Gulf were challenged by the American Baptist Churches and the United Church of Christ over the energy crisis in the United States in 1974. The churches argued that the energy crisis was a matter of deep and growing public concern and the role of the oil industry was central to the problem. In view of the urgency of the problem created by the oil shortage, it was the right of stockholders to have access to basic information on oil production and distribution and therefore a full written report was requested. The managements of both oil corporations urged stockholders to vote against the resolutions contending that information had already been provided through reports of all types, including Annual Reports and Interim Reports. Further, "much of the data requested in the Proposal and a great deal more information is being supplied by the Corporation to a number of Federal Governmental agencies and Congressional committees attempting to find solutions to the nation's energy shortage."[109] Further, management continued, information could be found in financial statements that had been prepared for the Securities and Exchange Commission. Therefore it was management's conviction that providing information beyond that required by the U.S. government would be detrimental to the best interests of the corporation's stockholders.[110]

Equal Employment Opportunities and Labor
Practices in the United States

This concern focused on J. P. Stevens, as well as General Electric, IBM, and Xerox. J. P. Stevens responded to the proponents of the resolutions for data on equal employment statistics and certain labor practices by stating that Stevens viewed the shareholder resolutions as part of the AFL-CIO boycott action which was commenced in June 1976 and asserted that the adoption of the resolutions would only aid the boycott effort.[111] General Electric had been asked by the Episcopal Church for specific details on its program of equal employment opportunities for minorities and women. General Electric did not see any value in furnishing raw data on numbers of women and minority groups for each of the company's facilities. GE had no objection to furnishing general data on its equal employment program, but felt that the very selective data could be subject to misinterpretation.[112] IBM responded to the proposal filed by the National Council of Churches with regard to its employment practices covering women and minorities by asserting that it believed it was providing equal employment opportunities for women and minorities and that it was properly discharging its responsibility in this connection.[113] Xerox responded to the United Methodist Church's proposal asking for detail concerning women on their sales force by contending that its commitment to equal employment was well known and clearly demonstrated and, therefore, the preparation of such a report would serve no useful purpose and could, in fact, slow progress.

Political Contributions in the United States

The Episcopal Church filed shareholder resolutions with the Phillips Oil Company and the 3M Company over the donation of corporate funds to a Presidential Campaign Committee in violation of Federal criminal statutes. The resolutions asked that the companies implement internal procedures to assure that such illegal contributions could not be made again in the future. 3M management agreed with the proposal and it received 97.7 percent of the vote.[114] Phillips did not disagree with the intent of the proposal but felt it was redundant. Phillips felt that appropriate and decisive remedial action had already been put into place which demonstrated the company's firm resolve to avoid any recurrence of a violation of the law. It was the conviction of the management of Phillips that the useful objectives of the proposal had already been accomplished through firm company action and nothing further would be achieved by the adoption of the proposal.[115]

Redlining/Urban Community Revitalization

Chemical New York Bank was petitioned in 1978 and 1979 and the First National Bank of Boston in 1979 by the United Methodist Church with proposals to commit the banks to revitalizing the urban communities in which they were situated by establishing a Community Reinvestment Review Committee.[116] The work of the committee, according to the proponents, would lead to an increased availability of residential mortgages in local urban communities and would create new programs of reinvestment. Both banks rejected the suggestion and said that the adoption of such a proposal would serve no real purpose as banks must have flexibility to meet credit demands wherever they may arise and that are consistent with the obligations of the bank to its depositors and to all stockholders of the corporation. By mandating credit allocations through actions of the Committee, this would, in essence, impose strictures on the bank. Bank management averred that they were in full compliance with the Community Reinvestment Act and were making regular public reports. It was the judgment of some bankers that certain regulations already in place controlling actions of the banks and designed to prevent redlining, have in actuality substantially increased home mortgage costs and have placed unnecessary burdens on lending institutions which in turn have harmed disadvantaged borrowers.

Strip Mining and Detrimental Effects of Other Mining Operations

A number of shareholder resolutions were filed with corporations over reclaiming land which had been affected by mining operations as well as over the environmental effects of strip mining. The churches argued that strip mining was the most destructive method of extracting coal and generated social, economic and ecological problems for the peoples who were affected by these operations. Churches therefore requested disclosure on such activities. The response of the corporations followed the theme that the preparation of a report as requested would cover only a minor part of the company's business, was burdensome, and would be of interest to only a few.[117] The preparation of such reports was an unnecessary expenditure of time and money in view of the fact that these data were already on file with state and federal agencies and were also available to those who have legitimate interest in such data.[118] The management of mining companies asserted that they have complied fully with all applicable laws and have provided adequate reclamation processes for surface-mined lands and have kept the public fully informed as to its reclamation policies.[119]

Nomination of a Woman to Board of Directors

The Christian Church filed a resolution with the American Fletcher Corporation (a bank) and argued that the bank had consistently nominated only men to the Board of Directors. Management responded to this contention by declaring that if such a resolution was adopted it would imply that the election of a corporate director would be heavily influenced by sex and not by the qualifications of the individual. This kind of action, in their opinion, would be discriminatory. Further, management did not feel that stockholders should mandate the selection of members of the board by sex, race, color or creed. "It is the continuing policy to recommend for election directors who are the most highly qualified individuals," the bank declared. These qualifications would include "a management and professional skill, community involvement and interest, business background and acumen and a dedicated interest in insuring that the Corporation is in sound financial condition and properly managed."[120]

Impact of Television Advertising on Children's Nutrition

The Church of the Brethren had filed a shareholder resolution with Pillsbury in 1979 over certain advertising of Burger King, a subsidiary. The resolution asked that the company voluntarily adopt the guidelines on advertising to children as outlined by the Federal Trade Commission. The church withdrew the resolution when advised by Pillsbury that the company's advertising to children was to be phased out. Food manufacturers are not convinced, however, that it is the advertising per se that contributes to possible poor diets on the part of children for several reasons: (a) there is little available proof that establishes a connection between poor diets and television advertising; (b) the focus on the use of highly sugared products may not be appropriate in that tooth decay and health problems may be due to the frequency of the consumption more so than the specific sugar content of a particular food; (c) it is the responsibility of parents to govern what foods are used by their children; and (d), there is a question of age-old issue of censorship, who should say "yes" or "no" to what is to be marketed.

Stereotypical Images of Women in Advertising

The United Church of Christ filed a resolution in 1976 with Colgate-Palmolive and the United Presbyterian Church filed a resolution with Procter and Gamble. Both requested a report concerning the advertising done by these companies. The churches felt that the preparation of such a report would allow a review of the images presented of women in advertising. Management disagreed that such a report would be of any value to shareholders. Colgate-Palmolive, for example, unequivocally stated that no other company had a record superior to Colgate's in casting women in a wide diversity of roles in its advertising. They contended that their advertising has included women portrayed as executives, designers, athletes, educators, mothers, and homemakers. The company was proud that it was a recognized leader in promoting women in sports and in awarding prize money equal to that earned by men. They argued that they had expanded women's participation in advertising and had made contributions in altering the thinking of many members of the public with regard to the role of women in the world today.[121]

Sponsoring Television Programs Containing Violence

Three shareholder resolutions were filed in connection with sponsoring television programs containing violence, and these involved McDonald's, Pillsbury, and Sears, Roebuck. All were withdrawn when the companies agreed to avoid placing advertisements with broadcasting companies that permitted television programs to be aired that contained excessive and gratuitous violence. Although broadcasting companies are taking steps to reduce excessive violence, this does not necessarily indicate that they are in complete agreement with the proponents of the resolutions. Business does not feel that the entire issue is as clear cut as the churches would like to suggest. However, with increasing pressures on the part of the public in general for a decrease in gratuitous violence, both the sponsors of television shows and the programmers themselves appear to be impacted by pressures for less violence on television.

Nuclear Weapons Production

There were three shareholder resolutions filed during 1979 on the issue of nuclear weapons production and these involved General Electric, Monsanto and Union Carbide. All resolutions were withdrawn after the companies agreed to furnish the information that was requested. The debate over the use of nuclear power, in different configurations whether for bombs or creating electrical energy, is bound to heat up during the decade of the 1980s. The use of nuclear fuels by utility companies will be a special target. The churches no doubt will continue a strong degree of opposition to the utilization of nuclear power for generating electric energy. Management of utilities, however, will argue that the expansion of nuclear power is the only practical option available which can help meet urgent energy requirements. Business, in assessing the potential of producing energy from such sources as fusion, solar and geothermal power, feel that none of these will result in commercially significant additions to the U.S. electric power supply in this century. Therefore, companies such as General Electric will continue to argue that the use of nuclear power is essential as part of a balanced U.S. energy program. Business will argue

154 *Business Responses*

that there must be growth in energy supplies in order to maintain or improve the standard of living, and the only viable and meaningful alternative to fossil fuels is resorting to nuclear power. Not only is nuclear power a realistic alternative, but can prove to be cheaper. The positions of the critics of nuclear power are well-known and are powerful. Nuclear power plants are potential health and environmental risks and until these risks can be minimized to a better degree than they have thus-far, the controversy will continue to rage.

Business Policy Modifications in Response to Pressures on Social Issues

Pressures brought to bear on corporations for changes in policy relative to social issues were generated from various sources. The Protestant churches were a distinct force. However, even though their efforts were unique and distinguishable, they were for the most part in concert with others. Therefore, it is not practical, or even fair, to attribute corporate policy changes to the efforts of the Protestants alone.

It is, however, possible to survey the impact of the pressures for corporate policy changes during the decade of the 1970s as it involved social concerns, and to note what progress has been made with relation to these issues, especially those that were of concern to the Protestant churches.

The primary tool utilized by the Protestant churches to bring pressure on American corporations during the 1970s was the use of shareholder resolutions. In viewing the voting results of the numerous proposals submitted by the churches, however, one could easily conclude that the churches had suffered consistent and overwhelming defeat. It would, however, be facile to draw such a conclusion for the church shareholder proposals had far greater impact than the voting results would imply. A Securities and Exchange Commission report issued in 1978 contained the following remark relative to the influence of church-initiated proposals:

> A broad mix of commentators, including many corporations, indicated that in their experience shareholder proposals exert pressure on management to defend its present policies, and have often resulted in significant revisions of these policies. Generally, these commentators pointed out that even though a proposal may not receive sufficient votes to compel management actions, factors external to the voting process, such as unfavorable publicity from the revelation of facts and views brought out in the proposal, as well as management's concern for its reputation and image with its shareholders and with the public at large, appear in many instances to have deterred management from continuing certain practices or to have influenced the adoption of certain policies.[122]

A representative of Union Carbide concurred in this assessment, adding that resolutions were an effective device "by which shareholders can compel management to discuss matters of shareholder interest that are reasonably related to corporate activity."[123] He emphasized the "the machinery has had a substantial impact on corporate action" even though the number of votes cast in favor of the proposals had been small. A General Electric Company representative remarked that shareholder proposals had provided guidance to boards of directors concerning issues to which they should give attention, especially as they related to equal employment opportunities, apartheid in South Africa, and nuclear energy concerns.[124] Frank Hudson, an executive from American Telephone & Telegraph Company, remarked that his company had voluntarily adopted several shareholder proposals and that it was his belief that many proposals relating to socially significant matters "have generated meaningful discussions and positive actions by managements of other corporations."[125] Roger R. Conant of the teacher's retirement fund TIAA-CREF, observed that shareholder proposals helped to induce General Motors to take steps to improve the structure of its board and to act favorably on certain social and environmental issues.[126]

Vogel noted in his book *Lobbying the Corporation* that corporations do take citizen demands seriously, especially when they are presented in the form of stockholder resolutions. These shareholder proposals are now considered part of the business environment and must be considered now as an essential requirement of doing business in America.[127] The very act of filing a shareholder resolution provides considerable leverage. Once the resolution is filed with the Securities and Exchange Commission, the proponent is always in position to negotiate with the corporation involved. At times the request involves disclosure of certain detail, on equal employment opportunities as an example, and corporations can meet this request without the need for such a proposal to reach the stockholders for vote. Corporations obviously will strive to have the proposals withdrawn lest their annual meetings become dominated with social issue themes, for as Vogel noted "the last thing most corporations want is a story about a criticism of their social performance on the front page of the *New York Times* or in a report of their annual meeting."[128] Vogel also sees shareholders' resolutions causing business executives to become more attuned to pressures and concerns of the "outside world." And while the resolutions in themselves may have had a minimal impact, the resolutions have had to force top decision makers to adopt a broader perspective. In some cases top executives became more aware of the working conditions of their employees in foreign countries. Just the exercise of coming to an annual meeting thoroughly prepared forced many top executives to evaluate their companies' policies relative to the social impact they may have engendered. As a minimum, it compelled "senior executives at least to think about the social and political dimensions of their profit-seeking efforts."[129]

Juanita Kreps, former Secretary of Commerce for the United States government, opined that many corporations responded to and sometimes anticipated public concern by improving their social performance.[130] She recognized this as an acceptance on the part of corporations that they cannot operate in the current business environment without regard to the social impact of their operations. She quotes John Filer, Chairman of Aetna Life and Casualty, as saying: "Large corporations cannot be single purpose institutions directed solely to economic results. All must . . . be visibly attentive to the public—to the public interest as the public views it.[131] Kreps also recalled the words of Walter A. Haas, Chairman of the Board of the Levi Strauss Company:

> We believe that a corporation must become actively involved in facing and solving the social problems of America. Today's corporation must develop practical means of giving human needs the same status as profit and production. . . . In the long run, this new task of the corporation will be in its own best interest, since it cannot prosper as fully or as long in a society frustrated by social ills and upheaval.[132]

Kreps noted that in the past fifteen years corporations have devoted increased attention to acts of social responsibility. In 1977, for example, 456, or 91.2 percent of the Fortune 500 Industrial firms published information about their social performance in the annual reports, according to an Ernst and Ernst survey. This is nearly twice the number of firms that did so in 1971.[132a]

A study by Henry Eilbirt and I. Robert Parket showed that the drive by churches and other activist groups were having a definite effect in the business world—that indeed corporate social responsibility had become part of the total corporate function.[133] Eilbirt and Parket gathered data from a sample of major U.S. corporations as they related to their activities in the area of social responsibility. The study revealed that "all of the responding firms were engaged in some form of effort."[134] In their summation they noted:

> To speculate whether the business goal is "merely" amelioration of social ills or acquiring good will through neighborliness, or a combination of these and other reasons, appear to be fruitless. Whatever the motives, our findings show, for a number of important firms corporate social responsibility is becoming an integral and expanding corporate function.[135]

In a Levi Strauss & Company publication entitled *Social Responsibility* Milton Moskowitz noted some significant changes in corporate attitude toward social responsibility since 1967. Moskowitz makes poignant contrasts between 1967 and 1977:

> In 1967, there wasn't a single industrial corporation in the land that had a Black or member of any other minority group sitting on its board of directors. Today, the number of major companies with such representation exceeds 100.
>
> In 1967, only a handful of companies had women directors—and they were, for the most part, descendants of founders or relatives of owner-managers. Today, the number of corporations with females on the board is nearing the 300 mark.
>
> In 1967, only seven of the nation's top 100 corporations discussed social responsibility in their annual reports. Today, covering in this area in the annual report is so common that it's exceptional to see it missing.
>
> In 1967, companies automatically rejected from consideration any proxy resolution not closely related to the nuts-and-bolts of the business. Today, companies accept resolutions dealing with many social issues, from investment in South Africa to the portrayal of women in television commercials.
>
> In 1967, social responsibility questions were not part of any portfolio analysis. Today, there are two mutual funds where social responsibility is a determining factor and many church organizations can scan their holdings with a social lens.
>
> In 1967, comedian Dick Gregory said, "When I become President, I will order all television networks to hire more Negroes for commercials. I am tired of looking at television and seeing no Black folks getting Excedrin headaches . . . and we're the ones who should be getting them." Today, Blacks do get Excedrin headaches—and appear in many commercials.
>
> In 1967, there were only four Black-owned companies with sales in excess of $5 million a year. Today, there are 40. Two-thirds of the nation's 100 largest Black-owned firms were organized *after* 1968.
>
> In 1967, there were 19 Black-owned commercial banks—and the largest had assets of $27 million. Today, there are 43 Black-owned banks across the country—and the largest has assets of $61 million.
>
> In 1967, the largest Black-owned life insurance company had assets of $90 million. Today, it has assets of $145 million.
>
> In 1967, corporations did not go out of their way to buy goods and services from minority-owned companies. Today, many of them do that—and nearly 900 participate in the National Minority Purchasing Council and expect to make purchases of $1 billion from minority firms in 1977. Their 1973 total: $273 million.[136]

One of the efforts of the Protestant churches during the 1970s was the drive for broader representation on the boards of directors of major corporations. The Chamber of Commerce of the U.S.A. reported in 1980 some significant changes in the composition of the corporate board over the past decade. The Chamber of Commerce observed that these changes were made voluntarily and without the necessity of corporate reform through an Act of Congress or a rule issued by the Securities and Exchange Commission.[137] The Chamber's report noted that an increasing number of corporations are opposing the appointment of their bankers or legal counsel to their boards. There are decreasing numbers of appointments of retired or former officers, outside lawyers, investment bankers, and commercial bankers to the board. Conversely, there are increasing numbers of appointments of former government officials and academicians. Academicians were found on 47 percent of the top 1,300 boards in 1977, as contrasted with only 11.5 percent of the boards in 1974. Further, in a 1971–1978 study of the 646 leading companies conducted by Heidrick and Struggler, it was learned that 12 percent of corporate boards had one minority director (black, Hispanic, Asian, or American Indian); 2.6 percent had two or more minority directors; 18 percent had one woman director; 2.7 percent had two or more women directors. Out of the nation's largest 1,300 corporations in 1977, 202 women served on boards of 228 companies.[138] This reflects a dramatic increase from 1976, when only 147 women served on 175 of these boards of directors.

The Chamber further noted that in a Touche-Ross survey of the new, young, female, or minority directors of the top 500 corporations that: (a) 68 percent believed they had made significant impact on corporate priorities, policies and decisions; (b) 96 percent felt that the role of the corporate board director had changed in the last decade; and (c) 84 percent could see continuing change in the role of the corporate director.[139] In the same survey, but based on reports received from long-standing directors and board officers of the top 500 companies, the following emerged: (a) 89 percent reported that significant changes had taken place in the role of director; (b) 40 percent attributed the change to a greater awareness of liabilities and responsibilities; (c) 38 percent indicated that directors must devote more time and make a greater commitment to their activities; and (d) 88 percent predicted continual changes in the role of the director, citing a broadening range of activities and responsibilities.[140]

In a study conducted in 1975 by Vernon M. Buehler and Y. K. Shetty of 232 major corporations listed in *Fortune's* compilation of the largest industrial and nonindustrial firms, it was discovered that 160 had formulated corporate policies on the nature and extent of company involvement in one or more areas of corporate responsibility.[141] Approximately three-fifths of the 232 companies had a high level executive with specific responsibilities in the area of social responsibility and who reported to the President or the Chief Executive Officer. The study also revealed that the larger the company, the greater the degree of concern and commitment that was expressed, largely because these companies were more visible to the public scrutiny than smaller firms. The authors noted:

> We found a consistent relationship between an organization's commitment to corporate responsibility and the number of its stockholders. The larger the number of stockholders the more committed was the company to social responsibility. This could be due to at least two related reasons. First, ownership dispersion may lead to increased corporate concern about favorable climates for the company among all concerned, particularly among stockholders. Second, the more stockholders, the more likely are stockholder pressures and proposals for change and action.[142]

In an 1978 *New York Times* article entitled "How to Make 'Ethical' Investments," author Weiss opined that "many stockholder proposals have had a considerable impact on corporate activities because management often takes such proposals quite seriously."[143] Some of the successes he cites are: (a) a substantial number of major corporations have responded to suggestions for publication of information about equal employment opportunity programs including such data in reports to shareholders; (b) many corporations, stung by church-sponsored proposals directed at their activities in South Africa, increased job opportunities for Blacks in that country; (c) General Motors, responding to shareholder pressures, added a Black, a woman, and a scientist to its board of directors; and (d) Exxon supported a stockholder proposal calling for a special report about the company's plan to mine coal in the American West. It was Weiss's judgment that large corporations responded to stockholder proposals because management was sensitive to those events which could impact on its public image and also because such proposals tended to increase the visibility of some troublesome areas within the corporation. Many times executives were not aware of day-to-day operations and, therefore, experience a rude shock when some irresponsible activity surfaces and is brought to the attention of the public through a proxy statement.

A *Harvard Business Review* article authored by Theodore V. Purcell, the chairman of the Jesuit Advisory Committee on Investor Responsibility since its beginning in 1974 and a professor of management in the School of Business Administration at Georgetown University, furnished a number of interesting observations relative to stockholder proxy resolution pressures on management during the 1970s. It was his opinion that important changes had become apparent in the attitudes on both the part of the proponents and recipients of the resolutions. "First, let me say that many companies are taking important steps toward the effective solution of social problems, quite by their own management initiative."[144] He cites as examples: (a) Leon Sullivan, a black member of General Motors' Board of Directors, developed six principles for affirmative action in South Africa. Both Chairman Thomas A. Murphy of GM and Chairman Frank T. Cary of IBM helped persuade 120 American companies to agree to carry out these principles; (b) in 1978, Beatrice Foods and Standard Brands adopted nutrition responsibility policies similar to those of General Foods, which developed out of discussions between the companies and shareholder groups; (c) in 1978, Gulf agreed to a church resolution, and thus withdrawn, to adopt a policy prohibiting political contributions in South Korea; (d) many corporations cooperated with church groups in providing requested reports on employment statistics of minorities and women, as well as wages and working conditions in developing countries; (e) the insistent and consistent proposals covering apartheid in Southern Africa were having a demonstrable effect in that modest improvement for blacks in South Africa was recognizable, an easing up of segregation of facilities was noticeable, and there was better access to skills training and housing; and (f) cooperation was evidenced from insurance companies such as Connecticut General, ITT's Hartford Insurance, and Sears' Allstate, in stamping out redlining in the issuance of insurance.[145] Purcell notes:

> A look at the past five years leaves little doubt that the public interest shareholder proposal movement has affected corporate management, raised its consciousness about a number of ethical issues, and caused it to do some things it would not otherwise have done.[146]

The Committee on Social Responsibility in Investment in a report to The Executive Council of The Episcopal Church in 1977 rhetorically asked the question: "What is the value of shareholder proposals?" They furnished the following answers. They concluded that: (a) corporate behavior is being changed for requested information is being provided, wage scales are being increased, and advertising practices changed; (b) management and directors are becoming aware of points of view that differ from theirs and are willing to discuss the issues and to consider ethical issues; (c) the shareholders have demonstrated a better use of a vehicle (the shareholder resolutions) to express their concerns about the corporations' activities and the ways in which their investments are used; (d) employees are given encouragement and support for their efforts to help move business toward more enlightened policies and practices; and (e) the larger public is becoming more aware of how our economic system works and is better able to participate in the ongoing public policy discussions.[147]

The Episcopal Church report spells out specific accomplishments relative to shareholder resolutions filed in connection with the apartheid situation in Southern Africa. It is the opinion of the Church that the wages and fringes paid to blacks were improved in South Africa when American management learned of the prevailing wages and working conditions in that country. In the case of Namibia, at the Newmont mining operation location as an example, the constant pressure from the United Church of Christ undoubtedly was responsible not only for some increases in wages, but also for the start of a program to permit at least some African employees to live with their families at the mine site, as contrasted to previous dormitory housing in cement slab cubicles. Again, in Namibia, the churches were largely responsible for a consortium of oil companies abandoning their exploratory concessions which had been obtained in violation of international law and State Department policy. Churches' efforts have resulted in eight banks in the United States halting loans to the South African government. General Motors, an early target of Episcopal South African resolutions, advised that they would not expand their operations in South Africa until that country's pressing social problems had been resolved. Ford announced that it would condition any further expansion on its ability to achieve equalization in the workingplace.[148]

The Episcopal Report continued with additional items. IBM, at its 1977 annual meeting, announced that it would not bid for business where they believed the products would be used to abridge human rights. Exxon supported a resolution in connection with strip mining which asked for a full disclosure on strip mining operations. Pittston Corporation, following a discussion with church representatives, established a policy calling for stronger regulations of strip mining in Virginia. The 3M Company altered its corporate bylaws relative to political contributions so that a stronger Audit Committee of the Board of Directors would police any violation of its statutes. The Phillips Petroleum Company, too, made fairly extensive bylaw changes to insure that there were no violations of political contribution laws.[149]

The Episcopal Report also contended that progress was made relevant to enhancing equal employment opportunities for minorities and women. The Church opined that many of the larger corporations voluntarily disclosed employment statistics and it was believed that this has forced corporations into closer adherence to the laws of the land currently in force relative to employment rights and policies. The Report also reflected that due to pressure from several denominations, various sponsors of television programs have negotiated with these church groups to withdraw their resolutions and, in turn, would establish policies of limiting the amount of violence contained in shows that they sponsored.[150]

Finally, the Episcopal Report opined: "Perhaps the major goal of the churches' shareholder resolution activities has been to add another dimension to management's decision making process."[151] This is perhaps one of the most positive statements that can be made relative to the significance of the churches' challenges during the decade of the 1970s. It is not the scattered examples of "successes" that can be attributed to this or that effort of any one religious group that adds up for total effect. Rather it is the overall impact upon the business community which has resulted in subtle and unannounced changes in the manner in which American corporations view social issues. Corporations seldom acknowledge that changes in policies have been instituted because of church pressures or for "moral reasons."

4

Summary and Conclusions

The following dialogue is an exchange between executives of Control Data Corporation and representatives of Protestant leadership over the issue of apartheid in the Republic of South Africa.[1]

Timothy Smith, Director of the Interfaith Center on Corporate Responsibility, remarks:

> The reason we wanted the meeting today as shareholders was that we think that the best step Control Data can take at this time is to develop a policy as Polaroid has [of making no further sales or leasing of equipment to the South African government]. We're convinced that in South Africa today there would be very few sales that could be made that wouldn't contribute to the oppression of the people there.

William C. Norris, Chairman of the Board of Control Data Corporation, taking full note of the implications of Smith's statement, replies:

> You're looking for a macrosolution. Like the problem of unemployment everyone's looking for a macrosolution. There isn't one. We've got to get down to the microlevel and grub for each job and save the job you've got. Speaking of not selling to the government, one of the dedications I have is to bring computer-based education to South Africa. There is no other way that you'll ever close the enormous educational gap in South Africa except through the use of the computer. If I say today that I'm not going to sell the government a computer, then I can't go down there and try to solve the educational problem.

William Thompson, President of the National Council of Churches, counters, "I would prefer not to have you do it than to do it through the present government."

Frank P. White, a founder of the Interfaith Center for Corporate Responsibility, adds, "Could the government use computer-based education programs to educate the military? What possible kinds of restrictions would be placed on that?"

Norris answers, "You can't place restrictions on a computer that you put in someone else's country."

164   Summary and Conclusions

Smith retorts, "But if you are concerned about human rights, but can't determine how your computer would be used, isn't the best thing not to sell computers?"

Norris reacts, "Well, then, you wouldn't be selling many computers in this world. You do the best you can, and that's exactly what we're doing. I can sell you toothpicks that are used in the dining room and you can push them in people's eardrums and kill them."

The dialogue continued for some two hours, but with no meeting of the minds. Thompson finally offered the following proposition: "I see no hope for evolution in South Africa. The time is past. I am asking you not to support the oppressors which you are now doing despite your pronouncements to the contrary."

Norris, answers "I take very direct issue with that!"

When sharp differences of opinion continued with no reconciliation in sight, Smith finally presented the challenge, "We don't question the motivation of Control Data, but are very skeptical about how the government might use your computers. We'll file a shareholder resolution and then you please take a look at it."

In January of 1978 a shareholder resolution was filed with Control Data requesting that Control Data make no further sales or leases or lease renewals to the South African government. The resolution was defeated.

This scenario has been repeated over and over in many dialogues between Protestant leadership and business corporate management during the 1970s. First the discussions and then the filing of shareholder resolutions when no satisfactory conclusions were reached. In some cases, through negotiations and mutual agreement, the Protestant churches withdrew the shareholder resolutions.

During the ten-year period of 1970 to 1979, Protestant churches by direct involvement and with the support of the National Council of Churches of Christ in the U.S.A., and the assistance of the Interfaith Center on Corporate Responsibility, directly challenged corporations on the issues of corporate social responsibility.

This book has described the specific issues that were presented as social concerns to American corporations during 1970 to 1979 by Protestant churches and has discussed the ways in which those issues were brought to the attention of corporate management. This was accomplished primarily through the filing of shareholder resolutions. There was participation in three boycotts and the churches made other direct contacts by entering into dialogues with management, either in face-to-face encounters or dialogue via written communications.

The book has described the business responses to these challenges

Summary and Conclusions 165

and commentary was offered as to what business practices reflected some change during the 1970s in response to the pressures engendered by the Protestant churches.

The method employed to develop the data presented in this study was to review every shareholder resolution that was sponsored or cosponsored by a Protestant denomination or the National Council of Churches during the period of 1970 to 1979, and to describe the social issues involved, enumerate the corporations targeted, and list the Protestant denominations filing the resolutions. Boycotts and other direct contacts were also described.

Background data was furnished describing the rationale for the Protestants' involvement over the social concerns. Records and publications of the Securities and Exchange Commission, the American Society of Corporate Secretaries, the Investor Responsibility Research Center, the Interfaith Center on Corporate Responsibility, and the Council of Economic Priorities, were examined. In addition, careful study was made of annual reports, committee minutes, policy statements, newsletters, special interest publications of the ten Protestant denominations under study, as well as those of the National Council of Churches. The positions of managements concerning the social issues under study in this paper were secured primarily from the proxy statements, as well as documents issued by the corporations involved, and articles in various business publications which are listed in the *Business Periodicals Index.*

Protestant churches placed the heaviest emphasis on the apartheid issue in Southern Africa. More than half of the shareholder resolutions filed with American corporations were filed in connection with this particular issue. Other issues that captured the attention of the Protestant churches during the decade of the 1970s were: colonialism in Angola, Guinea-Bissau and Mozambique; and human rights concerns in Chile, the Dominican Republic, Guatemala, Korea and the Philippines. Particular social concerns of developing countries gripped the Protestant churches and these focused on employment practices of American firms doing business in those countries, foreign military sales, the distribution of infant formula, questionable corporate payments overseas, and the development of needed farm technology for small farms. The social concerns involving issues within the United States included the energy crisis, equal employment opportunities for women and minorities, political contributions, redlining and reinvestment by banks, strip mining, the nomination of women to boards of directors, stereotypical images of women in advertising, the impact of television advertising on children's nutrition, and nuclear weapons production.

There were ten Protestant denominations, plus the National Council of Churches, who were actively engaged in sponsoring or cosponsoring shareholder resolutions. These were, in order of frequency of participation, the United Church of Christ, United Methodist Church, Episcopal Church, United Presbyterian Church in the U.S.A., Christian Church (Disciples of Christ), American Baptist Churches, National Council of Churches, Reformed Church in America, Church of the Brethren, Lutheran Churches of America, and the Presbyterian Church U.S.

There were 221 shareholder resolutions filed with 71 corporations by Protestant churches during the decade of the 1970s. More than half (53.4) percent of these resolutions involved the issue of apartheid in Southern Africa. The next three issues, dropping precipitously from the 53.4 percent frequency for the apartheid issue, were concerns over equal employment opportunities for women and minorities (7.2 percent), the ecological effects of strip mining (6.3 percent), and questionable corporate payments overseas (6.3 percent). The balance of the issues had a frequency ranking of 2.7 percent or less. Six or less shareholder resolutions out of a total of 221 were filed pertaining to any one issue. The majority of the corporations involved with Protestant shareholder resolutions had to cope with three resolutions or less in the ten-year span of 1970 to 1979. No corporation received more than nine shareholder resolutions from Protestant churches during the 1970s.

The particular social issues involved are described in the following paragraphs. In each of these paragraphs the position of the Protestant churches on the social issues involved are delineated. This is then followed by the responses of corporate managements. In almost every case, corporations opposed the proposals that were being made by the churches and the stockholders consistently followed the recommendations of corporate executives and overwhelmingly defeated church proposals. However, it should be noted at this point that the defeat of church proposals did not mean that the shareholder resolutions were without effect. The resolutions did have impact and this impact is described further on in this summary.[2]

As has already been noted, the issue precipitating the most Protestant inspired shareholder resolutions was by far the issue of apartheid in Southern Africa, particularly in the countries of the Republic of South Africa, Namibia, and Rhodesia. The churches argued that apartheid was an abhorrent system installed by the white-dominated governments in those countries. The apartheid system was responsible for wide discrepancies in the standard of living of the black people when contrasted with the white minority. It placed travel restrictions on the Black populace, deprived them of land ownership, limited union organizing rights, provided deficient education, and in many other ways violated the human rights of the blacks. Further, these harsh rules were enforced with a network of repressive laws and police power. The Protestant churches, in sympathy with the blacks in Southern Africa, approached American corporations who were doing business in that part of Africa and asked that they discontinue their operations there, or at least, not expand business operations in Southern Africa. It was the Protestants' contention that foreign monies flowing into Southern Africa buttressed the oppressive regimes. Managements of various corporations doing business in Southern Africa did not agree with the Protestants' position and argued that doing business in that part of the world did not necessarily constitute a general endorsement of local laws or local social or economic policies. Further, business argued, United States foreign policy should be controlled by the United States government and not by corporations. Business looked upon the Protestants' arguments as being subversive in that business decisions would be subordinated to the foreign goals of particular shareholders. Business also had another worry, the failure to expand investments in Southern Africa could jeopardize its ability to maintain a competitive position which, in time, could result in substantial losses to the shareholders, especially if the closing of the operations were necessitated. Contrary to the view of the churches, business felt that its presence in Africa was beneficial to the populace.

Another issue involving Southern Africa was that of colonialism: the Portuguese control of Angola, Guinea-Bissau and Mozambique. At the time of the filing of the shareholder resolutions, all three territories were struggling for independence and the Protestant churches sought to support the independence movement by asking American corporations to withdraw from these countries so that the Portuguese government would not have the benefit of American taxes and royalty payments and this would hasten the end of the Portuguese domination. Business responded to the requests for withdrawal by stressing that: (a) corporations were guests and have no right to meddle in political affairs; (b) American business was contributing to the social progress of the people there; and (c) activists were attempting to use corporations as political tools.

In Chile the churches were concerned about the military dictatorship which they claimed systematically violated human rights in that country. Shareholder resolutions were filed with several American corporations doing business in that country asking that there be no expansion of business there, that no computer equipment be sold to that country, and that no political contributions be permitted. Business answered these requests by stating: (a) Chilean employees were being treated fairly and equitably; (b) corporations had prohibitions against political contributions; and (c) there was no way that any corporation could police the use of equipment sold in a foreign land.

Reports of low wages and malnutrition in the Dominican Republic produced church-instigated resolutions arguing that large investments in export crops such as sugar, in a country suffering shortages of food staples, were bound to cause problems as the poor received only a small portion of the income that resulted from the export shipments. Business categorically rejected that they were exploiters of the Dominican people or their resources. They contended that they paid fair wages, promoted good labor-management relations, created new jobs, taught new skills, developed better housing and health care, and attempted to diversify the crops.

The issue of a franchised bottler in Guatemala came to the attention of the churches. The bottler was accused of poor labor practices and the company based in the United States was petitioned to establish a code of minimum labor standards that would be required of its franchised bottlers. The intent, of course, was to impact upon the Guatemalan bottler. Management rejected the suggestion and declared that the company's bottlers were independent and it would be an improper and unnecessary intrusion on the part of the Corporation to dictate labor policies to its bottlers. Finally, management noted, the proxy statement is not the proper forum in which labor relations should be discussed, especially between independent bottlers and their employees.

A letter from a missionary concerning certain labor conditions in South Korea alarmed Protestant constituents at home and shareholder resolutions were filed with a corporation that had a plant located in that country. The company was requested to furnish information concerning wages paid, working conditions, and relations with trade unions. The owner of the Korean plant rejected the need for disclosure feeling that such a report would be of value to competitors and union organizers. The company asserted that adequate information had already been provided to shareholders.

Because of the dictatorship in the Philippines which prevented the peoples of that country from expressing their convictions, the churches petitioned an American corporation doing business in that country to provide information concerning its current and past operations in the Philippines. The patent purpose was to appraise the stockholders of the validity of their investment in a dictatorship-controlled environment. Management responded to this request declaring that the preparation of special reports should not be determined by the vote of stockholders. Further, management perceived that the proponents were not seeking just for information, but in reality were asking for changes in the Philippines' social and political structure; hence, the company averred that it could not interfere with the internal affairs of that country, but rather had to operate in accordance with its laws.

One corporation was challenged as to its relations with employees located in Third World countries such as Costa Rica, Ecuador, Honduras, Nicaragua, Philippines and Thailand. The churches asked that a report be prepared as to wages and working conditions in each of these countries. Business executives of the corporation advised that the preparation of such a report would be difficult and expensive and would be of interest to very few shareholders. Further, it was management's perception that the proponents of the resolutions were attempting to press the corporation into effecting changes in the social and cultural milieu of foreign countries which were beyond the company's ability. The company declared that it believed that it best fulfills its social responsibilities by operating in these countries in a manner which would insure its continuance in those countries and deplored the tendency of certain elements of society who attempted to malign the company through innuendo, distortion and outright misstatements.

Protestant churches, concerned over the easy availability of military equipment which they claimed made the world a less secure place in which to live, filed shareholder resolutions with a major manufacturer and requested the formation of a Corporate Policy Committee that would evaluate human rights situations in those countries who were negotiating for military equipment. The Committee would establish criteria and would decline sales to any country that did not meet such criteria. Management responded to this suggestion by stating that foreign military sales are, quite appropriately, controlled by the U.S. government so as to insure that they were consistent with the international goals of the United States and its strategic interests. Management declared that substituting corporate for government judgment seemed to be presumptuous as by law all military sales must be approved by the U.S. government.

Because of the deleterious effects of the improper use of infant formula in Third World societies, Protestant churches supported other groups in an effort to bring an end to all promotion of infant formulas. Through the filing of shareholder resolutions and participation in a boycott, the churches asked manufacturers of infant formulas to cease advertising the formula in areas where social, economic and environmental conditions are such that the formula was apt to damage the health and well-being of the infant. The churches also asked that "milk nurses" be removed from hospitals and clinics and that the giving of special incentives to doctors and health professionals be terminated. The churches were disturbed that the manner in which the formula was promoted implied that it was superior to breastfed milk. Further, the vigorous promotions also tended to undermine the Third World governments' breast feeding campaigns and nutrition programs. The manufacturers of infant formulas did not agree with these contentions and stated that while they did not dispute the nutritionally superior qualities of mothers' milk, the decision as to the actual distribution of the formula in foreign countries was the prerogative of foreign governments and that medical personnel of the foreign countries were in the best position to decide on its proper use. Further, the manufacturers felt that their promotional materials adhered to sound medical practices. The companies argued that the promotion of their products was subject to international codes of ethics and that the codes do provide for: (1) product information and labeling recognizing breast milk as the feeding of choice; (2) restraints on product claims that imply superiority over breast milk; and (3) supplying the user with explicitly worded instructions and demonstrations of the product. The manufacturers stated that they were convinced that there is a need for infant formula products throughout the world, including the undeveloped countries.

Shocking disclosures of corporate payments overseas used to influence commercial transactions and public policies in foreign countries triggered a rash of Protestant-sponsored shareholder resolutions. The proposals asked corporations to establish policies that would prohibit the use of corporate assets for the purpose of influencing the election of political candidates, for the purchasing of favors for its own operations in foreign lands, and for helping any one group or person gain or retain governmental power. Corporations responded by assuring the church groups that control procedures were in place to insure that improper or illegal contributions would not be made.

One Protestant denomination, concerned over the emphasis on the production of only large farm machinery, petitioned a farm-equipment manufacturer, in which it held stock, to consider the fabricating of smaller equipment for use in undeveloped countries. The manufacturer rejected the suggestion noting that the main purpose of the proponent in submitting the resolution was to seek shareholder support for certain views held by that denomination about the needs of developing countries. Therefore, the purpose of the resolution was only to test the company's acceptance of the church's views. It was the judgment of the corporation that a major commitment of resources to develop and produce farm machinery specially tailored for the small farm was not justified. Further, there was small farm machinery already being manufactured and distributed worldwide by a Japanese manufacturer.

Two oil companies were confronted over the energy crisis of 1974. The companies were reminded that the shortage of energy fuels was a matter of deep and growing concern in the United States and in view of the fact that oil company profits were increasing substantially in the face of fuel shortages, there was an important need for the corporations to release basic information concerning their operations. The companies asserted that they fully recognized and accepted responsibility to communicate essential information to shareholders. However, from their vantage point, adequate information had already been provided to those interested. In addition, detailed information had also been provided to governmental agencies, such as the Form 10-K supplied to the Securities and Exchange Commission, and these were available for public inspection.

Protestant churches also filed shareholder resolutions over a concern relative to equality in the recruitment, employment, training, and promotion of minorities and women. One company, who was already involved in warding off boycott activities, termed these resolutions as outright support of the boycott actions. Another corporation affirmed that it had properly discharged all its responsibilities in providing adequate detail concerning its equal employment opportunity programs; others did not see any particular value in compiling raw data for each of the company facilities and occupation categories and releasing this to the public. One company declared that its commitment to equal employment was well known and clearly demonstrated and therefore the preparation of such a report would serve no useful purpose.

Illegal contributions in the United States in the form of donations to a presidential campaign provoked one Protestant denomination to file a shareholder resolution with an oil company to amend its bylaws to the effect that if any employee failed to comply with federal and state laws relative to political contributions, he would be subject to disciplinary action, including termination. The corporation responded by affirming that it had taken appropriate and decisive remedial action and therefore the shareholder's proposal was redundant. Another corporation, petitioned on the same grounds, agreed with the churches' proposal and in a rare act recommended that shareholders vote in the affirmative.

Two large banks, one in New York and one in Boston, were requested to establish a Community Reinvestment Review Committee which would help to revitalize deteriorating urban communities. The Committee would strive to increase the availability of residential mortgages for the local communities and to create new programs for community reinvestment. The suggestion was rejected and management averred that the adoption of such a proposal would serve no real purpose as banks must have flexibility to meet credit demands wherever they may arise and that are consistent with the obligations of the bank to its depositors and to all stockholders of the corporation.

A number of shareholder resolutions were filed with corporations with mining activities over the environmental and social effects of strip mining and other forms of mining operations. The churches argued that strip mining was the most environmentally destructive method of extracting coal. Further, there were social, economic and ecological adverse effects on the peoples in those areas where surface mining was in progress. The resolutions asked for disclosure concerning these mining operations. Management responded by declaring that they were complying with federal and state laws, were acting in a responsible way to care for the environment, were furnishing information to the public, as well as filing necessary reports with state and federal agencies. Management contended that the compiling, printing, and mailing of information to thousands of stockholders was an unwarranted expense in view of the fact that there would be only a very few that had interest in such data.

A Protestant denomination filed a resolution with a bank in a midwest community protesting the fact that the bank had consistently nominated only men to the board of directors. The denomination asked that a woman be nominated. Management responded to this suggestion with the argument that if the appointment was influenced primarily by the sex of the appointee, it would be discrimination. They affirmed that the bank's policy was to appoint individuals based on the qualifications of the nominee; such qualifications would include management and professional skill, community involvement and interest, business background and acumen, and a dedicated interest in insuring that the bank remained in sound financial condition.

Two large manufacturers of household items were recipients of shareholder resolutions relative to the charge that their advertising tended to stereotype women. Women were portrayed in minor, if not subordinate, roles which did not accurately reflect the diverse participation and accomplishments of women in modern society. The manufacturers disagreed with these contentions and declared that they have always striven to cast women in a wide range of life roles such as executives, designers, athletes, educators, mothers, and homemakers. In fact, these companies felt that they had contributed materially to a change of thinking of many members of the public with regard to the role of women in the world today.

Another target in the field of advertising was the churches' objections to advertising which tended to promote heavily sugared food products to children under the age of twelve. It was the churches' feeling that this kind of advertising contributed to malnutrition as children would be influenced by the advertising and would tend to favor such foods. Only one shareholder resolution was filed in this connection by a Protestant denomination and the manufacturer advised that such advertising was in the process of being phased out and the Protestant groups withdrew the resolution.

Three shareholder resolutions were filed in connection with sponsoring television programs containing violence. All were withdrawn when the companies agreed to state publicly and to instruct their advertising agencies that it was their policy to avoid the sponsorship of programs that contained gratuitous violence or antisocial material. The churches did not dispute the fact that the American public evidently had a great appetite for adventure programming that contained a great deal of violence, but they did not want companies in which they were part owners to become associated with such programming.

There were three shareholder resolutions filed during 1979 on the issue of nuclear weapons production by Protestant churches. All resolutions were withdrawn after the companies agreed to furnish the information that was requested.

In a brief look, on a year-to-year basis, from 1970 to 1979, of activities of the Protestant churches with American corporations over social issue concerns, the following essential items can be noted. While no shareholder resolutions were filed by a Protestant denomination during the year of 1970, the campaign waged by a group with General Motors over corporate social responsibility, set up a model for others to follow. Campaign GM, as it was called, demonstrated how corporate machinery could be marshalled to influence public opinion by effectively using shareholder resolutions. To one member of the GM board of directors, the 1970 shareholders' meeting appeared to him as an adversarial proceeding with Campaign GM speakers acting as prosecuting attorneys. In 1971 Protestant churches commenced filing shareholder resolutions: four were filed, two having to do with environmental concerns over coal mining, one with the apartheid situation in South Africa, and one with colonialism in Southern Africa. The years of 1972 and 1973 marked a trend toward more joint action on the part of the churches. The joint effort focused on attempting to change corporate policies on those issues that impacted on human rights as contrasted with a focus on economic issues which usually was the content of shareholder resolutions filed by other persons and groups. In 1974 the churches hammered away at the apartheid situation in Southern Africa. There were also other social concerns such as strip mining, equal employment opportunities for minorities and women, political contributions, the energy crisis in the United States, and human rights violations in the Philippines. The year of 1975 was a less active year than the preceding year as far as shareholder resolutions were concerned. New concerns, in this year, included employment practices in

South Korea as well as strip mining in Appalachia. In 1976 there was a dramatic increase in the filing of shareholder resolutions; familiar items reappeared such as the apartheid concern in Southern Africa, political contributions, and strip mining. In addition, concerns expanded to infant formula distribution in undeveloped countries, stereotypical images of women in advertising, and the need for appropriate farm technology in Third World countries. In 1977, other items were added to the host of familiar concerns and these related to overseas labor practices, foreign military sales, and sponsorship of television programs containing violence. In 1978, apartheid in Southern Africa still continued as the number one item. There was also a repetition of familiar items such as infant formula distribution, labor practices in developing countries, and political contributions. A new concern emerged over the need for banks to be concerned about making mortgage money available in urban communities for urban revitalization. Finally, in 1979, the last year covered in this study, the apartheid issue dominated all other issues, which for the most part, were similar to prior years. In that year, for the first time, Protestant shareholder resolutions were filed with relation to the concern over nuclear power—in this case the production of nuclear weapons.

During the period of 1970 to 1979 Protestant churches engaged in three boycotts. One involved the Gulf Oil Company because of that company's continuing operations in Angola—a country which at the time was struggling for its independence from Portugal. The second boycott involved the Nestle Company who was being accused of fostering malnutrition in Third World infants by virtue of its intensive zeal in selling infant formula which it manufactured. The third boycott action focused on the J. P. Stevens company because of that company's failure to bargain in good faith with unions legally voted for by Stevens' employees.

The issue with Gulf was over the proceeds from oil extracted from Angolan ground. Taxes and royalties were paid by Gulf to the Portuguese in accordance with contractual arrangements. These funds, according to the supporters of the liberation fighters, were being funneled back into Angola to strengthen military action against the insurgents. Thus, the churches contended that such payments of taxes and royalties were tantamount to supporting the suppression of the people of Angola. As an act of support for the liberation fighters which consisted of an attempt to have Gulf Oil withdraw from Angola, one Protestant denomination urged its members to boycott Gulf. Members were exhorted to return their credit cards to Gulf as a visible demonstration of their displeasure of Gulf's continuing presence in Angola. Gulf reacted to the implications of the boycotters and threatened a lawsuit. The lawsuit did not materialize. Instead Gulf chose to try to placate the black community in the United

States and others who were supporting the liberation of Angola. They hired a black public relations firm who offered various suggestions to Gulf in an attempt to defuse the boycott. Throughout the boycott Gulf maintained the position that as a company they were politically neutral, and as would be the case of any of their operations in a foreign country, they must abide by the laws of the host countries. Further, they felt that their presence in Angola was beneficial to the local populace. The matter was finally resolved when the Salazar dictatorship came to an end in Portugal, and Angola was allowed to assume its own independence.

The J. P. Stevens boycott was over the issue of that company's adamant refusal to allow any form of collective bargaining at any of its plants. The company steadfastly resisted efforts by their employees to elect union representation and to engage in a bargaining process. Employees had attempted to unionize in 1963 and the company used various tactics to discourage unionization and in the process reaped a series of accusations. The company was accused of intimidating its employees, of selective enforcement of rules, of appeals to racial prejudices, and the illegal termination of those employees who demonstrated pro-union tendencies. Stevens had been brought before various courts of law during the 1970s and a number of judgments were won against Stevens, but legal efforts did not bring any fruitful results. In view of the lack of any move toward the collective bargaining process, the Amalgamated Clothing and Textile Workers Union instigated a boycott. The boycott action was subsequently supported by various Protestant denominations. The churches felt that there was a real need to support the boycott action in view of the fact that the rights of Stevens's workers had been continually abused and that effective remedies through the legal system were not working. Toward the end of the 1970s the J. P. Stevens Company backed off its hardrock stand and began to revise its unimpressive record in litigation. Its labor policy was modified so that rather than take every union-related dispute to court, it made an effort to maintain a low profile and allow only sure cases to reach the National Labor Relations Board and the appellate courts. Finally, on October 19, 1980, a settlement was reached between organized labor and the J. P. Stevens Company that ended 17 years of open warfare. While the settlement was not an overwhelming victory on the part of the union because of its limitations, nevertheless it was a significant victory. In the long term this victory could have significant impact on labor relations in the South.

With regard to the Nestle boycott, the Nestle company had manufactured infant formula for many years. However, in the early 1970s concerns began to emerge over the use of infant formula in Third World countries and Nestle's formula product became the center of a storm of protest. The infant formula was being accused of fostering malnutrition in that it was being substituted for breastfeeding. In undeveloped countries unwitting mothers were mixing the powdered formula with contaminated water—or to save money, were diluting the product far too much. Warnings were issued by various health organizations concerning the misuse of the formula and manufacturers were urged to limit the promotion of the product. When it became apparent that manufacturers, such as Nestle, did not take adequate steps to restrain the promotion of infant formula, a boycott action was initiated and was coordinated by a group called the Infant Formula Action Coalition (INFACT). This coalition organized the activities of those who opposed the distribution of the formula and challenged companies involved in the preparation of this product. Protestant churches joined in these efforts and were aided by the Interfaith Center on Corporate Responsibility. Nestle, in reaction to mounting boycott actions, made some modifications in their promotion programs, but not enough to satisfy the boycotters. Nestle is not in disagreement that breast milk is superior to the formula. However, the company feels that the formula is an excellent supplement when the mother is ill, does not produce sufficient milk, or prefers not to breast feed. Nestle attempted to improve the labeling of the product and to adjust its methods of distribution to satisfy its critics. However, the "critics" do remain critical and the boycott continues. In 1981 the World Health Organization formed an international code which would restrict advertising and marketing of baby formula. The code, eight pages in length, is a nonbinding document. It urges a global ban on the promotion and advertising of the formula, distribution of free samples, and dispensing of gifts for recommending the use of the product. Inasmuch as the code is nonbinding, it is left to the individual governments to translate code into national law.

In addition to the wide use of shareholder resolutions and limited use of boycott actions, Protestant churches have also challenged American corporations on the issues of corporate responsibility in face-to-face dialogues, in group meetings, at symposiums, and by utilizing open letters, letters of inquiry and mass mailings. The Protestant churches also registered their protests relative to certain corporate policies by closing bank accounts, divesting of stock, engaging in legal actions, and utilizing the media. The social issues were the same as those already mentioned in connection with shareholder resolutions. In fact, a good part of these contacts and dialogues were in connection with a potential shareholder resolution or the possibility of withdrawing a resolution already filed with the Securities and Exchange Commission. In numerous meetings with hundreds of companies during the decade of the 1970s, many matters were discussed and amicably settled. Many companies were persuaded to disclose data or accommodate the churches in their particular requests and thus avoid a shareholder resolution. These face-to-face meetings were effective as evidenced by the fact that numerous shareholder resolutions were withdrawn by the churches after being satisfied by the companies' promised actions.

Letters were also used in several ways. Letters were used to make inquiries or to suggest meetings to discuss certain issues that were troubling the Protestant churches. Letters were used in mailings to corporations relative to a particular issue—such as the letter written to fifty U.S. companies who had investments in South Africa. The letter voiced the churches' objections to the continuance of these companies in apartheid South Africa. Letters were used in mass mailings—such as a letter sent to 281 corporations inquiring as to what written policies were in effect that would control the use of corporate assets that could possibly be diverted for partisan political purposes.

The symposium was another avenue for face-to-face contact between business and church representatives. These meetings were more structured in form with prepared agendas and could last a full day or longer. The merit of these meetings was that they provided both business and church leaders with the opportunity to present their views on particular social issues. One example was the day-long symposium held in Bartlesville, Oklahoma where oil company executives and church people exchanged views over the energy concern.

Representatives of Protestant groups have also presented testimony from time to time to governmental agencies. For example, delegates appeared before the Securities and Exchange Commission arguing for the desirability of companies disclosing socially significant matters in their annual reports. Testimony was also offered before committees of the United Nations, especially in connection with the apartheid situation in Southern Africa.

The closing of a bank account as an act of protest on the part of Protestant groups occurred from time to time. The National Council of Churches in 1978, for instance, closed its checking account with the Continental Illinois National Bank because of that bank's refusal to adopt a policy prohibiting loans to South Africa.

Protestant groups have joined in legal actions on occasion to support social causes. A case in point is a Protestant denomination that joined in litigation proceedings against the Securities and Exchange Commission on the side of environmentalists who sought to have corporations provide environmental data in their reports to the public.

Finally, certain Protestant denominations used investments in a creative fashion by investing money on the basis of a social motive rather than a profit one. Minority banks and business were assisted and mortgages and loans provided in worthy instances where the return on investment was not the very best, but the cause was.

Conclusions

The challenges by Protestant churches to American corporations in the 1970s had impact. Even though practically all of the Protestant shareholder proposals were badly defeated in the proxy votes, their effectiveness cannot be judged purely on a statistical basis. Churches and business commentators have noted that the proposals exerted pressure on corporate management to defend their policies and have resulted in some revisions of corporate policies. The very act of filing a shareholder resolution provided the churches with considerable leverage. Corporations obviously sought to resolve the issues in an amicable way and to avoid proxy votes lest their annual meetings become dominated with social-issue themes. Shareholder resolutions have influenced business executives to become more attuned to the concerns of the "outside world" and to sensitize top decision makers to adopt broader perspectives. Senior executive officers of major corporations no doubt now take into consideration the social and political dimensions of their profit-seeking efforts. Positive reports indicate that progress was made in corporate social responsibility on some of the issues which were of concern to Protestant churches; as examples, wages and fringes paid to blacks were improved in South Africa; housing was improved in South Africa; some companies agreed to halt expansion in South Africa and some banks consented to halt loans to the South African governments; a few companies altered their corporate bylaws to prohibit polical contributions; progress was made in equal employment opportunities for minorities and women; and certain sponsors of television programs agreed to petition broadcasters to limit violence in programming.

Businessmen have viewed church advocates of business social responsibility in three basic ways. First, some have been openly critical of the churches for being involved in business activities. They have regarded activists as anticapitalists and socialists. Church activists are considered by this group of businessmen as being overly simplistic in their approach to business problems and of attempting to force a transfer of money and assets of business to selected peoples, such as minorities. Activists are considered by these same businessmen as no more than agitators who file shareholder resolutions not to uplift unfortunate people, but to indict the business establishment. Second, the business community at large, however, did not adopt such a harsh stance but avoided a frontal attack on their critics and reaffirmed the classical or traditional view of business relative to corporate social responsibility. This view simply was that the business of business was business and that business had no business in social programs. The business executive had only one purpose and that was to maximize the profits for the corporation and to insure an adequate return for the investors. He was not to make forays into social activities using stockholders' money. The manner in which the business executive could best discharge social responsibility was to run an efficient and profitable business that generated jobs and uplifted the community. Indulgence in social actions would only prove detrimental to a company and in time would detract from the efficiency and profitability of the business. Inefficiency and nonprofitability ultimately would be destructive to society at large as jobs would be sacrificed and productive capacity would be dampened. Last, a third group of businessmen, a growing number, have gone on record with the declaration that they are convinced that there are shortcomings in the classical or traditional view of corporate social responsibility and are persuaded that there is a need for business to engage in certain citizen-like activities which go beyond the strict legal dictates of the corporate charter. These executives aver that corporations must be informed and sensitive to the new demands of society and that adaptations should be made when feasible to accommodate particular social needs. At the same time the business executive must fully protect the interests of the corporations' owners.

In contrast to these three views of business relative to corporate social responsibility, Protestant churches disputed the business view that the profit motive should be the cornerstone of all business activity. Rather, they reasoned, there should not only be one bottom line, profits, but bottom lines which would incorporate not only profits, but various aspects of social responsibility. The churches were convinced that large corporations cannot take a defensive position behind a shield of a 200-year tradition of laissez faire originally proclaimed by Adam Smith. Adam Smith, from the viewpoint of church activists, never conceived of the free enterprise system operating as it does today in a business environment laden with mammoth corporations who dominate not only the local markets but the world scene as well. Adam Smith perceived small businesses competing with other small businesses and this kind of competition would bring about a high degree of productivity as well as a fair pricing system. Large corporations, from the churches' viewpoint, have brought about distortions in the laissez faire system. Protestants would argue that in the 200-year span of American business history, business has suffered abuses which have emerged out of private and selfish initiatives coupled with unbridled competition. Short-term profits have remained paramount with total disregard for the long-term impacts upon society. Used corrosive chemicals, for example, have indiscriminately been dumped onto public lands with no consideration given to the long-term damaging effects of these chemicals on surrounding environments. The churches contend that any system which encourages and rewards selfishness is bound to create abuses. Therefore, there is a real need to put the profit objective into better perspective and to insist that corporate decision making give consideration to social factors as well as economic. The Protestant churches take the position that the corporation must be considered a social institution as well as an economic one for its impact upon society goes far beyond economics alone. The redefinition of the role of the American corporation as a social institution, as well as an economic one, establishes a new set of criteria by which a corporation's performance can be judged. Churches would judge a corporation by its social performance as well as its economic accomplishments. Business, of course, rejects this view and reaffirms that the corporation is solely a financial institution and is to be judged only by its economic performance. The differences in the perception of the role of the corporation in American society underlie the reasons why corporate managements have persistently disagreed with the proposals submitted by the churches and have, with only very few exceptions, urged shareholders to vote no to Protestant proposals. Even the most liberal of businessmen find that it is not easy for corporations to meet the wide spectrum of demands placed upon corporations from a host of special interest groups.

Business has been critical of the manner in which the churches have utilized shareholder resolutions. They argue that corporations are being charged with responsibilities or injustices which they neither created nor can they correct. Shareholder resolutions filed over the issue of apartheid in Southern Africa is one good example. Business asserts that corporations are not in position to resolve political issues. Solutions to human rights violations in foreign lands must be instigated by the United States government and must have the cooperation of the host governments in foreign lands. Proxy proposals, therefore, submitted in connection with apartheid in Southern Africa are considered as being misused. Business perceives that the only reason for the submission of these proxies is to provoke debate on social issues at stockholders' meetings and to use the proxy statements as public relations vehicles. Business would argue that debate over social issues is more appropriate in the assemblies of legislators and not at stockholders' meetings. The churches obviously chose very large corporations for confrontations to generate high visibility for social causes they espoused. Consequently some business executives feel that the hit list of large corporations drawn up by the Protestant churches are at best arbitrary and that corporations selected for proxy attack were no less socially responsible than others. It is ironic to note that the corporations which the churches selected for attack were the very same corporations which earlier they deemed reputable as they invested their money in those corporations. The irony becomes compounded when one considers that corporations who possibly were more flagrant in their corporate social responsibility performances went competely unscathed as the churches held no stock in those corporations.

Business, further, questions whether church shareholders represent the viewpoint of shareholders-at-large. Regardless of the churches' arguments for a greater voice on the part of shareholders, there does seem to be inadequate evidence which would affirm that shareholders want to become involved in the intricacies of corporate management and policies. In the view of the business community, most shareholders chose to be inactive. The stockholders' primary purpose for making investments is for financial gain and not because they wish to become part of the decision making processes of the corporation. If stockholders are not content with the performance of any corporation, they normally will sell the stock and invest elsewhere. While there have been expressions of some concern on the part of a small segment of stockholders relative to the protection of the environment and product safety, by and large it is the economic factor that governs the actions of the stockholders. This appears to be substantiated by the stockholders' overwhelming endorsement of the recommendations of management. The heavy vote in favor of managements' recommendations as regards the proposals submitted by Protestant churches indicates that they, the stockholders; (a) supported the actions of management; (b) did not want management to make forays into social ventures; and (c) underscored the primary concern as an economic one and not a social one. A large portion of the shareholder resolutions submitted by the Protestant churches were requests for additional information concerning corporate operations. Based on the voting of the stockholders, there appeared to be little support for the churches' contentions that such information was needed. These requests were overwhelmingly defeated consistently through the period of 1970 to 1979. Stockholders were persuaded that the social issues raised by Protestant churches did not have economic impact on their investment and, therefore, rejected Protestant proposals for additional corporate information. It should be said at this point, however, that while the Protestant churches witnessed a very heavy vote against their resolutions, they did contend that the present system of shareholder ownership is slanted very heavily in favor of management and there is little opportunity for the small shareholder to promote his point of view. The churches argue that there is no effective way that the small shareholder can rebut managements' views and because of this, stockholders do not receive a full presentation of the problems propounded.

While businesss in some instances recognized the validity of some of the arguments of the Protestant churches when presenting shareholder resolutions for inclusion in proxy statements, they disagreed as to how societal changes should be effected. One such instance is the apartheid situation in Southern Africa. Business did not agree that the multinational corporation was the proper vehicle for effecting the mitigation of the apartheid situation in that part of the world even though they (business) would affirm their repugnance of the apartheid system. More than half of the Protestant shareholder resolutions revolved around the apartheid issue in Southern Africa and business' consistent rebuttal was that: (a) only the United States government can set foreign policy and not corporations; (b) it is not within the province of the charter of corporations to attempt to dictate foreign policy or force alterations in foreign political structures by use of economic power; (c) they were guests in a foreign country and were obliged to abide by the host's laws; (d) they abide by United States laws in all their international dealings; (e) the closing down of plants would only hurt the peoples of the countries involved and would not necessarily weaken the host governments; and finally (f) there could be severe economic losses to the corporations which would impact upon American stockholders.

Not only did business disagree with the churches as to how societal changes should be effected, they also concluded that Protestant churches demonstrated a lack of understanding as to how corporations really work or some of the problems that they face. In the case of questionable payments overseas, for example, business contends that the issue was overstated. Certain payments had to be made to do business in certain foreign lands. Critics of business should have differentiated between illegal and questionable payments as in many cases certain payments were not only legal but were a requirement for doing business in certain countries. Many of the cases involved only small payments which did not reflect adversely on the quality of corporate mangement nor were they given for personal gain. Payments were made as part of the routine of doing business and to allow the American corporation to get a fair chance in getting foreign business when in competition with corporations around the world who had no prohibition against making such payments. Father Theodore V. Purcell, part of the religious community and a strong corporate social responsibility advocate, perceived that some of the resolutions that were submitted by the churches were unrealistic. He agreed with the criticism that the churches, at times, demonstrated a lack of knowledge of business and the problems that business faces. He surmised that some of the proposals that were submitted by the churches were for symbolic purposes only.

> Symbols are obviously important. But, to become meaningful, symbols must be related to practical reality. The symbolism syndrome is very likely to be counterproductive. Important socio-economic and ethical issues can surely be approached by accurate and realistic means in a resolution. Management cannot be expected to accept unrealistic means and clauses in resolutions. When it makes a policy decision, management is not game playing or merely dealing with words. Management has to say, "If we are to accept this, can we do it?"[3]

The choice of social issues by Protestant churches during the ten-year period of 1970 and 1979 does not demonstrate any master design or intent. The churches apparently were willing to join in certain efforts master minded by the Interfaith Center on Corporate Responsibility. The result was lopsided in favor of the apartheid concern in Southern Africa. The figures show that the Protestant churches expended 53.4 percent of their efforts with regard to the apartheid matter in Southern Africa. The next area in which they actively participated was the concern over equal employment opportunities for women and minorities, and this participation (as judged by a count of shareholder resolutions sponsored or cosponsored) dropped to 7.2 percent, then to 6.3 percent for concerns over strip mining and questionable corporate payments overseas. The balance of the issues, as far as participation of Protestant churches in sponsoring or cosponsoring shareholder resolutions is concerned, showed an activity of 2.7 percent or less. This translates into the fact that six or less Protestant sponsored or cosponsored resolutions had been filed in the ten-year period over any one particular issue. The majority of the 71 corporations with which Protestant churches had become involved received only three resolutions or less in the ten-year span of 1970 to 1979. This can hardly represent any pattern or master plan. Father Theodore V. Purcell was also critical of the fact that there was a lopsided stress on South Africa. Although there were resolutions involving other countries, he asks nevertheless, "Why is there emphasis on South Africa as a nation violating human rights? Do not many other countries violate human rights—for instance, Soviet Russia, China, Argentina, Iran and Uruguary? Why are the sponsors silent about those countries."[4]

There is evident division among the Protestant denominations as to how to approach business. The study has indicated that there were a limited number of Protestant groups involved in shareholder resolutions, boycotts, and other direct contacts. Many denominations chose not to get involved. In fact, some Protestant denominations openly opposed Protestant involvement with American business. The participation of Protestant churches on certain issues did not follow a firm pattern and at times was erratic—some participating and some choosing not to support certain issues. It is evident that not all Protestant denominations, for example, joined the boycott actions. In fact, only a select few chose to be involved. Parishioners back home in local churches also found church involvement with corporations somewhat confusing. Some were not convinced that the churches' actions with corporations were appropriate. For example, while the church members may have recognized the seriousness of the apartheid system in South Africa, they possibly did not fully understand the reasoning of the churches in attempting to force foreign-based American corporations out of host countries and in this way bring an end to apartheid constrictions. The Presbyterian Panel, a group that surveys Presbyterian opinion, in a February 1979 Questionnaire entitled "Social Policy: Activities and Attitudes Among Presbyterians" reported that a "greater portion of members and elders 'disagree' rather than 'agree' with the call for 'discussions and stockholders' actions that urge business to discontinue operations in South Africa.' " (p. 38).

Comments and Suggestions

The large corporation will always remain an essential part of the American way of life. It will always be needed to produce required goods and services. In accomplishing the production of such goods and services to the public, it must at the same time provide an adequate return on investment so that stockholders will continue to invest. If investments in corporations cease, corporations cease. This emphasizes the fact that the primary thrust of business is, and will always remain, economic. All other reasons, including those of corporate social responsibility, will remain secondary. This does not mean, however, that the churches should not have interest in monitoring the affairs of business. The churches have, in fact, taken great interest in the conduct of business as evidenced by their activities in the 1970s. The actions of the Protestant churches during the 1970s in their confrontation with the business community calls for reflection and the following suggestions are offered:

1. While Protestant churches have made good use of the shareholder resolution, they have in essence narrowed their relationship with business management to an adversarial role. As a suggestion, the Protestant churches may want to consider a shift to a broader base in their contacts with business by using their good offices in three ways. First, urge cor-

porations to include social issues in their strategic and operating plans. In this way executive compensation would be gauged by social as well as economic performance. Second, seek changes in corporate governance such as encouraging corporations to include women, minorities, and consumers, in the make-up of the Boards of Directors. Third, search for cooperative efforts wherein churches could join hand-in-hand in some efforts with corporations in promoting the social good, such as aiding in Junior Achievement programs, promoting the purchasing from minority-owned firms, finding jobs for hardcore unemployed, and similar efforts.

2. The churches have overemphasized the negative side of corporate activities during the 1970s with little, or no mention, of the good corporations are now doing in social endeavors. While there is a need to point out acts of malfeasance, there is also a need for fair play in reporting business activities. The portraying of negative business acts, without also indicating positive social acts on the part of business, has the possibility of generating an attitude among some of the churches' memberships that business, and large corporations especially, are potentially evil. We are not suggesting that business is blameless or that capitalism is without fault, but we do suggest that the reporting become more fairly balanced. As this book has reported, both conservative Protestant church peoples and conservative business persons have perceived some words and deeds of the Protestant churches as verging on the advocacy of socialism as a replacement for capitalism. Whether the perception is accurate or not, it does remain that such a perception has arisen among some church folks and some business people.

3. As a suggestion, Protestant churches could consider devoting more attention to areas in which they best perform: preaching on Sundays and church discussion groups. Many of the executives of large corporations are in the pews of Protestant churches every Sunday morning. The churches may want to examine their own ministries to determine whether they are being as effective as they can in reaching these business executives with the message of corporate social responsibility from the pulpit or in discussion groups.

4. The approach to corporations on the part of Protestant churches by use of shareholder resolutions, boycotts, and other direct contacts, may be at best a very simplistic one. Corporate social responsibility is a very complex matter and in order for the Protestant churches to do a more effective job, they may have to join with others in finding answers to some very difficult questions with regard to the social responsibility of corporations. Some of these questions could include: (a) What are the guidelines for corporations' involvement in social responsibility? Honest consideration has to be given to the fact that business executives operate

under many constraints and are not free to dispense corporate funds in accordance with their own inclinations. The guidelines, further, must be consistent from one corporation to another. (b) What is the division of responsibility between business and government in areas formerly never considered within the province of business, such as apartheid? What actions in the area of social responsibility are more those of government than business? (c) How does one measure the economic impact on the corporation when social ventures are advocated? The stockholders must know what it is costing the corporation for social activities. (d) In what ways can the impact of corporate social action be measured as it affects the quality of life? What form of measurement can be devised to judge in a fair manner that a corporation has or has not been socially responsible? Or, to phrase the question in another way, can a socio-economic operating statement be developed acceptable to corporations? In sum, how can we determine that a company has done an effective job in the area of corporate social responsibility?

Melvin Anshen in his recent book *Corporate Strategies for Social Performance* has more questions:

> (1) What responses to social needs can be feasibly undertaken by a single company under the constraints of its unique competitive position and unique resources, (2) What responses are feasible only through some type of cooperative effort among firms in a single industry or geographic location, and (3) What responses require some type of government intervention to which business may be able to contribute valuable guidance.[5]

Further on, Anshen adds these questions:

> Who defines the bounds and specific content of the responsibility of a corporation to deliver benefits to society? Is the implementation of social responsibility a course of action determined by a corporation's chief executive officer, possibly in consultation with his board of directors? What about the effect of such action on costs and therefore on profits and return on investment? How does a reasonable manager mediate the conflicting claims among elements of the society whose objectives and priorities are not identical? Does a company's social responsibility extend to the amelioration of social ills not caused by its own actions, or even by the business system?[6]

If Protestant churches are to gain the respect of the business world, some effort should be devoted to seriously grappling with some of these questions before filing shareholder resolutions or taking other direct actions.

5. There is a wide divergence of opinion and practice from one Protestant group to another worldwide. This is especially notable relative to the practice of apartheid. One Protestant denomination, the Nederduitse Gereformeerde Kerk, strongly supports the apartheid system, while other

Protestant groups vehemently oppose it. A recent United Methodist publication entitled *New World Outlook*, dated December 1981, called attention to the fact that the foundation of apartheid was established some 100 years ago when Protestant whites inaugurated four racially separated churches.[7] The Protestant denomination that established these racially segregated churches was the Nederduitse Gereformeerde Kerk. As one business executive wryly commented to this researcher: "Protestants originated the apartheid system—not American corporations." It would appear that there remains a great deal of work still to be done on the level of Protestant to Protestant worldwide. Perhaps more effort can be directed to influencing other Protestants on the same social issues that are being directed to American corporations.

Even though business criticizes the church and the church criticizes business, there still remains a need for the churches to participate in and to influence the business community. The business community must be reminded of important social values that sometimes appear to get lost in the scramble for profits. The churches certainly can play a part as monitors of human behavior in the business world and certainly can make valuable contributions to the development of a viable and workable business ideology. It is not a matter of imposing "Christian solutions" on business problems, but rather it is a matter of Christians

> participating in the various realms of the secular world in which they are involved in such a way as to support all movements in these realms which are struggling to overcome structures that threaten man's humanity and to develop more human patterns of common life and work. . . . When Christians become deeply involved in such struggles, they soon discover that . . . the calling to be servant and witnesses in the secular world is not an empty phrase or an easy lot.[8]

Western Religions have traditionally attempted to direct people out beyond themselves and have urged generosity toward one's neighbors based on reverence for God and for a loving concern for others. However, the chore of the religious community to influence the business world is not an easy lot. It is a chore that is constantly beset with frustrations. Liston Pope sums these frustrations admirably in *Millhands and Preachers*:

> Nearly everybody has notions about the proper role of the church in economic affairs. Businessmen and labor leaders, laymen and ministers disagree emphatically, and frequently accuse each other of apostasy. On the one hand, the church is admonished to confine its attention to the spiritual needs of its parishioners lest its inclusive fellowship be broken or its gospel compromised. On the other hand, ministers are summoned to fearless proclamation of the Kingdom of God in social terms, with less retreat into surplices and cloisters and more attention to practices of factory and market place. The church is blamed for its indifference and praised for minding its

188   Summary and Conclusions

own business, commended as an agent of social salvation and denounced as a haven for meddlers, acclaimed as a guarantor of social stability and cursed as an insidious peddler of dope.[9]

Suggestions for Additonal Research

There is need for additional research as to whether the present method of approach to the business community by Protestant churches should be continued in its present form (through shareholder resolutions, boycotts, and other contacts as described in this study) or whether there is need for modification and change.

Some of the challenging questions that could be incorporated in additional studies are:

1. Are American corporations moving toward less investment in certain Third World societies in order to avoid potential church action in the United States? In view of the fact that there are limited corporate funds for overseas capital investments, will corporations choose to invest in stabilized countries that are less controversial? (See chapter 5.)

2. Is there a role for Protestant churches to play in encouraging corporate giving? Corporate contributions are now at the rate of 1 percent of pre-tax domestic income or in excess of two billion dollars per year. Inasmuch as the Internal Revenue Service will permit contributions up to 5 percent as tax deductions, can the churches help release the multi-billion dollar potential?

3. Should the Protestant churches recognize more openly what corporations are now doing in participation in social causes? Can the churches develop a distinct role in encouraging and enlarging the participation? Can an alliance of business executives and church leadership suggest new and exciting avenues for corporate participation in social causes which still remain within the constraints of corporate charters? Are there projects in which churches and corporations can work jointly together dealing with problems such as those associated with inner cities, the resettling of refugees, the employment of teenagers, and the like?

5

Observations: The Transnational Corporations

The transnational corporation (TNC)[1] has inspired both enthusiastic support and cries of outrage and alarm. It is considered a global integrator that spreads scientific knowledge and expertise to parts of the world where no other agency can reach and is extolled as a real hope for progress in the world. Critics look upon the TNCs as "hydra-headed economic monsters that imperil the political sovereignty of nations, as Machiavellian manipulators that dump their outdated technology on hapless nations in return for extravagant profits."[2] Transnationals have been subjected to increasing pressures from special interest groups, labor unions, economists, religious and academic critics, as well as governments and minorities of host countries.

Criticisms of the transnationals fall into several general areas. TNCs have been accused of exporting jobs outside of the country, exploiting less developed countries, spurring the growth of monopolistic practices, manipulating currencies causing monetary instability, and interfering with the sovereignty of national states.

Despite the criticism and failures of TNCs, large international corporations have distinct capabilities which do serve mankind. They have the ability to tap financial, physical, and human resources around the world and combine them into economically feasible and commercially profitable activities which as an end result can help the people of less developed countries in a manner that no other agency can duplicate.

Pressure groups, while accomplishing a great deal in guiding corporations into a consciousness of social needs, should exercise caution not to cut off the effectiveness and benefits that can accrue to people of less developed countries. Unthinking and passionate thrusts against the TNCs can possibly cause large corporations to shift their resources to less troublesome areas. No multinational corporation has unlimited resources at its command. Consequently corporations choose carefully among the many investment opportunities which are open to them—weighing both the risks and prospective returns. When long-term investments are being considered out of the home country, large corporations are vitally concerned that at least the "rules of the game" affecting foreign investments will remain relatively stable or at least predictable.

It is estimated that more than $300 billion has been invested by the TNCs throughout the world and developing countries are best served by getting their share of this investment. International companies have the capital, trained personnel, and entrepreneurial capacity to assist developing countries and to integrate them into the world economic structure. There are no other substitutes that are as effective. The United Nations can finance some limited projects, but can offer no organizational counterpart as large corporations.

In 1973 Emilio G. Colado, Executive Vice President of Exxon Corporation, commented that the transnational corporations are not in business, either at home or abroad, to earn quick returns, recover their capital and then get out of business in a given project or country. On the contrary, decisions to make additional investments for expansion and modernization, for example, are likely to follow the initial capital commitments so that the project is in a nearly constant state of evolving growth.[3] World corporations are extraordinary vehicles for stimulating ideas and deed. They are the principal agents for the peaceable transfer of technology and ideas from one part of the world to another. Since no developing nation can hope to achieve self-sufficiency in industrial or agricultural skills purely on its own efforts, the continuous exchange of men, money and ideas is vitally necessary if the world's standard of living is to be improved.

The history of America bears testimony to its dependence in its early life on outside sources of capital and technology. Our earliest commercial enterprises were launched under royal charters and were funded by British merchants. Long after gaining political independence, the United States remained financially dependent on European capital for industrial and agricultural growth. Scottish and English investors, for example, poured over $30 million into the development of ranches in the American Southwest. Without a steady flow of capital from offshore investors, we could not have achieved the rapid expansion of our canals, railways and other vital services that were so necessary to our national growth. By drawing freely on foreign capital and applying it to develop the abundant natural resources at home, the United States economy has flourished so that today America provides capital and technology throughout the world. The spreading of capital and technology is not only an "American challenge," as it has been characterized, but it is a contribution being made by many corporations of other industrialized nations. In fact, the earliest world corporations to become international in scope were European.

Today, the less developed countries, as well as church activists domiciled in the United States, are making specific demands on large industrial corporations. These are to be expected and should not be ignored or brushed aside as no other problem more urgently requires the imagination and constructive attention of business. However, nations of the world, large and small, developing or emerging, are economically interdependent—and becoming more so. Therefore, it requires vision and patience to reconcile the varied interests and developmental needs of both emerging and advanced economies. When that reconciliation is achieved, it can result in unhampered access to vigorous, competitive, global markets that will help to develop local resources.

The religious community has done well in applying pressures to alert large corporations to social responsibility. At the same time they will want to encourage—not discourage—the international giants to use their vast skills to deploy the world's resources so that poor countries can become the beneficiary of the latest technology and can be helped to be integrated into the global economic structure. Christian idealists, hard headed businessmen, and foreign governments, can work together, for each, in their own way, seek to fill the basic needs of people. Resources can be redeployed to areas of the world that need it most—and this surely can be done where there is mutual respect and cooperation.

Notes

Notes for Chapter 1

1. "The Corporate Image: PR to the Rescue," *Business Week,* January 22, 1979, p. 47.
2. Ibid.
3. Jensen, Michael C. "Dissident Stockholders Begin to Get Somewhere At Last," *New York Times,* May 16, 1977, p. 43, col. 2.
4. Ibid.
5. Ibid.
6. Gerald F. Cavanagh, *American Business Values in Transition* (Englewood Cliffs, N.J.: Prentice-Hall, 1976), p. 178.
7. Milton Friedman, "The Social Responsibility of Business Is to Increase Its Profits," *New York Times Magazine,* September 13, 1970, title of article, sec. 6, p. 32.
8. Lee E. Preston and James E. Post, *Private Management and Public Policy* (Englewood Cliffs, N.J.: Prentice-Hall, 1975), see pp. 38–39.
9. John G. Simon, Charles W. Powers and Jon P. Gunnemann, *The Ethical Investor* (New Haven: Yale University Press, 1972), p. 48.
10. David Vogel, *Lobbying The Corporation* (New York: Basic Books, Inc., 1978). Vogel points out that "those seeking to change the policies and challenge the prerogatives of managements were not confining their efforts to pressuring the government: they were taking many of their grievances directly to the firm." (p. ix). The book contains some excellent examples of activist confrontation of corporations on social issues during the late 1960s and the early 1970s.
11. The phrase "Protestant churches" used throughout this study refers to ten Protestant denominations who actively participated in shareholder resolutions and other contacts (see "Limitations of the Study"). These are: American Baptist Churches in the U.S.A., Christian Church (Disciples of Christ), Church of the Brethren, Episcopal Church, Lutheran Church in America, Presbyterian Church in the United States, Reformed Church in America, United Church of Christ, United Methodist Church, and the United Presbyterian Church in the U.S.A. These ten Protestant denominations are members of the National Council of Churches of Christ in the U.S.A.

12. "Other direct contacts" were primarily face-to-face meetings with corporate executives in dialogue prior to filing shareholder resolutions. These contacts included sending letters to management, attendance at shareholder meetings, sponsoring symposiums which brought together representatives of church and business, and similar events.
13. "Social issues" refers to concerns which involve human rights contrasted to concerns which involve economic issues with which American corporations have been primarily associated. (See "Definitions.")
14. The Protestant churches, as outlined in note 11 previously, received the cooperation and assistance of the National Council of Churches in Christ in the U.S.A. and its sponsor-related affiliate the Interfaith Center on Corporate Responsibility.
15. "Targeted corporations" refers to those corporations selected by Protestant churches for direct action.
16. George A. Steiner, "Should Business Adopt the Social Audit," *The Conference Board Record*, May 1972, p. 8.
17. Nathan H. VanderWerf, *The Times Were Very Full* (New York: National Council of Churches of Christ in the U.S.A., 1975), p. 5.
18. Eleanor Craig, *A Shareowners' Manual* (New York: Interfaith Center on Corporate Responsibility, 1977), p. 15.
19. *Letters on Social Ministry: A Guide to the Congregation* (New York: Lutheran Church in America, 1963), p. 7.
20. Charles H. Hopkins, *The Rise of the Social Gospel in American Protestantism, 1865–1915* (New Haven: Yale University Press, 1940), p. 3.
21. Gaylord B. Noyce, *Power for the Local Church* (New York: United Church of Christ, 1966), p. 2.
22. Richard J. Niebanck, *Social Statements: Their Purpose and Development* (New York: Lutheran Church of America, 1974), p. 3.
23. Herman Nickel, "The Corporation Haters," *Fortune*, June 16, 1980, p. 126.
24. Ibid. The reference to Riverside Drive implicates the National Council of Churches and the Interfaith Center on Corporate Responsibility who are located at 475 Riverside Drive, New York, N.Y.
25. Ibid.
26. Edgar C. Bundy, "Corporate Responsibility: The Attack on American Industry—Subversion by Proxy," *News and Views* (Chicago: National Laymen's Council of the Church League of America), June 1978, p. 1.
27. Harvey G. Cox, "The 'New Breed' in American Churches: Sources of Social Activism in American Religion," *Religion in America*, edited by Wm. G. McLoughlin and Robert N. Bellah (Boston: Beacon Press, 1966), p. 368. Cox points out:

> The New Breed has brought to the fore a style of theology and a political vision that have lain dormant for some years although they have deep sources in the Christian tradition and in the American religious experience. In Buffalo, Philadelphia, Kansas City, Chicago, Oakland, and dozens of other cities, the New

Breed can be found organizing welfare unions, tenant's councils, rent strikes, and school boycotts. Wherever they are at work, they have evoked opposition, both inside and outside the churches. (p. 368).

28. I. J. Kirchoff, in a reply to comments in the *Presbyterian Layman*, December 1979–January 1980, p. 8.

29. Carmine Saginario, General Overseer, Christian Church of North America, Sharon, Pa., in a letter dated June 1, 1980, addressed to this researcher. This letter contained comments similar to those received from other conservative Protestant groups in reply to this researcher's query as to their view of Protestant activism. Mr. Saginario stressed that "emphasis is on the 'Living Bread' and the 'Water of Life,' rather than on the 'social implications' of the Gospel."

30. "Corporate Critics Build Steam for Anti-MNC Campaigns Throughout Third World," *Business International*, October 17, 1980, p. 329.

31. E. A. Wallis Budge, *Babylonia Life and History*, 2nd ed. (London: Religious Tract Society, 1925). The Hammurabi Code, for example, contained a stipulation relative to liability: "The mason who builds a house which falls down and kills an inmate shall be put to death." (p. 130). Also, "If a wine merchant allows riotous men to assemble in his house and does not expel them, he shall be killed." (p. 126).

32. Plato, *The Laws of Plato*, trans. A. E. Taylor (London: Dent, 1934), 847B. Plato comments: "If a native stray from the pursuit of goodness into some trade or craft, they shall correct him by reproach and degradation until he be brought back again into the straight course." (p. 235).

33. Aristotle, "Politics," *Basic Works of Aristotle*, ed. Richard McKeon (New York: Random House, 1941). Aristotle observes: "Citizens must not lead the life of mechanics or tradesmen for such a life is ignoble and inimical to virtue. Neither must they be husbandmen, since leisure is necessary for the development of virtue and the performance of political duties." (p. 1141).

34. Quoted by R. H. Tawney, *Religion and The Rise of Capitalism* (New York: Mentor, 1947), p. 83.

35. Max Weber, *The Protestant Ethic and the Spirit of Capitalism* (New York: Scribner's 1930), pp. 111–12.

36. Ibid. pp. 70–73.

37. Gerald F. Cavanagh, *American Business Values in Transition* Englewood Cliffs, N.J.: Prentice-Hall, 1976), p. 40.

38. Ibid.

39. Quoted by Max Weber, op. cit., pp. 48–50.

40. Ibid. p. 175.

41. Ibid.

42. Fred Luthans and Richard M. Hodgetts, *Social Issues in Business* (New York: Macmillan, 1972), p. 6.

43. Adam Smith, *The Wealth of Nations: An Inquiry into the Nature and Causes of the Wealth of Nations* (New York: The Modern Library, 1937). See p. 421.

44. Ibid.

45. Howard R. Bowen, *Social Responsibilities of the Businessman* (New York: Harper & Brothers, 1953), p. 17.

46. Ibid., p. 20.

47. Ibid., p. 21.

48. The Federal Power Act (1930) regulated electric utilities to insure reasonable rates; The Norris-LaGuardia Act (1932) insured labor's right to organize, strike, boycott and picket; the National Industry Recovery Act (enacted in 1933 but repealed in 1935) restrained competition through production, price and wage controls. The Securities Act of 1933 required public disclosure and widespread dissemination of information regarding securities to prevent fraud. The Glass-Stengall Act (1933) separated investment banking from commercial banking and also established the Federal Deposit Insurance Corporation to guarantee deposits up to $5,000 and thus forestall runs on banks in crises. The Securities Exchange Act of 1934 extended the "truth-in-securities" rule and created a commission to set disclosure of information requirements and establish rules of exchange. The Federal Communications Act of 1934 gave the Federal Communications Commission jurisdiction over rates, services, charges, practices, classifications and licensing of telegraphic and telephonic communications. The National Labor Relations Act of 1935 provided freedom to form, join, and assist labor organizations. The Public Utility Holding Company Act of 1935 regulated the issue, sale and alteration of securities. The Internal Revenue Act of 1935 allowed corporations up to five percent deduction on their taxable income for corporate contributions to charitable and educational institutions. The Robinson-Patman Act (1936) prevented manufacturers and other producers of goods and services from discriminating in price among wholesale or retail purchasers. The Wheeler-Lea Act (1938) protected the consumer from unfair or deceptive acts or practices in commerce and false advertising. The Federal Food, Drug and Cosmetic Law was enacted in 1938 to protect public health and safety by prohibiting adulteration, mislabeling and misbranding of drugs. The Natural Gas Act of 1938 regulated the interstate transportation of natural gas by pipelines. The Fair Labor Standards Acts of 1938 established minimum wages, maximum hours, and restriction of the use of child labor.

49. Other examples in the 1960s: The National Traffic and Motor Vehicle Safety Act of 1966 provided standards of safety for the automobile industry. The Federal Fair Packaging and Labeling Act of 1966 (Truth-in-Packaging Act) provided industry guidelines and standards for packing and disclosing accurate information regarding contents. The National Environmental Policy Act of 1969 promoted efforts to prevent or eliminate damage to the environment and biosphere and stimulate health and welfare of man.

50. These examples of major Federal laws which regulate business out of concern for the public's health and welfare, were suggested by Charles S. Clark in his Ph.D. dissertation "Corporate Social Responsibilities and Management Perception," University of Washington, 1975, pp. 61-62.

51. Juanita M. Kreps, "Statement of Secretary of Commerce Juanita M. Kreps for the State, Justice, Commerce and Judiciary Subcommittee of the House Committee on Appropriations, January 23, 1978, Washington, D. C.," p. 2.

52. John D. Rockefeller, Jr., *The Personal Relation in Industry* (New York: Boni and Liveright, 1923), p. 21.
53. Elton Mayo, *The Human Problems of an Industrial Civilization* (New York: Macmillan, 1933).
54. "The Moral History of U.S. Business," *Fortune,* pp. 143–46, 148, 150, 152, 156 and 158.
55. Bernard W. Dempsey, S. J., "The Roots of Business Responsibility," *Business and Religion,* ed. Edward C. Bursk (New York: Harper, 1949), pp. 101–18.
56. Bowen, *Social Responsibilities of the Businessman.*
57. Ibid. p. xi.
58. *The Conference Board Record,* April 1964, pp. 7–17.
59. Rachel Carson, *Silent Spring* (New York: Houghton-Mifflin, 1962).
60. Phillip T. Drotning, "Organizing the Company for Social Action," *The Unstable Ground: Corporate Social Policy in a Dynamic Society,* ed. S. Prakash Sethi (Los Angeles: Melville Publishing, 1964), p. 256.
61. Jules Cohn, "Is Business Meeting the Challenge of Urban Affairs?" *Harvard Business Review,* 48:68–82 (March-April 1970).
62. William L. Kandel, "The Social Conscience in Hard Times," *Business and Society Review/Innovation,* 5:17–20 (Winter 1973).
63. *Social Responsibilities of Business Corporations* (New York: Committee for Economic Development, 1971), p. 16.
64. Arjay Miller, "The Social Responsibility of Business," an address before the White House Conference on the "Industrial World Ahead," Washington, D.C., February 7, 1972.
65. Mayo J. Thompson, "Free Enterprise and Free Men: A Prayer for the Future," commencement address by the Commissioner of the Federal Trade Commission to the mid-year graduating class of Texas A & M University, College Station, Texas, December 15, 1973.
66. Gerald F. Cavanagh, *American Business Values in Transition* (Englewood Cliffs, N.J.: Prentice-Hall, 1976), p. 139.
67. Ibid. p. 140.
68. Leonard Silk and David Vogel, *Ethics and Profits* (New York: Simon & Schuster, 1976), p. 21.
69. The study of the Stanford Research Institute was reported by William J. Bolce in "The Development of a Profile for Evaluating the Level of Corporate Social Responsibility," unpublished dissertation for the Ph.D., The American University, 1974, p. 37.
70. Harry F. Ward, *The Social Creed of the Churches* (New York: Abingdon Press, 1914), p. 5.
71. Ibid.

Notes for Chapter 1

72. Ibid., p. 9.

72a. Ibid.

73. Ibid.

74. Worth M. Tippy, ed. *The Socialized Church* (New York: Eaton and Mains, 1908), pp. 276–77.

75. Liston Pope, "Religion as a Social Force in America," *Social Action,* 19:2–15, May 1953.

76. Harry F. Ward, "Organized Religion, the State, and the Economic Order," *Annals of the American Academy of Political and Social Science,* 256:76, March 1948.

77. From the introductory section of "Policy," issued by the Office of Research, Evaluation and Planning of the National Council of Churches, May 1979.

78. Dennis E. Shoemaker, *The Global Connection* (New York: Friendship Press, 1977), p. 85.

79. Ibid.

80. See p. 193.

81. Shoemaker, *Global Connection,* p. 91.

82. Ibid.

83. Thomas C. Campbell, Jr., "Capitalism and Christianity," *Business and Religion,* ed. Edward C. Bursk (New York: Harper, 1959), p. 166.

84. Ibid.

85. Ibid., p. 168.

86. Ibid.

86a. From the "Investment Policy and Guidelines" of the General Assembly Mission Board of the United Presbyterian Church in the U.S.A., adopted on March 20, 1976. This is an excellent document which presents a very lucid argument from a theological view relative to the meaning of the churches' involvement with corporations, especially as it relates to the churches' investments and social responsibility of the corporations in which they have invested.

87. F. Ernest Johnson and Arthur E. Holt, *Christian Ideals In Industry* (New York: Methodist Book Concern, 1924), p. 110.

88. Ibid. p. 113.

89. Ibid., p. 112.

90. Ibid., p. 114. The writers liken the unloading of a troublesome security upon someone else to a minister who said midway in his discourse, "And, now having looked the difficulty square in the face, let us pass on." They also tell another story, on p. 112, of a friend who wanted to buy a bond, but before doing so, wanted to be sure he approved of the labor policy of the concern in question. A ring on the telephone brought the perplexed retort, "What has the labor policy to do with buying a bond?" "You see," it was explained, "this gentleman does not want to put his money into

a concern whose labor policy he does not approve." The authors comment that this elicited many expressions of disgust.

91. Ibid.
92. Horace E. Gale, "Why Are Churches Getting Involved in Investments?" *Corporate Responsibility and Religious Institutions* (New York: Corporate Information Center, National Council of Churches, 1973), p. 34.
93. Ibid. p. 35.
94. A list of these denominations is provided on p. 193 of this study.
95. Information in this segment is based on the Spring 1979 I & S Kit of The United Presbyterian Church in the U.S.A., dated September 1979, a four-page pamphlet.
96. Minutes of the 183rd General Assembly (New York: General Assembly of the United Presbyterian Church in the U.S.A., 1971), p. 596.
97. *Christian Responsibility In Investments* (Valley Forge, Pa.: American Baptist Churches, U.S.A., no date), p. 5.
98. From a statement developed and approved by the Council of Finance and Administration of The United Methodist Church in 1973.
99. From a report of the Committee on Financial Investment of the United Church of Christ, October 1970.
100. "Investment Guidelines," Church of the Brethren, 1972.
101. "Investment Policies," Christian Church, no date, pamphlet.
102. "Report of Social Criteria for Investments," Sixth Biennial Convention, 1972, Lutheran Church in America.
103. From the "Guidelines for Missions Investments," adopted by the Governing Board of the National Council of Churches of Christ, March 1973.
104. Frank White and Tim Smith, "Corporate Responsibility and the Church," *The Unstable Ground*, S. Prakash Sethi, ed. (Los Angeles: Melville Publishing Company, 1974), p. 523.
105. Ibid. pp. 523–24. These options suggested by the authors.
106. See "Research Questions" in this chapter for sub-questions.
107. The "direct contacts" were primarily face-to-face meetings with corporate executives in dialogue prior to filing shareholder resolutions. The contacts also included sending letters to management, attendance at shareholder meetings, sponsoring symposiums which brought together representatives of church and business, and similar events.

Notes for Chapter 2

1. The phrase "Protestant churches" used throughout this study refers to ten Protestant denominations who actively participated in shareholder resolutions, boycotts and other contacts. These are: American Baptist Churches in the U.S.A., Christian Church (Disciples of Christ), Church of the Brethren, Episcopal Church, Lutheran Church in America, Presbyterian Church in the United States, Reformed Church in America,

Notes for Chapter 2

United Church of Christ, United Methodist Church, and the United Presbyterian Church in the U.S.A. These ten Protestant denominations are members of the National Council of Churches of Christ in the U.S.A.

2. "The Role of the Shareholder," *Economic Priorities Report,* 2:3, April–May 1971.
3. H. Lee Silverman, "The Shareholder Comes to Life," *Finance Magazine,* November 1970, p. 28.
4. Howard R. Bowen, *The Social Responsibilities of the Businessman* (New York: Harper, 1953), p. 48.
5. John G. Simon, Charles W. Powers, and Jon P. Gunneman, *The Ethical Investor* (New Haven: Yale University Press, 1972), p. 48.
6. Ibid. p. 57.
7. Ibid., p. 51.
8. *Notice of Annual Meeting and Proxy Statement* (New York: Union Carbide Corp., 1974), Item No. 6.
9. "The Church Speaks," *Church & Society,* 67:23, January–February 1977.
10. Ibid.
11. Ibid.
12. "South Africa: The Heart of the 'White Redoubt,' " *Church & Society,* 57:16, January–February 1977.
13. "Namibia: South Africa Once Removed," *Church & Society,* 67:17–18, January–February 1977.
13a. *Notice of Annual Meeting & Proxy Statement* (New York: Mobil Oil Corp., 1977), Proposal No. 3.
14. Ibid.
15. *Notice of Annual Meeting and Proxy Statement* (New York: Mobil Oil Corp., 1978), pp. 24–25.
16. *Notice of Annual Meeting and Proxy Statement* (San Francisco: Standard Oil Co. of California, 1979), Proposal No. 4.
17. Ibid.
18. *Notice of Annual Meeting and Proxy Statement* (New York: Union Carbide Corp., 1976), Proposal No. 5.
19. James Munves, *Minding the Corporate Conscience* (New York: Julian Messner, 1974), p. 113.
20. See pp. 106–8 of this study for further detail on this boycott.
21. "Gulf Oil and Portugal: Partners in Colonialism," *CIC BRIEF,* April 1974, p. 3A. The *CIC BRIEF* is a publication of the Interfaith Center on Corporate Responsibility.
22. *Notice of Annual Meeting and Proxy Statement* (New York: Exxon Corporation, 1974), p. 21.

23. Ibid. p. 22.
24. This shareholder resolution was slated for inclusion in the *Notice of Annual Meeting and Proxy Statement* of the Bethlehem Steel Corporation, 1974. However, the resolution was filed too late for inclusion and information was obtained from material published by the Church Project on United States Investments in Southern Africa, 475 Riverside Drive, New York, N.Y.
25. Ibid.
26. *Notice of Annual Meeting and Proxy Statement* (Detroit: General Motors Corp., 1976), Item No. 5.
27. Ibid.
28. *Corporate Examiner,* July 1976, p. 4. Published by the Interfaith Center on Corporate Responsibility, New York.
29. *Notice of Annual Meeting and Proxy Statement* (New York: International Telephone and Telegraph Corporation, 1977), Item No. 10.
30. *Notice of Annual Meeting and Proxy Statement* (New York: International Telephone and Telegraph Corporation, 1978), Item No. 5.
31. *Notice of Annual Meeting and Proxy Statement* (New York: Gulf & Western Industries, Inc., 1976), Proposal No. 6.
32. Father Thomas E. Scheetz, "Gulf & Western in the Dominican Republic," *CIC BRIEF,* October 1975, p. 3A. The *CIC BRIEF* is a publication of the Interfaith Center on Corporate Responsibility.
33. *CIC BRIEF,* November–December 1976, p. 3D.
34. *Notice of Annual Meeting and Proxy Statement* (Atlanta: The Coca-Cola Company, 1979), Proposal No. 4.
35. Ibid.
36. *Notice of Annual Meeting and Proxy Statement* (Schaumburg, Ill.: Motorola, Inc., 1976), p. 13.
37. Ibid.
38. Ibid.
39. *Notice of Annual Meeting and Proxy Statement* (Dearborn, Mich.: Ford Motor Co., 1974), Proposal No. 5.
40. Ibid.
41. *Notice of Annual Meeting and Proxy Statement* (Honolulu: Castle & Cooke, Inc., 1979), Proposal No. 1.
42. *Notice of Annual Meeting and Proxy Statement* (Honolulu: Castle & Cooke, Inc., 1977), pp. 15–16.
43. Excerpts from "Statement Made At Annual Stockholders' Meeting of Castle & Cooke, Inc., Thursday, April 21, 1977, 4:00 p.m. at the Ilikai Hotel, Honolulu, Hawaii." Taken from an unpublished document issued by the United Church Christ, New York, N.Y., not dated.

44. *Notice of Annual Meeting and Proxy Statement* (Fairfield, Conn.: General Electric Co., 1977), Proposal No. 3.
45. *Notice of Annual Meeting and Proxy Statement* (Fairfield, Conn.: General Electric Co., 1978), Proposal No. 6.
46. Ibid.
47. Ibid.
48. *Notice of Annual Meeting and Proxy Statement* (Houston, Texas: Tenneco Oil Co., 1972), Proposal No. 2.
49. Ibid.
50. Ibid.
51. *Notice of Annual Meeting and Proxy Statement* (Moline, Ill.: Deere & Company, 1976), p. 8.
52. Ibid.
53. *Notice of Annual Meeting and Proxy Statement* (New York: Exxon Corporation, 1974), p. 25.
54. Ibid.
55. *Corporate Challenges, 1974* (New York: Interfaith Center on Corporate Responsibility, 1974), p. 6.
56. See pp. 108–10.
57. *Notice of Annual Meeting and Proxy Statement* (Bartlesville, Okla.: Phillips Petroleum Company, 1974), Proposal No. 2.
58. *Notice of Annual Meeting and Proxy Statement* (Bartlesville, Okla: Phillips Petroleum Company, 1975), Proposal No. 5.
59. *Notice of Annual Meeting and Proxy Statement* (New York: Chemical New York Corporation, 1979), Proposal No. 4.
60. *Notice of Annual Meeting and Proxy Statement* (New York: American Metal Climax, Inc., 1971), Proposal No. 2.
61. Ibid.
62. *Notice of Annual Meeting and Proxy Statement* (New York: American Metal Climax, Inc., 1974), Proposal No. 2.
63. *Notice of Annual Meeting and Proxy Statement* (Stamford, Conn.: Continental Oil Company, 1974), Proposal No. 2.
64. *Notice of Annual Meeting and Proxy Statement* (Indianapolis, Ind.: American Fletcher Corp., 1977), Proposal No. 4.
65. *Notice of Annual Meeting and Proxy Statement* (New York: Colgate-Palmolive Co., 1976), p. 5.
66. Judy Klemesrud, "Feminist Shareholders Challenge the Corporate Structure," *New York Times,* May 15, 1975, p. 52, col. 1.

Notes for Chapter 2   203

67. "GM's Ordeal May Set the Fashion," *Business Week,* May 30, 1970, p. 84.
68. Ibid.
69. *Business Week,* May 30, 1970, p. 84.
70. Ibid.
71. Ibid.
72. *Business Week,* February 13, 1971, p. 86.
73. "The American Corporation Under Fire," *Newsweek,* May 24, 1971, p. 78.
74. "Companies Feel the Wrath of the Clergy," *Business Week,* March 18, 1972, p. 84.
75. Ibid.
76. Barbara B. Carool, "Activists, Better Organized, Plan Even More Activity at Annual Meetings," *Industry Week,* March 19, 1973, p. 15.
77. *Business Week,* March 31, 1973, p. 76.
78. "Proxy Statements Feel the Watergate Ripples," *Business Week,* April 13, 1974, p. 89.
79. *Notice of Annual Meeting and Proxy Statement* (Dearborn, Mich.: Ford Motor Co., 1974), Proposal No. 5.
80. *Notice of Annual Meeting and Proxy Statement* (New York: Gulf Oil Corp., 1974), Proposal No. 10.
81. John C. Perham, "Annual Meetings: Back to Basics," *Dun's Review,* April 1975, p. 106.
82. *Notice of Annual Meeting and Proxy Statement* (Armonk, New York: International Business Machines Corp., 1975), Proposal No. 8.
83. *Notice of Annual Meeting and Proxy Statement* (Bartlesville, Okla: Phillips Petroleum Company, 1975), Proposal No. 5.
84. *Notice of Annual Meeting and Proxy Statement* (New York: Union Carbide Corp., 1976), Proposal No. 5.
85. *Notice of Annual Meeting and Proxy Statement* (New York: International Telephone and Telegraph Corporation, 1976), Proposal No. 5.
86. Ibid.
87. *Corporate Examiner,* July 1976, p. 4.
88. *Notice of Annual Meeting and Proxy Statement* (New York: Colgate-Palmolive Co., 1976), p. 5.
89. For further detail over the concern of infant formula distribution in Third World countries, see the Boycott Section of this study.
90. *Notice of Annual Meeting and Proxy Statement* (Moline, Ill: Deere & Company, 1976), p. 7.
91. *Notice of Annual Meeting and Proxy Statement* (New York: J. P. Stevens & Co., Inc., 1977), Proposal No. 5.

92. *Notice of Annual Meeting and Proxy Statement* (Fairfield, Conn.: General Electric Co., 1977), Proposal No. 3.
93. *Notice of Annual Meeting and Proxy Statement* (New York: Chemical Bank, 1978), p. 31.
94. Ibid.
95. Ibid.
96. "Engagement in Boycotts: Preliminary Considerations," *Church & Society*, 29:12, May–June 1979.
97. Ibid.
98. *Boycotts: Policy Analysis and Criteria* (New York: General Assembly Mission Council, The United Presbyterian Church in the U.S.A., 1979), p. 1.
99. Ibid. p. 5.
100. Ibid., p. 5.
101. Ibid.
102. Ibid., p. 6.
103. Ibid.
104. Ibid.
105. Ibid.
106. Ibid., p. 7.
107. Ibid., p. 9.
108. Quoted in *People/Profits: The Ethics of Investment*, ed. Charles W. Powers (New York: Council on Religion and International Affairs, 1972), p. 172.
109. Ibid.
110. "Gulf Oil and Portugal: Partners in Colonialism," *CIC Brief*, 1974, p. 3B.
111. David Vogel, *Lobbying the Corporation* (New York: Basic Books, Inc., 1978), p. 188. Vogel makes the following observation:

> The denouement of the controversy is replete with irony. Following the overthrow of the Salazar dictatorship in Portugal, the new government moved to give independence to its African colonies. At the same time, Gulf began private negotiations with the leaders of the Popular Movement for the Liberation of Angola which de facto controlled the land upon which Gulf's refinery was situated. The rebels assured Gulf that they had no present intention of expropriating its property; Gulf's management was more than happy to comply; they had indicated all along that they were indifferent as who ruled Angola, and now they were able to demonstrate the consistency of their conviction.
>
> During the civil war that followed Portugal's withdrawal, Gulf found itself on the opposite side from that of the United States government. Dutifully Gulf was sending its royalty checks to the Soviet-supported MPLA, while the CIA was funding its Western-backed opponents. The company's payments, in fact, were larger than those of the CIA. Under pressure from the State Department, Gulf

agreed to place its royalties in an escrow account for the duration of the conflict. Following the MPLA's victory, the payments were unfrozen, and Gulf resumed the payments of royalties to the Republic of Angola. (pp. 188–89).

112. Quoted in *Fabric of Injustice: The Struggle at J. P. Stevens* (New York: National Council of Churches, 1978), pp. 23–24.

113. See "On the Dispute Between the J.P. Stevens Company and the Amalgamated Clothing and Textile Workers Union," a report published in 1979 by the Advisory Council on Church and Social Special Task Force of the United Presbyterian Church in the United States of America. The report took this position:

> The Biblical narrative portrays the creation as a condition in which human beings live freely and fully in relationship with each other and with God. According to the creation story, life for human beings created in the image of God is life together. Created in God's image we are to realize our own being not in isolation but in interaction and mutual support with others, in community and in communities, in the context of God's love. That is the basis of human dignity. This life together is made to reflect God's own internal love through relationships of love between and among people; it is intended to reflect the sanctity of God's creation through human relationships characterized by justice, relationships in which the worth and dignity of each group and each individual are respected. To be fully human is to share the joys, sorrows and struggles of life with others. The Bible makes clear that the vision of just and loving human relationships is inherent in God's creation. But as the Genesis account portrays so vividly, relationships between and among human beings and between God and his people are flawed. The basic flaw is in our human inclination to deny our own mortality, to live our lives as though we were God and to exploit our relationships with other human beings to further our own personal ends and desires. It is this basic condition, the condition of sin, from which we have redemption, that is both within and beyond history. While we even now experience the first fruits of our redemption, nevertheless we recognize also that we still are subject to the corrupting effects of pride. No one is good save God and therefore no one can be trusted with extensive, unchecked power over others. This applies to all areas of life including the area of industrial relations. (pp. 3–4).

114. *Fabric of Injustice: The Struggle at J. P. Stevens* (New York: National Council of Churches, 1978), pp. 1–2.

115. As quoted in "Stevens' Campaign to Polish Its Image," *Industry Week*, December 10, 1979, p. 27.

116. Ibid.

117. Ibid.

118. Ibid.

119. "A Special Communication to Presbyterian Pastors," *PPS* (New York: United Presbyterian Church in the U.S.A., October 28, 1980), p. 3.

120. Excerpted from an excellent brochure entitled "Infant Formula," published by the Church of the Brethren, no date.

121. "The Nestle Boycott Kills Babies," *The Wall Street Journal,* November 1, 1979, editorial page.
122. Ibid.
123. "Letters to the Editor," *The Wall Street Journal,* January 26, 1981.
124. Letter issued by David E. Guerrant, President of the Nestle Company, White Plains, New York, undated.
125. "A Boycott Over Infant Formula," *Business Week,* April 23, 1979, p. 137.
126. "Nestle Boycott," *Church & Society,* 64:20, May–June 1979.
127. "Report to the 12th General Synod of the United Church of Christ on 1977–1979 Corporate Social Responsibility Actions," published by the United Church of Christ, 1979, p. 6.
128. Eleanor Craig, *A Shareowners' Manual* (New York: Interfaith Center on Corporate Responsibility, 1977), pp. 152–58.
129. "Report on DMNA Actions re IBM operations in South Africa," Church & Society Section, Exhibit CS-C, of a report by Franklin L. Jensen addressed to the Executive Council of the Lutheran Church in America, Division for Mission in North America, p. 1. Report dated September 18–20, 1975.
130. Included in the Report of the Executive Director, Division for Mission in North America, Lutheran Church in America, dated Feb. 10–12, 1977, p. 22.
131. As reported in "Minutes, Corporate Social Responsibility," Lutheran Church in America, p. 680, dated May 4–6, 1978.
132. "Contacts with Corporations," General Assembly Mission Council Minutes, United Presbyterian Church in the U.S.A., 1978, p. 160.
133. "Report to the 12th General Synod of the United Church of Christ on 1977–1979 Corporate Social Responsibility Actions," published by the United Church of Christ, 1979, p. 16.
134. Quoted in "Nurturing Corporate Policy Improvements Through Management Discussions," *Church As Shareholder,* Fall 1978, p. 1.
134a. Ibid.
135. "Symposium on Specific Issues, "General Assembly Mission Council Minutes, The United Presbyterian Church in the U.S.A., 1978, p. 160.
136. Ibid.
137. Eleanor Craig, *A Shareowners' Manual* (New York: Interfaith Center on Corporate Responsibility, 1977), pp. 157–58.
138. "Report to the 12th General Synod of the United Church of Christ on 1977–1979 Corporate Social Responsibility Actions," published by the United Church of Christ in 1979, p. 19.
139. Craig, *Shareowners' Manual,* p. 153.
140. *Corporate Examiner,* December 1977, p. 5.

141. "Report to the Eleventh General Synod of the United Church of Christ on 1975–1977 Corporate Social Responsibility Actions, With Special Emphasis on Southern Africa," published by the United Church of Christ, February 1, 1977, p. 4.
142. Ibid.
143. *Corporate Examiner,* May 1976, p. 5.
144. Craig, *Shareowners' Manual* pp. 152–58.
145. *Corporate Examiner,* October 1978, p. 1.
146. Craig, *Shareowners' Manual,* p. 156.
147. *The Corporate Examiner,* December 1974, p. 1.
148. Craig, *Shareowners' Manual,* p. 159.
149. Ibid.
150. Ibid., p. 152.
151. Press Release dated April 29, 1977 issued by Lillian Moir, Director of News Services of the Christian Church (Disciples of Christ), Indianapolis, Ind.
152. Press Release dated April 28, 1978 issued by Lillian Moir, Director of News Services of the Christian Church (Disciples of Christ), Indianapolis, Ind.
153. As quoted in "General Assembly Mission Council Minutes," the United Presbyterian Church in the U.S.A., p. 161.
154. Ibid.

Notes for Chapter 3

1. Robert S. Diamond, "What Business Thinks, The Fortune 500-Yankelovich Survey," *Fortune,* February 1970, pp. 118–19, 171–72. Diamond reports that the study showed that corporate leaders responding to a survey almost to the person conceded that they had responsibility when dealing with environmental problems as contrasted with other social concerns which were ranked far lower on the scale.
2. *The Private Sector Contribution to a Clean Environment* (Washington, D.C.: Chamber of Commerce of the U.S.A., February 1980), pp. 1–2.
3. The multinational corporation is also known as a transnational corporation in that such a corporation operates manufacturing plants in one or more locations outside of the continental United States.
4. William R. Dill, "Private Power and Public Responsibility," *Running the American Corporation,* William R. Dill, ed. (Englewood Cliffs, N.J.: Prentice-Hall, 1978), p. 26.
5. Lewis H. Young, "The Claimants for Influence with the Corporation," *Running the American Corporation,* William R. Dill, ed. (Englewood Cliffs, N.J.: Prentice-Hall, 1978), p. 38.
6. Ibid. p. 39.
7. Ibid.
8. Ibid.

Notes for Chapter 3

9. Donald E. Schwartz, "Reforming the Corporation from Within," *Corporate Social Policy,* Robert L. Heilbroner and Paul London, eds. (Reading, Mass.: Addison-Wesley Publishing, 1975), p. 12.
10. Herman Nickel, "The Corporation Haters," *Fortune,* June 16, 1980, p. 126.
11. Ibid.
12. Ibid.
13. Ibid.
14. Ibid., p. 128.
15. Ibid.
16. John C. Boland, "Saints and Sinners?" *Barrons,* May 5, 1980, p. 26.
17. Ibid. Mr. Boland observes that Mr. Smith was a contributor and member of the *Southern Africa* magazine, published by the Southern Africa Committee.

    The magazine of those days was devoted to features on the "liberation" armies that won control of Angola, Guinea-Bissau and Mozambique. In 1973, he was a leader of the Committee for a Free Mozambique, a group supporting FRELIMO (Front for the Liberation of Mozambique), the Marxist insurgents who succeeded the Portuguese. . . . The Southern Africa Committee itself sprang out of the National Council of Churches, as a late-Sixties project of a National Council group called the University Christian movement. Early copies of *Southern Africa,* then a newsletter, were published under the Council's auspices out of the Riverside Drive headquarters. Sometime in that fractious period, the University Movement went out of business and the Southern Africa Committee became independent. (p. 26).

18. Michael J. Jensen and William H. Meckling, "Can the Corporation Survive," first published in May 1976 by the Center for Research in Government Policy and Business, the Graduate School of Management, University of Rochester, Rochester, N.Y. and republished in the *ERC Transcript,* Series No. 5, May 1977 (West Vancouver, B.C.: ERC Publishing Company), p. 1.
19. Ibid.
20. Ibid.
21. Deane Carson, "Companies as Heroes? Bah! Humbug!", *New York Times,* December 25, 1977, sec. 3, p. 10, col. 3.
22. Ibid.
23. Ibid.
24. "Corporate Responsibility: The Attack on American Industry, Subversion by Proxy," *News & Views* (Chicago: The Church League of America, 1978), p. 1.
25. Ibid.
26. Ibid., p. 30.
27. Ibid.
28. Sidney Jaffe, "American Businessmen Must Understand the Soviet Propaganda At-

tack on Corporations," *Special Report* (Chicago: Church League of America, 1979), p. 1.

29. Ibid. p. 2.
30. Ibid.
31. Ibid.
32. Milton Friedman, *Capitalism and Freedom* (University of Chicago Press, 1962), p. 133.
33. "The 'Responsible' Corporation: Benefactor or Monopolist?" *Fortune*, November 1973, p. 56.
34. Friedman, *Capitalism and Freedom*, p. 13.
35. Luther H. Hodges, Jr. and Milton Friedman, "Does Business Have a Social Responsibility?" *The Magazine of Bank Administration*, April 1971, p. 13.
36. Ibid. p. 15.
37. Friedman, *Capitalism and Freedom*, p. 133.
38. Theodore Levitt, "The Dangers of Social Responsibility," *Harvard Business Review*, 26:46, September–October 1958.
39. Ibid.
40. Ibid.
41. Ibid., p. 48.
42. Andrew Hacker, "A Country Called Corporate America," *The Corporation in the American Economy*, ed. Harry M. Trebing (Chicago: Quadrangle Books, Inc., 1970), p. 39.
43. Ibid. p. 40.
44. John Humble, *Social Responsibility Audit* (New York: AMACOM, 1973), p. 2.
45. As quoted by Alden G. Lank in "The Implementation of Corporate Social Policies: A Study of the Process of Securing Organization Commitment to Social Philosophies, Social Foci and Social Policies in Two Corporations" (DBA dissertation, Harvard University, 1974), p. 2. of appendix D.
46. E. Kastenholz, "An Accountant's View of Corporate Responsibility," *Financial Executive*, 44:68, April 1974.
47. Comment made by Albert T. Sommers, member of the Conference Board's Office of the Chief Economist, in the book review section, p. 7, *The Conference Board Record*, November 1979.
48. Keith Davis, "The Case For and Against Business Assumptions of Social Responsibility," *Academy of Management Journal*, 16:312–23, June 1973.
49. Edward H. Bowman and Mason Haire, "A Strategic Posture Toward Corporate Social Responsibility," *California Management Review*, 20:59, Winter 1975.
50. Jerry L. Kinard, "A Survey of Industrial Corporate Executives' Attitudes Toward Corporate Social Responsibility" (DBA dissertation, Mississippi State University, 1971), p. 151.

51. Peter F. Drucker, *Management: Taxes, Responsibilities, Practices* (New York: Harper & Row, 1974).
52. John L. Paluszek, *Business and Society: 1976–2000* (New York: AMACOM, 1976), p. 1.
53. Ibid. p. 3.
54. George A. Steiner, "Should Business Adopt the Social Audit," *The Conference Board Record,* May 1972, p. 8.
55. Charles S. Clark, "Corporate Social Responsibilities and Management Perception," (Ph.D. dissertation, University of Washington, 1975), p. 13.
56. Steven C. Dilley, "What is Social Responsibility?" *CA Magazine,* 103:26, November 1974.
57. Henry G. Manne and Henry C. Wallich, *The Modern Corporation and Social Responsibility,* Rational Debate Series of the American Enterprise Institute (Washington, D.C.: American Enterprise Institute for Policy Research, 1972), p. 4.
58. Dan H. Fenn, Jr., *Business Responsibility in Action* (New York: McGraw-Hill, 1960), p. v.
59. Edmund R. Gray, "Social Responsibility—What's It All About?" *Current Concepts in Management,* ed. O. Jeff Harris (Baton Rouge: Division of Research, College of Business Administration, Louisiana State University, 1972), p. 17.
60. *The Corporation in Transition* (Washington, D.C.: Chamber of Commerce of the U.S.A., 1972), p. 92.
61. R. Joseph Monsen, Jr., *Business and the Changing Environment* (New York: McGraw-Hill, 1973), p. 121.
62. John G. Simon, Charles W. Powers and Jon P. Gunneman, *The Ethical Investor* (New Haven, Conn.: Yale University Press, 1972), p. 18.
63. Ibid.
64. Alden G. Lank, "The Implementation of Corporate Social Policies: A Study of the Process of Securing Organizational Commitment to Social Philosophies, Social Foci and Social Policies in Two Corporations," (DBA dissertation, Harvard University, 1974), p. 36.
65. Quoted in *What Direction? Corporate Philanthropy* (Washington, D.C.: National Chamber Foundation, 1978), p. 7.
66. Ibid.
67. Data obtained from *Measuring Business Social Performance: The Corporate Social Audit,* ed. John J. Corson and George A. Steiner, and was prepared for The Committee for Economic Development, an independent research and educational organization made up of two hundred business executives and educators.
68. *Notice of Annual Meeting and Proxy Statement* (Minneapolis, Minn.: Control Data Corp., 1978), pp. 8–9.
69. *Notice of Annual Meeting and Proxy Statement* (New York: Citicorp, 1977), Proposal No. 4.

Notes for Chapter 3   211

70. *Notice of Annual Meeting and Proxy Statement* (New York: Phelps Dodge Corporation, 1977), Proposal No. 3.
71. *Notice of Annual Meeting and Proxy Statement* (New York: Manufacturers Hanover Trust Co., 1978), Proposal No. 4.
72. *Notice of Annual Meeting and Proxy Statement* (Pittsburgh, Pa.: United States Steel Corp., 1979), Proposal No. 8.
73. *Notice of Annual Meeting and Proxy Statement* (Armonk, N.Y.: International Business Machines Corp., 1975), Proposal No. 8.
74. Ibid.
75. *Notice of Annual Meeting and Proxy Statement* (Bartlesville, Okla.: Phillips Petroleum Company, 1975), Proposal No. 5.
76. *Notice of Annual Meeting and Proxy Statement* (Stamford, Conn.: Continental Oil Company, 1974), Proposal No. 1.
77. Ibid.
78. *Notice of Annual Meeting and Proxy Statement* (Los Angeles, Calif.: Getty Oil Co., 1974), p. 9.
79. *Notice of Annual Meeting and Proxy Statement* (Bartlesville, Okla.: Phillips Petroleum Company, 1974), Proposal No. 1.
80. *Notice of Annual Meeting and Proxy Statement* (New York: Union Carbide Corp., 1976), Proposal No. 5.
81. *Notice of Annual Meeting and Proxy Statement* (New York: Mobil Oil Corp., 1978), Proposal No. 4.
82. Ibid.
83. "The Case of Gulf Oil and Angola: A Manager, His Critics, and His Supporters," remarks by Russell G. Connolly of Gulf Oil Company, *People/Profits,* ed. Charles W. Powers (New York: Council on Religion and International Affairs, 1972), p. 172.
84. Ibid.
85. *Notice of Annual Meeting and Proxy Statement* (New York: Exxon Corporation, 1974), pp. 22–23.
86. *Notice of Annual Meeting and Proxy Statement* (New York: General Motors Corp., 1976), Proposal No. 5.
87. *Notice of Annual Meeting and Proxy Statement* (New York: International Telephone and Telegraph Corporation, 1978), Proposal No. 5.
88. *Notice of Annual Meeting and Proxy Statement* (Houston, Texas: Superior Oil Company, 1979), Proposal No. 4.
89. *Notice of Annual Meeting and Proxy Statement* (New York: Gulf & Western Industries, Inc., 1975), Proposal No. 5.
90. Ibid.
91. Ibid.

Notes for Chapter 3

92. *Notice of Annual Meeting and Proxy Statement* (New York: Gulf & Western Industries, Inc., 1979), Proposal No. 6.
93. Ibid.
94. *Notice of Annual Meeting and Proxy Statement* (Atlanta, Georgia: The Coca-Cola Company, 1979), Proposal No. 4.
95. Ibid.
96. *Notice of Annual Meeting and Proxy Statement* (Schaumburg, Ill.: Motorola, Inc., 1976), pp. 13–14.
97. *Notice of Annual Meeting and Proxy Statement* (Dearborn, Michigan: Ford Motor Co., 1974), Proposal No. 5.
98. *Notice of Annual Meeting and Proxy Statement* (Honolulu, Hawaii: Castle & Cooke, Inc., 1977), pp. 16–17.
99. Ibid.
100. *Notice of Annual Meeting and Proxy Statement* (Fairfield, Conn.: General Electric Co., 1977), Proposal No. 3.
101. Ibid.
102. *Notice of Annual Meeting and Proxy Statement* (New York: American Home Products Corp., 1978), Proposal No. 2.
103. *Notice of Annual Meeting and Proxy Statement* (New York: American Home Products Corp., 1978), Proposal No. 2.
104. Affirmations of having policies in place relative to the prohibition of illegal and improper payments for political purposes were found in the *Notices of Annual Meetings and Proxy Statements* of Gulf Oil (1976), Exxon Corporation (1976), Ford Motor Company (1976), Merck & Co., Inc. (1976), and Tenneco, Inc., (1977), which corporations had received a Protestant sponsored or cosponsored resolution.
105. *Notice of Annual Meeting and Proxy Statement* (Rahway, N.J.: Merck & Co., Inc., 1976), Proposal No. 7.
106. Ibid.
107. *Notice of Annual Meeting and Proxy Statement* (Moline, Ill.: Deere & Company, 1976), p. 9.
108. Ibid.
109. *Notice of Annual Meeting and Proxy Statement* (Pittsburgh, Pa.: Gulf Oil Corp., 1974), Proposal No. 10.
110. Ibid.
111. *Notice of Annual Meeting and Proxy Statement* (New York: J. P. Stevens & Co., 1977), Proposal No. 5.
112. *Notice of Annual Meeting and Proxy Statement* (Fairfield, Conn.: General Electric Co., 1974), Proposal No. 3.

113. *Notice of Annual Meeting and Proxy Statement* (Armonk, New York: International Business Machines Corp., 1974), Proposal No. 2.

114. *Notice of Annual Meeting and Proxy Statement* (St. Paul, Minn.: Minnesota Mining & Mfg. Co., 1974), pp. 16–17.

115. *Notice of Annual Meeting and Proxy Statement* (Bartlesville, Okla.: Phillips Petroleum Company, 1974), Proposal No. 3.

116. *Notice of Annual Meeting and Proxy Statement* (New York: Chemical New York Corporation, 1978) and *Notice of Annual Meeting and Proxy Statement* (Boston, Mass.: First National Bank of Boston, 1979), Proposal No. D.

117. *Notice of Annual Meeting and Proxy Statement* (Greenwich, Conn.: The Pittston Company, 1976), Proposal No. 2.

118. *Notice of Annual Meeting and Proxy Statement* (New York: American Electric Power Co., 1975), pp. 14–15.

119. Ibid.

120. *Notice of Annual Meeting and Proxy Statement* (Indianapolis, Ind.: American Fletcher Corp., 1977), Proposal No. 4.

121. *Notice of Annual Meeting and Proxy Statement* (New York: Colgate-Palmolive Co., 1976), p. 5.

122. *Re-Examination of Rules Relating to Shareholder Communications, Shareholder Participation in the Corporate Process and Corporate Governance Generally* (Washington, D.C.: Securities and Exchange Commission, 1978), p. 17.

123. Ibid.

124. Ibid.

125. Ibid.

126. Ibid.

127. David Vogel, *Lobbying the Corporation* (New York: Basic Books, Inc., 1978), p. 205.

128. Ibid.

129. Ibid. p. 208.

130. Juanita M. Kreps, "Statement of Secretary of Commerce Juanita M. Kreps for the State, Justice, Commerce and Judiciary Subcommittee of the House Committee on Appropriations, January 23, 1978, Washington, D.C.," p. 3.

131. Ibid.

132. Ibid.

132a. Ibid.

133. Henry Eilbirt and I. Robert Parket, "The Practice of Business: The Current Status of Corporate Social Responsibility," *Business Horizons*, 18:5–14, August 1973.

134. Ibid. p. 5.

135. Ibid., p. 14.

136. Milton Moskowitz, "Corporate Social Responsibility 1967–1977: An Overview," *Social Responsibility* (San Francisco: Levi Strauss & Co., 1977), pp. 3–4.

137. "The Changing Corporate Board," prepared by the National Economic Development Division, Chamber of Commerce of the U.S.A., February 1980.

138. The Heidrick and Struggler survey referred to by the Chamber of Commerce was reported in the *Wall Street Journal*, January 19, 1977, p. 6.

139. The Touche-Ross survey included in the Chamber of Commerce's report was based on interviews with the board members of Fortune 500 companies in August 1978.

140. See n. 139 above.

141. Vernon M. Buehler and Y. K. Shetty, "Managing Corporate Social Responsibility," *Management Review*, 64:5–14, August 1975.

142. Ibid. p. 7

143. Elliott J. Weiss, "How to Make 'Ethical' Investments," *New York Times*, July 30, 1978, sec. 3, p. 14, col. 3.

144. Theodore V. Purcell, "Management and the 'Ethical' Investors," *Harvard Business Review*, 57:26, September–October 1979.

145. Ibid. pp. 29–30.

146. Ibid., p. 30.

147. "Report of the Committee on Social Responsibility In Investments to the Executive Council of the Episcopal Church, for the Year Ending August 31, 1977" (New York: The Episcopal Church, 1977), p. 17.

148. Ibid. pp. 4–5.

149. Ibid., pp. 6–7.

150. Ibid., p. 7.

151. Ibid., p. 8.

Notes for Chapter 4

1. This conversation was reported by Robert J. Flaherty in an article, "Revolution, Sayeth the Churchman: One Soul At a Time, Says a Businessman," *Forbes*, February 6, 1978, pp. 31–33. The participants in the discussion from Control Data Corporation were William C. Norris, Chairman, Norbert R. Berg, Senior Vice President of Administration and Personnel, and Gary H. Lohn, Vice President, Human Resources Development and Public Affairs. Participants from the religious community were the Rev. Mr. William P. Thompson, President, National Council of Churches of Christ in the U.S.A., and Stated Clerk of the General Assembly, United Presbyterian Church in the U.S.A., the Rev. Mr. Timothy H. Smith, Director of the Interfaith Center for Corporate Responsibility and the Rev. Mr. Frank H. White, a founder of the Interfaith Center and Staff Aide for the United Presbyterian Church.

2. See pp. 178 ff.

3. Theodore V. Purcell, "Management and the 'Ethical' Investors," *Harvard Business Review*, 57:32, September–October 1979.
4. Ibid. p. 36.
5. Melvin Anshen, *Corporate Strategies for Social Performance* (New York: Macmillan, 1980), p. 11.
6. Ibid. p. 36.
7. "Mission Memo," *New World Outlook*, December 1981, no page number. This monthly magazine is published by the General Board of Global Ministries of the United Methodist Church.
8. Horst Symanowski, *The Christian Witness In An Industrial Society*, trans. George H. Kehm (Philadelphia, Pa.: Westminster Press, 1976), p. 27.
9. Liston Pope, *Millhands & Preachers* (New Haven: Yale University Press, 1942), p. vii.

Notes for Chapter 5

1. Transnational corporations (also known as multinationals) are enterprises that own or control production or service facilities outside the country in which they are based.
2. S. R. Madhu, "Multinational Corporations: Where Are They Now? Where Are They Going?" *SPAN*, March 1977, p. 6.
3. From a statement of Emilio G. Collado, Executive Vice President, Exxon Corporation, before the Group of Eminent Persons to Study the Impact of Multinational Corporations on Development and on International Relations, United Nations, New York, September 11, 1973.

Bibliography

Books

Abbott, Lyman. *Christianity and Social Problems.* New York: Houghton Mifflin, 1896.
Abt, Clark C. *The Social Audit.* New York: AMACOM, 1977.
Ackerman, Robert W. *The Social Challenge to Business.* Cambridge: Harvard University Press, 1975.
Ackerman, Robert W., and Raymond A. Bauer. *Corporate Social Responsiveness.* Reston, Va.: Reston Publishing Company, Inc., 1976.
Allen, Jerry K., Isolde Chapin, Shirley Keller, and Donna Hill. *Volunteers from the Workplace.* Washington, D.C.: National Center for Voluntary Action, 1979.
Andrews, C. F. *Christ and Human Need.* New York: Harper, no date.
Anshen, Melvin, ed. *Managing the Socially Responsible Corporation.* New York: Macmillan, 1974.
_____. *Corporate Strategies for Social Performance.* New York: Macmillan, 1980.
Anshen, Melvin and George L. Bach. *Management and Corporations 1985.* New York: McGraw Hill, 1960.
Aristotle. *Basic Works of Aristotle,* ed. Richard McKeon. New York: Random House, 1941.
Babson, Roger W. *Religion and Business.* New York: Macmillan, 1920.
Backman, Jules, ed. *Social Responsibility and Accountability.* New York: New York University Press, 1975.
Barber, Richard J. *The American Corporation, Its Power, Its Money, Its Politics.* New York: E. P. Dutton, 1970.
Barnes, Charles W. *Social Messages.* New York: Methodist Book Concern, 1915.
Barnet, Richard J. *The Crisis of the Corporation.* New York: AMACOM, 1975.
Barnet, Richard J. and Ronald E. Muller. *Global Reach.* New York: Simon & Schuster, 1974.
Barnett, John, ed. *Getting Involved: A New Challenge for Corporate Activists.* Princeton, N.J.: Dow Jones Books, 1972.
Batten, Samuel Z. *The Social Task of Christianity.* New York: Revell, 1911.
Bennett, John C. *Christian Ethics and Social Policy.* New York: Scribner's, 1946.
_____. *Social Salvation: A Religious Approach to the Problems of Social Change.* New York: Scribner's, 1935.
Bennett, John C., Howard R. Bowen, William A. Brown, Jr., and G. Bromley Oxnam. *Christian Values and Economic Life.* New York: Harper, 1954.
Berle, Adolph A. *Christianity and the Social Rage.* New York: McBride, Nast & Co., 1914.
Bodein, Vernon P. *The Social Gospel of Walter Rauschenbusch and Its Relation to Religious Education.* New Haven: Yale University Press, 1944.

Bowen, Howard R. *Social Responsibilities of the Businessman.* New York: Harper, 1953.
Brown, Charles R. *The Social Message of the Modern Pulpit.* New York: Scribner's, 1911.
Budge, E. A. Wallis. *Babylonian Life and History,* 2nd ed. London: Religious Tract Society, 1925.
Bursk, Edward C. *Business and Religion.* New York: Harper, 1959.
Business and Social Progress: Views of Two Generations of Executives. New York: Praeger, 1970.
Business Leadership in Social Change. New York: The Conference Board, 1971.
Campbell, R. J. *Christianity and the Social Order.* New York: Macmillan, 1907.
Carroll, Archie B., ed. *Managing Corporate Social Responsibility.* Boston: Little, Brown, 1977.
Carson, John J., and George A. Steiner. *Measuring Business's Social Performance: The Corporate Social Audit.* New York: Committee for Economic Development, 1974.
Carson, Rachel. *Silent Spring.* New York: Houghton Mifflin, 1962.
Cavanagh, Gerald F. *American Business Values in Transition.* Englewood Cliffs, N.J.: Prentice-Hall, 1976.
Chaffee, Edmund B. *The Protestant Churches and the Industrial Crisis.* New York: Macmillan, 1933.
Chatterton-Hill, George. *The Sociological Value of Christianity.* London: Adam & Charles Black, 1912.
Childs, Marquis W., and Douglas Cater. *Ethics in a Business Society.* New York: Harper, 1954.
Church and Society: Social Policy of The Episcopal Church, December 1967 to April, 1979. New York: The Executive Council of The Episcopal Church.
Clow, W. M. *Christ in the Social Order.* New York: Hodder & Stoughton, 1913.
Coffin, Henry Sloane. *A More Christian Industrial Order.* New York: Macmillan, 1920.
Commons, John R. *Social Reform and the Church.* New York: Thos. Y. Crowell, 1894.
Corporate Challenges, 1974. New York: Interfaith Center on Corporate Responsibility, 1974.
Corporate Responsibility and Religious Institutions: Information and Action Documents. New York: Corporate Information Center, National Council of Churches, October 1971.
Corporate Responsibility: The Attack on American Industry. Subversion by Proxy. Wheaton, Ill.: National Laymen's Council of the Church League of America, June 1978.
Crafts, Wilbur F. *Practical Christian Sociology.* New York: Funk & Wagnalls, 1907.
Craig, Eleanor. *A Shareowner's Manual: For Church Committees on Social Responsibility in Investments.* New York: The Interfaith Center on Corporate Responsibility, 1977.
Cripps, Stafford. *Toward Christian Democracy.* New York: Philosophical Library, 1946.
Cutting, R. Fulton. *The Church and Society.* New York: Macmillan, 1912.
D'Aprix, Roger M. *In Search of a Corporate Soul.* New York: AMACOM, 1976.
Darby, James E. *Jesus An Economic Mediator.* New York: Revell, 1922.
Davis, Jerome. *Christianity and Social Adventuring.* New York: Century, 1927.
Davis, Ozoras. *Preaching the Social Gospel.* New York: Revell, 1922.
Demant, V. A. *God, Man and Society.* Milwaukee, Wis.: Morehouse, 1934.
Dickinson, Charles Henry. *The Christian Reconstruction of Modern Life.* New York: Macmillan, 1913.
Diefendorf, Dorr F. *The Christian in Social Relationship.* New York: Methodist Book Concern, 1922.
Dill, William R., ed. *Running the American Corporation.* Englewood Cliffs, N.J.: Prentice-Hall, 1978.
Donaldson, Thomas, and Patricia H. Werhane, eds. *Ethical Issues in Business.* Englewood Cliffs, N.J.: Prentice-Hall, 1979.

Drucker, Peter F. *The Age of Discontinuity.* New York: Harper & Row, 1969.
_____. *Management: Taxes, Responsibilities, Practices.* New York: Harper & Row, 1974.
_____. *The Practice of Management.* London: William Heinemann, 1955.
Epstein, Marc, J., Eric G. Flamholtz, and John J. McDonough. *Corporate Social Performance: The Measurement of Product and Service Contributions.* New York: National Association of Accountants, 1977.
Everett, John R. *Religion in Economics.* New York: King's Crown Press, 1946.
Farmer, Richard N., and W. Dickerson Hogue. *Corporate Social Responsibility.* Chicago: Science Research Associates, 1973.
Fenn, Dan H., Jr. *Business Responsibility in Action.* New York: McGraw-Hill, 1960.
Foreign Investment and Employment: An Examination of Foreign Investments To Make 58 Products Overseas. New York: The Conference Board, 1975.
Friedman, Milton. *Capitalism & Freedom.* Chicago: The University of Chicago Press, 1962.
Galbraith, John Kenneth. *The New Industrial State.* New York: New American Library, 1971.
Gordon, Theodore, Dennis L. Little, Harold L. Strudler, and Donna D. Lustgarten. *A Forecast of the Interaction Between Business and Society in the Next Five Years.* Middletown, Conn.: Institute for the Future, April 1971.
Gram, Harold A. *Ethics & Social Responsibility in Business.* St. Louis: Concordia, 1969.
Greenwood, William T. *Issues in Business and Society: Readings and Cases.* 2nd ed. Boston: Houghton Mifflin, 1971.
Guide to Corporations: A Social Perspective. Chicago, Ill: The Swallow Press, 1974.
Guilliland, G. E., Jr., ed. *Readings in Business Responsibility.* Braintree, Mass.: D. H. Mark Publishing Co., 1969.
Haas, John J. *Corporate Social Responsibilities.* Brooklyn, New York: Theo. Gaus Sons, 1973.
Harris, James F., and Anne Klepper. *Corporate Philanthropic Public Service Activities.* New York: The Conference Board, 1976.
Hartzler, Richard H. *Justice, Legal Systems and Social Structure.* Port Washington, New York: Kennikat Press, 1976.
Heald, Morrell. *The Social Responsibility of Business: Company and Community, 1900–1960.* Cleveland: The Press of Case Western Reserve University, 1970.
Heilbroner, Robert L., and Paul London, eds. *Corporate Social Policy.* Reading, Mass.: Addison-Wesley, 1975.
Hershfield, David C. *The Multinational Union Challenges the Multinational Company.* New York: The Conference Board, 1975.
Hobson. J. A. *God and Mammon: The Relation of Religion and Economics.* New York: Macmillan, 1931.
Hopkins, Charles H. *The Rise of the Social Gospel in American Protestantism 1865–1915.* New Haven: Yale University Press, 1940.
How America Continues to Benefit from U.S. Business Investment Abroad in the '70s. New York: Business International Corporation, 1976.
Humble, John. *Social Responsibility Audit.* New York: AMACOM, 1973.
International Business Principles—Company Codes. Stanford: Stanford Research Institute, 1976.
Ivens, Michael, ed. *Industry & Values.* London: George G. Harrap, 1970.
Jacoby, Neil H. *Corporate Power and Social Responsibility.* New York: Macmillan, 1973.
Johnson, F. Ernest. *Economics and the Good Life.* New York: Association Press, 1934.
_____. *The Social Gospel Re-Examined.* New York: Harper, 1940.

Johnson, F. Ernest, and Arthur E. Holt. *Christian Ideals in Industry.* New York: The Methodist Book Concern, 1924.
Johnson, Harold L. *Business in Contemporary Society.* Belmont, Calif.: Wadsworth, 1971.
Johnson, M. Bruce, ed. *The Attack on Corporate America.* New York: McGraw-Hill, 1978.
Kapp, K. William. *The Social Costs of Private Enterprise.* New York: Shocken Books, 1971.
Kay, Lillian W., ed. *The Future Role of Business in Society.* New York: The Conference Board, 1977.
Kelley, James P. *The Economics of Christianity.* Boston: The Pilgrim Press, 1931.
Knight, Frank H., and Thornton W. Merriam. *The Economic Order and Religion.* New York: Harper, 1945.
Kuhn, James W., and Ivar Berg. *Values in a Business Society.* New York: Harcourt, Brace & World, 1968.
Letters on Social Ministry: A Guide to the Congregation. New York: Lutheran Church in America, 1963.
Levitt, Theodore. *The Third Sector.* New York: AMACOM, 1973.
Litschert, Robert J., and Edward A. Nicholson. *The Corporate Role and Ethical Behavior: Concepts and Cases.* New York: Petrocelli/Charter, 1977.
Lindsay, A. D. *Christianity and Economics.* London: Macmillan, 1933.
Linowes, David F. *Strategies for Survival.* New York: AMACOM, 1973.
―――――. *The Corporate Conscience.* New York: Hawthorn, 1974.
Luccock, Halford E. *Christian Faith and Economic Change.* New York: Abingdon Press, 1936.
Luthans, Fred, and Richard M. Hodgetts. *Social Issues in Business.* New York: Macmillan, 1972.
McBride, Thomas G. *Christian Ethics and Economics.* New York: Richard R. Smith, 1944.
McKie, James W. *Social Responsibility and the Business Predicament.* Washington, D.C.: Brookings Institute, 1975.
Madden, Carl H. *Clash of Culture: Management in an Age of Changing Value.* Washington, D.C.: National Planning Association, 1972.
Manne, Henry G., and Henry C. Wallich. *The Modern Corporation and Social Responsibility: Rational Debate.* Washington, D.C.: American Enterprise Institute for Public Policy Research, 1972.
Marty, Martin E. *Righteous Empire: The Protestant Experience in America.* New York: Dial Press, 1971.
―――――. *Second Chance for American Protestants.* New York: Harper & Row, 1963.
May, Henry F. *Protestant Churches and Industrial America.* New York: Harper, 1949.
Mayo, Elton. *The Human Problems of an Industrial Civilization.* New York: Macmillan, 1933.
Measurement of Corporate Social Performance. New York: American Institute of Certified Public Accountants, 1976.
Merrill, Harwood F., ed. *Classics in Management.* New York: American Association, 1970.
Minding the Corporate Conscience 1974. New York: Council on Economic Priorities, 1974.
Monsen, R. Joseph, Jr. *Business and the Changing Environment.* New York: McGraw-Hill, 1973.
Muelder, Walter G. *Religion and Economic Responsibility.* New York: Charles Scribner's Sons, 1953.
Multinational Corporations and National Elites: A Study in Tensions. New York: The Conference Board, 1976.
Munves, James. *Minding the Corporate Conscience.* New York: Julian Messner, 1974.

Must We Choose Sides? Oakland, Calif.: The Inter-Religious Task Force for Social Analysis, 1980.
Nader, Ralph, Mark Greene and Joel Seligman. *Taming the Giant Corporation.* New York: W. W. Norton, 1976.
Niebanck, Richard J. *Social Statements: Their Purpose and Development.* New York: Lutheran Church in America, 1974.
Noyce, Gaylord B. *Power for the Local Church.* New York: United Church of Christ, 1966.
O'Connor, James S. *The Corporation and the State.* New York: Harper & Row, 1974.
Organizing for Effective Public Affairs. New York: National Industrial Conference Board, 1969.
Our Economic Life in the Light of Christian Ideals. New York: Association Press, 1932.
Page, Kirby. *Christianity and Economic Problems.* New York: Association Press, 1922.
Paluszek, John L. *Business and Society: 1976–2000.* New York: AMACOM, 1976.
Perspectives for the '70s and '80s. New York: National Industrial Conference Board, 1970.
Plato. *The Laws of Plato.* A. E. Taylor, trans. London: Dent, 1934.
Pope, Liston. *Millhands & Preachers.* New Haven: Yale University Press, 1942.
Powers, Charles W., ed. *People/Profits: The Ethics of Investment.* New York: Council on Religion and International Affairs, 1972.
──────. *Social Responsibility and Investments.* Nashville: Abingdon, 1971.
Preston, Lee E. and James E. Post. *Private Management and Public Policy.* Englewood Cliffs, N.J.: Prentice-Hall, 1975.
Rasmussen, Albert T. *Christian Responsibility in Economic Life.* Philadelphia: Westminster Press, 1965.
Rauschenbusch, Walter. *A Theology for the Social Gospel.* New York: Macmillan, 1919.
Re-Examination of Rules Relating to Shareholder Communications, Shareholder Participation in the Corporate Process and Corporate Governance Generally. Washington, D.C.: Securities and Exchange Commission, 1978.
Reich, Charles A. *The Greening of America.* New York: Random House, 1970.
Rockefeller, John D. *The Second Revolution.* New York: Harper & Row, 1973.
Rockefeller, Jr., John D. *The Personal Relation in Industry.* New York: Boni and Liveright, 1923.
Role of Business in Public Affairs. New York: National Industrial Conference Board, 1968.
Root, Edward T. *The Bible Economy of Plenty.* New York: Harper, 1939.
──────. *"The Profit of the Many": The Biblical Doctrine and Ethics of Wealth.* New York: Revell, 1899.
Ross, Joel E., and Robert G. Murdick. *Management Update.* New York: AMACOM, 1973.
Samuelsson, Kurt. *Religion and Economic Action.* E. G. French, trans. New York: Basic Books, 1961.
Selekman, Sylvia K., and Benjamin N. Selekman. *Power and Morality in a Business Society.* New York: McGraw-Hill, 1956.
Sethi, S. Prakash, ed. *The Unstable Ground: Corporate Social Policy in a Business Society.* New York: McGraw-Hill, 1956.
──────. *Up Against the Corporate Wall.* Engelwood Cliffs, N.J.: Prentice-Hall, 1971.
Shoemaker, Dennis E. *The Global Connection: Local Action for World Justice.* New York: Friendship Press, 1977.
Silk, Leonard, and David Vogel. *Ethics and Profits.* New York: Simon & Schuster, 1976.
Simon, John G., Charles W. Powers and Jon P. Gunnemann. *The Ethical Investor.* New Haven: Yale University Press, 1972.
Smith, Adam. *The Wealth of Nations: An Inquiry into the Nature and Causes of the Wealth of Nations.* New York: The Modern Library, 1937.

Social Responsibilities of Business Corporations. New York: Committee for Economic Development, 1971.
Stamp, Josiah. *Christianity and Economics.* New York: Macmillan, 1938.
_____. *Motive and Method in a Christian Order.* New York: Abingdon, 1936.
_____. *The Christian Ethic as an Economic Factor.* London: Epworth Press, 1926.
Steiner, George A. *Business and Society.* New York: Random House, 1975.
Steiner, George A., and John B. Miner. *Management, Policy and Strategy: Text, Readings, and Cases.* New York: Macmillan, 1977.
Stone, Christopher D. *Where the Law Ends: The Social Control of Corporate Behavior.* New York: Harper & Row, 1976.
Sturdivant, Frederick D., and Larry M. Robinson. *The Corporate Social Challenge: Cases and Commentaries.* Homewood, Ill.: Richard D. Irwin, 1977.
Symanowski, Horst. *The Christian Witness in an Industrial Society.* George H. Kehm, trans. Philadelphia, Pa.: Westminster Press.
Tawney, R. H. *Religion and the Rise of Capitalism.* New York: Harcourt, Brace & Co., 1926.
The Church and Industrial Reconstruction. New York: Association Press, 1920.
The Corporation in Transition. Washington, D.C.: Chamber of Commerce of the U.S.A., 1972.
The Multinational Company: A Chronological Bibliography, 1966–1974. New York: Foreign Trade Council, 1975.
The Multinational Corporation: Studies on U.S. Foreign Investment. Washington, D.C.: U.S. Department of Commerce, 1972.
The Private Sector Contribution to a Clean Environment. Washington, D.C.: Chamber of Commerce of the U.S.A., 1980.
Tippy, Worth M., ed. *The Socialized Church,* New York: Eaton and Mains, 1908.
Troeltsch, Ernst. *The Social Teaching of the Christian Churches, Vols. 1 and 2,* Olive Wyon, trans. New York: Harper, 1960.
VanderWerf, Nathan H. *The Times Were Very Full.* New York: National Council of Churches of Christ in the U.S.A., 1975.
Vogel, David. *Lobbying the Corporation.* New York: Basic Books, Inc., 1972.
Votaw, Dow, and S. Prakash Sethi. *The Corporate Dilemma: Traditional Values Versus Contemporary Problems.* Englewood Cliffs, N.J.: Prentice-Hall, 1973.
Walton, Clarence, ed. *The Ethics of Corporate Conduct.* Englewood Cliffs, N.J.: Prentice-Hall, 1977.
Ward, Harry F. *The Social Creed of the Churches.* New York: Abingdon, 1914.
Weber, Max. *The Protestant Ethic and the Spirit of Capitalism.* New York: Scribner's, 1930.
Weissmann, Jacob, ed. *The Social Responsibilities of Corporate Management.* Hempstead, N.Y.: Hofstra University, 1966.
What Direction? Corporate Philanthrophy? Washington, D.C.: National Chamber Foundation, 1978.
Which Side Are We On? Oakland, Calif: The Inter-Religious Task Force for Social Analysis, 1980.
Wren, Daniel A. *The Evolution of Management Thought.* New York: Ronald, 1972.
Zeitlin, Maurice, ed. *American Society, Inc.* Chicago: Rand McNally, 1977.

Journals, Periodicals and Newspapers

"A Boycott Over Infant Formula." *Business Week,* April 23, 1979, p. 137.
Ackerman, Robert W. "How Companies Respond to Social Demands." *Harvard Business Review.* 51:88–98. July–August 1973.

"Activists Stir Up Their Annual Attacks." *Business Week,* March 31, 1973, pp. 76–78.
Alexander, Tom. "The Social Engineers Retreat Under Fire." *Fortune,* October 1972, pp. 132–48.
Andrews, Kenneth R. "Public Responsibility in the Private Corporation." *Journal of Industrial Economics.* 20:135–45. April 1972.
Andrews, Kenneth R. "Can the Best Corporations Be Made Moral?" *Harvard Business Review.* 51:57–64. May–June 1973.
"Annual Meeting Time." *Forbes,* April 15 1979, pp. 40, 42.
"Annual Meetings: Back to Basics, This Year Social Issues Are Yielding the Floor to Dollars and Cents." *Dun's Review,* April 1975, pp. 48–51, 106, 108, 110.
Anshen, Melvin. "Changing the Social Contract: A Role for Business." *Columbia Journal of World Business.* 5:6–14. November–December 1970.
Baker, Sr., Henry G. "Identity and Social Responsibility Policies." *Business Horizons.* 16:23–38. April 1973.
Bauer, Raymond A., and Dan H. Fenn, Jr. "What is a Corporate Audit?" *Harvard Business Review.* 5:137–48. January–February 1973.
Bell, Daniel. "The Corporation and Society in the 1970s." *Public Interest.* 42:5–31. Summer 1971.
Bergson, Lisa. "The Corporate World Is Her Beat." *New York Times,* March 25, 1979.
Beyer, Robert. "The 'Bottom Line' Is No Longer Where It's At." *New York Times,* September 24, 1972.
Boland, John C. "Saints and Sinners? Church-Sponsored Critics of Private Enterprise Gain a Following." *Barron's,* May 5, 1980, pp. 22–26.
Browne, M. Neil, and Paul F. Haas. "Social Responsibility: The Uncertain Hypothesis." *MSU Business Topics.* 22:47–51. Summer 1974.
Buehler, Vernon M., and Y. K. Shetty. "Managerial Response to Social Responsibility Challenges." *Academy of Management Journal.* 19:66–78. March 1976.
———. "Managing Corporate Social Responsibility." *Management Review.* 64:4–15. August 1975.
———. "Motivations for Corporate Social Action." *Academy of Management Journal.* 17:767–71. December 1974.
Bundy, Edgar C. "Corporate Responsibility: The Attack on American Industry—Subversion by Proxy." *News and Views,* June 1978, pp. 1–70. (Published by the National Laymen's Council of the Church League of America, Chicago, Illinois.)
Burck, Gilbert. "The Hazards of Corporate Responsibility." *Fortune,* June 1973, pp. 114–17, 214, 216, 218.
Burns, John. "Investors Warned Over South Africa." *New York Times,* July 13, 1978.
"Businesses Are Stepping Up Their Roles in Social Problems of Cities." *New York Times.* February 4, 1979.
"Business Ready to Support Public Interest. . . Once It's Defined." *Commerce America,* June 7, 1976, pp. 6–8.
Byrne, Harlan S. "GE Head Never Gets to Fiscal Forecast as War, Dirt Protesters Soil Meeting." *Wall Street Journal,* April 23, 1970, p. 8.
"Capitalizing on Social Change." *Business Week,* October 29, 1979, pp. 105–6.
Carroll, Archie B. "Social Responsibility and Management." *The Personnel Administrator.* 20:46–50. April 1975.
Carroll, Barbara B. "Activists, Better Organized, Plan Even More Activity At Annual Meetings." *Industry Week,* March 19, 1973, pp. 15–16.
Carson, Deane. "Companies as Heroes? Bah! Hambug!" *New York Times,* December 25, 1977.

Cohn, Jules. "Is Business Meeting the Challenge of Urban Affairs?" *Harvard Business Review.* 48:68–82. March–April 1970.
"Companies Feel the Wrath of the Clergy." *Business Week,* March 18, 1972, pp. 84–85.
Cook, James. "Is Charity Obsolete?" *Forbes,* February 5, 1979, pp. 49–51.
"Corporate Critics Build Steam for Anti-MNC Campaigns Throughout Third World." *Business International,* October 17, 1980, p. 329.
"Corporate Giving Goes Cultural." *Business Week,* December 11, 1978, pp. 136, 141–42.
Coult, Catherine. "Chief Executives Polled On Obligations to Society." *Financial Executive.* 43:8–9. March 1973.
Crittenden, Ann. "Philanthropy, The Business of the Not-So-Idle Rich." *New York Times,* July 23, 1978, p. 3.
Davis, Keith. "Five Propositions for Social Responsibility." *Business Horizons.* 18:19–24. June 1975.
———. "The Case for and Against Business Assumptions of Social Responsibility." *Academy of Management Journal.* 16:312–33. June 1973.
Diamond, Robert S. "What Business Thinks, The Fortune 500-Yankelovich Survey." *Fortune,* 1970, pp. 118–19, 171, 172.
Dierkes, Meinolf and Rob Coppock. "Europe Tries the Corporate Social Report." *Business and Society Review.* 25:21–24. Spring 1978.
Dilley, Steven C. "What Is Social Responsibility: Some Definitions for Doing the Corporate Social Audit." *CA Magazine.* 103:24–28. November 1974.
Dionne, Jr., E. J. "New York Churches Make Their Worldly Influence Felt." *New York Times,* May 28, 1978.
Dunnock, D. E. "Social Responsibility in Practice." *Cost and Management.* 47:6–13. October 1973.
Eilbirt, Henry, and I. Robert Parket. "The Current Status of Corporate Social Responsibility." *California Management Review.* 18:5–14, August 1973.
———. "The Practice of Business." *Business Horizons.* 16:5–14. August 1973.
Elkins, Arthur. "Toward a Positive Theory of Corporate Social Involvement." *Academy of Management Review.* 2:128–33. January 1977.
Emshoff, James R., and R. Edward Freeman. "Who's Butting Into Your Business?" *The Wharton Magazine.* 4:44–48, 58–59. Fall 1979.
"Engagement in Boycotts: Preliminary Considerations." *Church & Society.* 29:12–13. May–June 1979.
Fitch, H. Bordon. "Achieving Corporate Social Responsibility." *Academy of Management Review.* 1:38–46. January 1976.
Flaherty, Robert J. "Revolution, Sayeth the Churchman: One Soul At A Time, Says A Businessman," *Forbes,* February 6, 1978, pp. 31–33.
Fowler, Elizabeth M. "Helping Officers to Face Annual Meetings." *New York Times,* February 25, 1977.
Friedman, Milton. "The Social Responsibility of Business Is To Increase Its Profits," *New York Times Magazine,* September 13, 1970.
"GM's Ordeal May Set the Fashion." *Business Week,* May 30, 1970, p. 84.
Gelb, Betsy D., and Richard H. Brien. "Survival and Social Responsibility: Themes for Marketing Education and Management." *Journal of Marketing.* 35:3–9. April 1971.
Gottschalk, Jr., Earl C. "The Annual Trial By Stockholder Is About To Begin." *Wall Street Journal,* February 7, 1977.
"Gulf Oil and Portugal: Partners in Colonialism," *CIC Brief,* April 1974, p. 4. (Published by the Corporate Information Center in 1974 when part of the National Council of Churches of Christ in the U.S.A.)

Hacker, Andrew. "A Country Called Corporate America." *New York Times,* July 3, 1966, p. 122.
Hartley, William D. "More Concerns Willing to Enter Negotiations on Holder Resolutions." *Wall Street Journal,* March 23, 1977.
Henderson, Hazel. "Toward Managing Social Conflict." *Harvard Business Review.* 49:82–90. May–June 1971.
Hessen, Robert. "Are Shareholders Being Victimized?" *Nation's Business,* April 1980, pp. 75–78.
Hill, John W. "The Business of Business . . ." *New York Times,* October 6, 1976.
Hodges, Luther H., and Milton Friedman. "Does Business Have A Social Responsibility?" *The Magazine of Bank Administration.* 12:12–17. April 1971.
Holmes, Sandra L. "Executive Perceptions of Corporate Social Responsibility." *Business Horizons.* 19:34–40. June 1976.
"How Social Responsibility Became Institutionalized." *Business Week,* June 30, 1973, pp. 74–79, 82.
Humble, John. "A Practical Approach to Social Responsibility." *Management Review.* 67:18–22. May 1978.
Hunt, Stanley M. "Conducting A Social Inventory." *Management Accounting.* 55:15–16, 26. October 1974.
Ibrahim, Youssef M. "The Metamorphosis of the Shareholder Meeting." *New York Times,* April 9, 1978.
"Institutions that Balk at Antisocial Management." *Business Week,* January 9, 1974, pp. 66–67.
Jaffe, Sidney. "American Businessmen Must Understand the Soviet Propaganda Attack on Corporations." *Special Report,* 1979, pp. 1–2. (Published by the Church League of America, Chicago.)
Janssen, Richard F. "Maverick Broker Specializes in Stocks for 'Socially Responsible' Investment." *Wall Street Journal,* May 1, 1979.
Jensen, Michael C. "Dissident Stockholders Begin to Get Somewhere At Last." *New York Times,* May 16, 1977.
Jensen, Michael C., and William H. Meckling. "Can the Corporation Survive?" *ERC Transcript,* Series No. 5, May, 1977, pp. 1–4. (The *ERC Transcript* is published by the ERC Publishing Company of West Vancouver, B.C.)
Jones, Thomas M. "Stockholders and the Corporation: A New Relationship." *Journal of Contemporary Business.* 8:93–102. November 1979.
Kandel, William L. "The Social Conscience in Hard Times." *Business and Society Review/Innovation.* 5:17–20. Winter 1973.
Kastenholz, E. "An Accountant's View of Corporate Responsibility." *Financial Executive.* 44:68–70. April 1974.
Klemesrud, Judy. "Feminist Shareholders Challenge the Corporate Structure." *New York Times,* May 15, 1975.
Kristol, Irving. "No Cheers for the Profit Motive." *Wall Street Journal,* February 20, 1979.
Levy, Ferdinand K., and Gloria M. Shatto. "A Common Sense Approach to Corporate Contributions." *Financial Executive.* 46:36–40. September 1978.
Lipson, Harry A. "Do Corporate Executives Plan for Social Responsibility?" *Business & Society Review.* 12:80–88. Winter 1974.
Lodge, George Cabot. "Top Priority, Renovating Our Ideology." *Harvard Business Review.* 48:43–55. September–October 1970.
McGuire, Joseph W., and John B. Parrish. "Status Report on a Profound Revolution." *California Management Review.* 13:84–87. Summer 1971.

"Macy Shareholders Decide to Continue Donations to Charity." *Wall Street Journal*, November 29, 1978, p. 18.
Manne, Henry G. "The Myth of Corporate Responsibility." *Public Relations Journal*. 26:6–8. December 1970.
Mason, Alister K., and S. R. Maxwell. "The Changing Attitude to Corporate Social Responsibility." *The Business Quarterly*. 40:42–50. Winter 1975.
Miller, Judith. "New Activist Tactics." *New York Times*, April 9, 1978.
Moskowitz, Milton R. "Conscientious Corporations: A Record." *Sloan Management Review*. 13:25–30. Fall 1971.
Murphy, Patrick E. "An Evolution: Corporate Social Responsiveness." *University of Michigan Business Review*. 30:19–25. November 1978.
"Namibia: South Africa Once Removed." *Church & Society*. 67:17–19. January–February 1977.
"Nestle Boycott." *Church & Society*. 69:19–20. May–June 1979.
Nickel, Herman. "The Corporation Haters." *Fortune*, June 16, 1980, pp. 126–36.
Orr, Leonard H. "Is Corporate Social Responsibility a Dead Issue?" *Business & Society Review*. 25:4. Spring 1978.
Ostlund, Lyman E. "Attitudes of Managers Toward Corporate Social Responsibility." *California Management Review*. 19:35–49. Summer 1977.
Paluszek, John. "How Three Companies Organized for Social Responsibility." *Business & Society Review/Innovation*. 6:16–20. Summer 1974.
Perham, John C. "Annual Meetings: Back to Basics. This Year, Social Issues Are Yielding the Floor to Dollars and Cents." *Dun's Review*, April 1975, pp. 48–51, 106, 108, 110.
Pope, Liston. "Religion as a Social Force in America." *Social Actions*. 19:2–15. May 1953.
Post, James E. "The Challenge of Managing Under Social Uncertainty." *Business Horizons*. 20:51–60. August 1977.
"Proxy Statements Feel the Watergate Ripples." *Business Week*, April 13, 1974, p. 89.
Purcell, Theodore V. "Management and the 'Ethical' Investors." *Harvard Business Review*. 57:24–26, 30, 32, 36, 40, 44. September–October 1979.
Scheets, Thomas E. "Gulf & Western in the Dominican Republic." *CIC Brief*, October 1975. (*CIC Brief* was originally published by the Corporate Information Center when it was part of the National Council of Churches of Christ in the U.S.A.)
Schwartz, Kenneth. "How Social Activists See Business." *Business & Society Review*. 14:70–73. Summer 1975.
Sethi, S. Prakash. "The Corporation and the Church: Institutional Conflict and Social Responsibility." *California Management Review*. 15:63–74. Fall 1972.
"Shareholder Communications: Shareholder Participation in the Corporate Electoral Process and Corporate Governance Generally." *Federal Register*, December 14, 1978, pp. 58522–32.
Silverman, H. Lee. "The Shareholder Comes to Life." *Fortune*, November 1970.
Sloane, Leonard. "Social Role Urged on Business." *New York Times*, October 15, 1970.
Smith, Robert R. " 'Social Responsibility': A Term We Can Do Without." *Business & Society Review/Innovation*. 9:51–55. Spring 1974.
"Social Activists Stir-Up the Annual Meeting." *Business Week*, April 1, 1972, pp. 48–49.
"Social Activists Switch to Proxy Power." *Business Week*, February 13, 1971, pp. 86–87.
Sommer, Dale W. "Companies Without Social Concern Won't Make It." *Industry Week*, January 14, 1974, pp. 32–35.
"South Africa: The Heart of the 'White Redoubt.' " *Church & Society*. 57:15–17. January–February 1977.

Spitzer, Carlton E. "Does Business Need a Social Responsiveness Index?" *Public Relations Journal.* 34:8–11. June 1978.

―――. "Washington Toys with a Corporate Social Index." *Business & Society Review.* 25:25. Spring 1978.

Steiner, George A. "Should Business Adopt the Social Audit?" *The Conference Board Record,* May 1972, p. 8.

"Stevens' Campaign to Polish Its Image." *Industry Week,* December 10, 1979, p. 27.

Sturdivant, Frederick D., and James L. Ginter. "Corporate Social Responsiveness." *California Management Review.* 19:30–39. Spring 1977.

"The American Corporation Under Fire." *Newsweek,* May 24, 1971, pp. 74–79.

"The Corporation and Its Obligations." *Harvard Business Review.* 53:127–38. May–June 1975.

"The Corporate Image: PR to the Rescue." *Business Week,* January 22, 1979, pp. 47–50, 54, 56, 60–61.

"The Church Speaks." *Church & Society.* 67:22–28. January–February 1977.

"The Moral History of U.S. Business." *Fortune,* pp. 143–46, 148, 150, 152, 156, 158.

"The Moral Power of Shareholders." *Business Week,* May 1, 1971, pp. 76, 78.

"The Nestle Boycott Kills Babies." *Wall Street Journal,* November 1, 1979, editorial.

"The 'Responsible' Corporation: Benefactor or Monopolist?" *Fortune,* November 1973, pp. 55–59.

"The Role of the Shareholder." *Economic Priorities Report.* 2:3, April–May 1971.

van Pelt, III, John V. "The Social Costs of Social Benefits." *Management Accounting.* 55:11–14. October 1974.

Walter, Kenneth D. "Corporate Social Responsibility and Political Ideology." *California Management Review.* 19:40–51. Spring 1977.

Weiss, Elliott J. "How to Make Ethical Investments." *New York Times,* July 30, 1978.

Reports, Public Speeches, and Unpublished Items

"A Summary of American Churches' Actions, Policies and Investments and U.S. Corporations in Southern Africa." An outline prepared by the Corporate Information Center of the National Council of Churches, New York, July 1972. (Mimeographed.)

Biegler, John C. "Corporate Accountability and Credibility: Meeting the Public's New Expectations." Distributed by Price Waterhouse & Company of New York, dated September 20, 1977.

"Boycotts: Policy Analysis and Criteria." New York: The United Presbyterian Church in the U.S.A., 1979. (Small booklet.)

"Christian Responsibility in Investments." Valley Forge, Penn.: American Baptist Churches. No date. (Pamphlet.)

Ciocca, Henry G. "The Nestle Boycott as a Corporate Learning Experience." A talk presented to the Institute of Food Technologists, Northeast Section, March 18, 1980.

"Commerce Department Plans to Measure Social Performance of Nation's Business." Washington, D.C.: U.S. Department of Commerce, October 19, 1977. (Press Release.)

"Corporate Governance in America." A summary report of the Fifty-Fourth American Assembly, held April 13–16, 1979 at the Arden House, Harriman, New York. Conducted by The American Assembly of Columbia University, New York.

"Corporate Social Responsibility—Investment Policy Guidelines." Summary of Statement of the 183rd General Assembly of the United Presbyterian Church in the U.S.A., 1971. (Mimeographed.)

"Fabric of Injustice: The Struggle at J. P. Stevens." Statement by the National Council of Churches of Christ in the U.S.A., New York, 1978. (Booklet.)

Farley, James B. "The Board of Directors: An Effective Vehicle for Change." Statement of the President of Booz, Allen & Hamilton, Inc. before the Senate Commerce Committee, Hearings on the Rights and Responsibilities of Corporations, Washington, D.C., June 17, 1976.

"Guidelines for Mission Investment." Issued by the National Council of Churches of Christ in the U.S.A., New York, March 1973. (Mimeographed.)

Harness, Edward G. "View on Corporate Responsibility." Excerpts from a talk of the Chairman of the Board of Procter & Gamble Company at the year-end annual meeting of company management in Cincinnati, Ohio on December 8, 1977.

"Infant Formula." A Study/Action Guide. Issued by the Church of the Brethren, Elgin, Illinois. No date. (Pamphlet.)

"Investment Policies: Does Being Christian Matter?" Issued by the Christian Church, Indianapolis, Ind. No date. (Pamphlet.)

"Investment Policy and Guidelines." Issued by the General Assembly Mission Board of the United Presbyterian Church in the U.S.A., March 20, 1976. (Mimeographed.)

"Investments." Issued by the Women's Division of the Board of Global Ministries of The United Methodist Church, October, 1974. (One page.)

Jones, David. "Statement by David Jones for the United Church Board for World Ministries and the Office for Church and Society of the United Church of Christ before the Securities and Exchange Commission, October 25, 1977. (Mimeographed.)

Kreps, Juanita M. "Corporate Image and Social Performance." Washington, D.C.: U.S. Department of Commerce, October 19, 1977. (Press Release.)

—————. "Statement of Secretary of Commerce Juanita M. Kreps for the State, Justice, Commerce and Judiciary Subcommittee of the House Committee on Appropriations, January 23, 1978." Washington, D.C.: General Counsel of the U.S. Department of Commerce, February 1978.

Miller, Arjay. "The Social Responsibility of Business." An address before the White House Conference on the "Industrial World Ahead." Washington, D.C., February 7, 1972.

Moskowitz, Milton. "Corporate Social Responsibility 1967–1977: An Overview." Preface in a small booklet published by the Levi Strauss & Company, San Francisco, Calif., 1977.

"1978 Social Report of the Life and Health Insurance Business." A report issued by the Clearinghouse on Corporate Social Responsibility for insurance companies located in Washington, D.C.

"On the Dispute Between the J. P. Stevens Company and the Amalgamated Clothing and Textile Workers Union." A report issued by the United Presbyterian Church in the U.S.A., Advisory Council on Church and Society, Special Task Force, 1979. (Mimeographed.)

"Policy." New York: National Council of Churches of Christ in the U.S.A., May 1979. (One page.)

Reihm, John W. "Statement on the Role of the Corporation." Presented to the Senate Committee on Commerce. Issued by the Chamber of Commerce of the U.S., Washington, D.C., June 16, 1976.

"Report to the Eleventh General Synod of the United Church of Christ on 1975–1977 Corporate Social Responsibility Actions, With Special Emphasis on Southern Africa." Issued by the United Church Board for World Ministries, New York, February 1, 1977.

"Report to the 12th General Synod of the United Church of Christ on 1977–1979 Corporate

Social Responsibility Actions." Issued by the United Church Board for World Ministries, 1979.
"Social Policy: Activities and Attitudes Among United Presbyterians." Issued by the United Presbyterian Church in the U.S.A., February 1979. (A survey.)
"Some Questions Can't Be Answered: Trends in Management/Investor Relations." Booklet issued by Georgeson & Company, New York, September 1971.
Sparks, John A. "The Nestle Controversy-Anatomy of a Boycott." Issued by the Public Policy Education Fund, Inc., Grove City, Penn., No Date.
Stoner, Richard B. "Social Responsibility, Can We Measure Up?" A talk presented to the Machinery & Allied Products Institute, Hot Springs, Va., April 23, 1971.
"The Social Impact of United Church of Christ Invested Funds 1971–73." Issued by the United Church Board for World Ministries, New York, May 9, 1973.
Thompson, Mayo J. "Free Enterprise and Free Men: A Prayer for the Future." Commencement address by the Commissioner of the Federal Trade Commission to the Mid-Year Graduating Class of Texas A & M University, College Station, Texas. December 15, 1973.
Williams, Harold M. "Corporate Accountability and Corporate Power." A paper presented by the Chairman of the Securities and Exchange Commission at the Carnegie-Mellon University, Pittsburgh, Penn., October 24, 1979.
Young, Patricia. "Where Poverty is Norm: Inappropriate Use of Infant Formula in Developing Countries." Remarks in a debate with Nestle representatives at Maywood College. November 14, 1978.

Dissertations

Allyn, Compton. "Corporate Social Action. A Systems Model of the Decision Process." Ph.D. dissertation, University of Cincinnati, 1973.
Anstey, John R. "A Comparison of Chief Executive Leadership Styles and Personal Values with His Orientation Concerning the Firm's Social Responsibility in Air and Water Pollution." Ph.D. dissertation, University of Arkansas, 1974.
Baumhart, Raymond C. "An Exploratory Study of Businessmen's Views on Ethics in Business." Ph.D. dissertation, Harvard University, 1963.
Bolce, William J. "The Development of a Profile for Evaluating the Level of Corporate Social Responsibility." Ph.D. dissertation, The American University, 1974.
Brighton, Gerald D. "Social Responsibility of Public Accountants." Ph.D. dissertation, University of Illinois, 1953.
Brandon, III, Thomas N. "An Exploratory Study of the Social Responsibility Attitudes of Small Businessmen in South Louisiana." Ph.D. dissertation, Louisiana State University, 1974.
Callaghan, Dennis W. "Management of the Corporate Gift-Giving Function: An Empirical Study in the Life Insurance Industry." Ph.D. dissertation, University of Massachusetts at Amherst, 1975.
Cashman, Thomas E. "The Modern Corporation and Its Social Responsibilities: A Structural-Functional Model." Ph.D. dissertation, The University of Alabama, 1972.
Clark, Charles S. "Corporate Social Responsibilities and Management Perception." Ph.D. dissertation, University of Washington, 1975.
Durdan, Scott. "The Effect of Social Responsibility Upon the Management of Business." DBA dissertation, University of Oregon, 1966.

Farris, Roy S. "Social Responsibility Profile of Selected Retail Firms with Emphasis Upon Jackson, Mississippi." Ph.D. dissertation, The University of Mississippi, 1972.

Higgins, James M. "A Partial Application of an Inventory Model Social Audit of Equal Employment Opportunity Programs in Selected Commercial Firms from Two Urban Areas—with Special Emphasis on Recruitment, Selection and Affirmative Action Programs." Ph.D. dissertation, Georgia State University, 1974.

Holmes, Sandra L. "An Examination of Social Responsibilities in Large Corporations." Ph.D. dissertation, The University of Texas at Austin, 1975.

Hoyt, Richard W. "Testing a Social Responsibility Audit: A Case Study of the Las Vegas Board of Realtors." Ph.D. dissertation, University of Arkansas, 1977.

Hunnicutt, Garland G. "An Audit of Social Performance of Two Banks and Two Breweries: A Comparative Study." Ph.D. dissertation. University of Arkansas, 1977.

Ingram, Robert W. "The Impact of Social Responsibility Disclosures on Security Returns." DBA dissertation, Texas Tech University, 1977.

Jesaitis, Patrick T. "Corporate Strategies and the Urban Crisis: A Study of Business Response to a Social Problem." Ph.D. dissertation, Harvard University, 1969.

Kinard, Jerry L. "A Survey of Industrial Corporate Executives' Attitude Toward Social Responsibility." Ph.D. dissertation, Mississippi State University, 1971.

Lank, Alden G. "The Implementation of Corporate Social Policies: A Study of the Process of Securing Organizational Commitment to Social Philosophies, Social Foci, and Social Policies in Two Corporations." DBA dissertation, Harvard University, 1974.

Lewis, Stanley X. "An Analysis of the Costs Related to a Manufacturing Firm's Social Goals Using Goal Programming." Ph.D. dissertation, Mississippi State University, 1975.

Ludlum, Sara L. "The Social Performance of Large Commercial Banks in the United States." DSW dissertation, University of Utah, 1975.

McGraw, VanCook. "An Analysis of the Social Responsibility of Business Managers." Ph.D. dissertation, Louisiana State University, 1966.

Murray, Jr., Edwin A. "The Implementation of Social Policies in Commercial Banks." DBA dissertation, Harvard University, 1974.

Neubeck, Kenneth J. "Social Responsibility and the American Corporation: A Benefit-Cost Perspective." Ph.D. dissertation, Washington University, 1972.

Randall, Frederic D. "Corporate Strategies in the Drug Industry: A Study of Strategic Response to Social and Political Pressures." DBA dissertation, Harvard University, 1972.

Sanner, Richard E. "The Development of a Systems Paradigm for the Ethical Analysis of Corporate Behavior." ThD dissertation, Boston University School of Theology, 1977.

Sawyer, George C. "Social Responsibility, Social Balance & Social Costs." Ph.D. dissertation, New York University, Graduate School of Business Administration, 1972.

Schneid, Daniel L. "Social Responsibility: An Empirical Test of Significance." Ph.D. dissertation, The Ohio State University, 1974.

Snyder, Phyllis. "Church Investments and Corporate Social Accountability: A Study of the United Church of Christ, The United Methodist Church, and The United Presbyterian Church, 1970–1980." MDiv dissertation, Union Theological Seminary, New York, 1980.

Tipgos, Manuel A. "The Accounting Aspects of Corporate Social Responsibility." Ph.D. dissertation, The Louisiana State University, 1974.

Van Over, Harlan C. "A Study Concerning the Social Responsibility of Large Industrial Corporations to Contemporary Society in the United States." Ph.D. dissertation, St. Louis University, 1974.

Webster, John F. "Corporate Social Policy: An Empirical Investigation of the Effect of Structure and Procedure on Perceived Social Effectiveness." Ph.D. dissertation, University of Pittsburgh, 1975.

Bibliography 231

Notices of Annual Meetings and Proxy Statements

Proxy references are from the *Notices of Annual Meetings & Proxy Statements* of the corporations listed below.
American Electric Power Co., New York, N.Y., 1975; 1976; 1977.
American Fletcher Corp., Indianapolis, Ind., 1977.
American Home Products Corp., New York, N.Y., 1977; 1978; 1979.
AMAX, Greenwich, Conn., 1971; 1972; 1973; 1974.
Bank of America National Trust & Savings Assn., San Francisco, Calif., 1979.
Bethlehem Steel Corp., Bethlehem, Penn., 1974.
Bristol-Myers Co., New York, N.Y., 1976; 1979.
Castle & Cooke, Inc., Honolulu, Hawaii, 1977; 1978.
Caterpillar Tractor Co., Peoria, Ill., 1973; 1979.
Chemical Bank, New York, N.Y., 1978; 1979.
Citicorp, New York, N.Y., 1973; 1977; 1978; 1979.
Coca-Cola Company, The, Atlanta, Ga., 1979.
Colgate-Palmolive Co., New York, N.Y., 1976.
Continental Illinois National Bank & Trust Co. of Chicago, Chicago, Ill., 1978; 1979.
Conoco, Inc., Stamford, Conn., 1973; 1974; 1976.
Control Data Corp., Minneapolis, Minn., 1978; 1979.
Deere & Company, Moline, Ill., 1976.
Eastman Kodak Co., Rochester, N.Y., 1978; 1979.
Engelhard Minerals & Chemicals Corp., New York, N.Y., 1974.
Exxon Corporation, New York, N.Y., 1973; 1974; 1975; 1976; 1977.
First National Bank of Boston, Mass., 1978; 1979.
First National Bank of Chicago, Ill., 1979.
Foote Mineral Company, Exton, Penn., 1974.
Ford Motor Co., Dearborn, Mich, 1974; 1977; 1979.
General Electric Co., Fairfield, Conn., 1971; 1974; 1977; 1978.
General Motors Corp., New York, N.Y., 1972; 1976; 1979.
Getty Oil Co., Los Angeles, Calif., 1974.
Goodyear Tire & Rubber Company, Akron, Ohio, 1972; 1976; 1977.
Gulf Oil Corp., Pittsburgh, Penn., 1971; 1972; 1974; 1976.
Gulf & Western Industries, Inc., New York, N.Y., 1976; 1979.
International Business Machines Corp., Armonk, N.Y., 1973; 1974; 1975; 1976; 1977.
International Telephone & Telegraph Corporation, New York, N.Y., 1976; 1977; 1978; 1979.
Kennecott Corporation, Stamford, Conn., 1971; 1976; 1977.
Manufacturers Hanover Trust Co., New York, N.Y., 1977; 1978; 1979.
Merck & Co., Inc., Rahway, N.J., 1976.
Minnesota Mining & Mfg. Co., St. Paul, Minn., 1974.
Mobil Oil Corp., New York, N.Y., 1973; 1977; 1978; 1979.
Morgan Guaranty Trust Co. of New York, New York, N.Y., 1977; 1978; 1979.
Motorola, Inc., Schaumburg, Ill., 1975; 1976.
Newmont Mining Corp., New York, N.Y., 1972; 1973; 1974; 1976; 1977; 1978.
Phelps Dodge Corporation, New York, N.Y., 1977.
Phillips Petroleum Company, Bartlesville, Okla., 1973; 1974; 1975; 1979.
Pittston Company, The, Greenwich, Conn., 1976.
Southern Co., Atlanta, Ga., 1975; 1976; 1977; 1978.
Sperry Corporation, New York, N.Y., 1979.
Standard Oil Co. of California, San Francisco, Calif., 1974; 1976; 1977; 1978; 1979.

J. P. Stevens & Co., Inc., New York, N.Y., 1977; 1978.
Superior Oil Company, The, Houston, Tex., 1979.
Tenneco Oil Co., Houston, Tex., 1977; 1978.
Texaco, Inc., White Plains, N.Y., 1976; 1977; 1978; 1979.
Union Carbide Corp., New York, N.Y., 1974; 1975; 1976; 1977; 1978; 1979.
United States Steel Corp., Pittsburgh, Penn., 1978; 1979.
Wells Fargo & Co., San Francisco, Calif., 1979.

Index

ABC
  shareholder resolutions filed:
    television violence, 115;
    women in advertising, 115
activism, church
  churches listed by frequency of participation, 166
  conflict between church members regarding, 6-7,17-18
  corporations targeted, defined, 194 n.15
  defined, 194 n.13
  Social Creed of Churches, The, 15-16
  social gospel, 5,16-17
  social issues: 32-70,165,173-78; choice of, examined, 183-84; summarized, 71-78
  United Presbyterian Church, rationale, 20
  views on:
    AMA study, 135-36; Boland, John C., 128-29; business, 7,82-85,123-62, 178-83; business media, 82-85,89,136; Carson, Deane, 129; Eilbirt & Parket study, 156; Kirchoff, I. R., 7.
    See also direct contacts, other; investing; individual issues; shareholder resolutions
advertising. *See* nutrition, children's, impact of television advertisements on; television violence; women's issues
Aetna Life and Casualty Union, 117,156
Air Commerce Act of 1926, 11
Allstate Insurance Co.
  shareholder resolutions filed:
    redlining, 160
Amalgamated Clothing & Textile Workers Union, 109,175
  See also J.P. Stevens Corp., boycott
AMAX Corp.
  shareholder resolutions filed, 75:
    apartheid (Namibia), 40,41,44,83-86,97;
    number (1970-1979), 75; strip mining, 64-66,81,82,84,86,88
American Baptist Church, 20,118,120
  on Christian investing, 20
  involvement:
    apartheid, 35-39,41,44,84,86,88,89, 91,96,97,99,102,103,104; colonialism, 47,88; energy crisis (U.S.), 58,59, 88,149; equal employment opportunities (U.S.), 61,89; farm technology, developing countries, 58-59,93,148- 49; human rights (Chile), 48,103; strip mining, 66,93-94,97; television violence, 70,97
  shareholder resolutions, number filed (1970-1979), 74
American Baptist Home Mission Society, 120
American Electric Power Co.
  shareholder resolutions filed:
    number (1970-1979), 74; strip mining, 66,91,93.
American Enterprise Institute for Policy Research, 136
American Fletcher Corp.
  Christian Church involvement, 66,67,121
  shareholder resolutions filed:
    nomination of women to board of directors, 32,66-67,96,100,151; response to, 151-52
  summarized, 172
American Home Products Corp.
  shareholder resolutions filed:
    infant formula distribution, 50,56,94, 96,99,102,117; number filed with (1970-1979), 74; political contributions overseas, 55,94; response to, 147- 48
American Management Association (AMA), 134

survey on corporate responsibility, 135-36
American Metal Climax Corp. *See* AMAX Corp.
American Petroleum Institute, 118
American Society of Corporate Secretaries, 165
American Telephone & Telegraph Co.
  shareholder resolutions, view of, 155
Angola
  colonialism, 31,44-45,87,142-43
  Gulf Oil Corp. boycott, 44-45
  shareholder resolutions filed:
    Gulf Oil Corp., 83,88,204 n.11
  United Presbyterian Church involvement, 81.
  See also Gulf Oil Corp.
Anshen, Melvin, 186
apartheid. *See* Namibia, apartheid in; Rhodesia, apartheid in; South Africa, Republic of, apartheid in
Atonement Friars, 120
AT&T. *See* American Telephone & Telegraph Co.

Bank of America National Trust & Savings Assn.
  shareholder resolutions filed:
    apartheid (South Africa), 37,102,117;
    number (1970-1979), 75
banks/banking. *See* redlining/reinvestment (U.S.)
Beatrice Foods, nutrition policy, 160
Bennett, John, 5
Bethlehem Steel Corp.
  shareholder resolutions filed:
    colonialism, Mozambique, 47,74,88;
    number (1970-1979), 75
Blanchard, Right Reverend Roger, 81
Boland, John C., on church activism, 128-29
Borg-Warner Corp.
  shareholder resolutions filed:
    apartheid (South Africa), 39,75,103,117
Bowen, Howard, 12,57
boycotts, 2,3,104-14,165
  history of, 105-6
  United Presbyterian Church and, 104-6.
  See also Gulf Oil Corp., boycott; Nestle Co., boycott; J. P. Stevens Corp., boycott
Bristol-Myers Co.
  shareholder resolutions filed:
    infant formula distribution, 56,75,93,102,117,147
Buehler, Vernon and Y. K. Shetty, study on corporate response, 158-59
Bundy, Edgar, 6
Burger King. *See* Pillsbury Co.
Burlington Industries
  shareholder resolutions filed:
    South Africa, 119
Burroughs Corp.
  shareholder resolutions filed:
    apartheid (South Africa), 38,39,75,86,103
business
  changes in, during the 1970s, 21-26
  criticism of, 125-26
  free enterprise system, 10.
  See also Adam Smith
  historical view of, 8
  interaction with, suggestions for, 2,184-88
  Miller, Arjay on, 13
  profit motive, 180-81
  social responsibility of.
  See corporate social responsibility
  traditional position of, 2,131-33
Business International, 7
Business Periodical Index, 16
Business and Religion, 12
Business Responsibility in Action, 136
Business Week, 1,79-80
  on church activism, 82-85

Campaign GM, 79-80,120,126-27,173
Campbell, Thomas, 17-18
Carnation Corp.
  shareholder resolutions filed:
    South African investments, 119
Carson, Deane, on church activism, 129
Carson, Rachel, 12
Cary, Frank T., 160
Castle & Cooke Corp.
  shareholder resolutions filed:
    labor practices in developing countries, 7,53,96,99,104,117,146; number (1970-1979), 75; political payments overseas, 58
Caterpillar Tractor Co.
  shareholder resolutions filed:
    apartheid (South Africa), 35,37,85,86,102;
    number (1970-1979), 75
CBS
  shareholder resolutions filed:
    equal employment opportunity, 61;
    number (1970-1979), 75; television violence, 115; women in advertising, 69,97,104,115
Chamber of Commerce
  on corporate reform, 157
  Resources and Environmental Quality Division, 124
  on social responsibility, 137
Chase Manhattan Bank
  shareholder resolutions filed:
    South African loans, 115

Chemical Bank
  shareholder resolutions filed:
    number (1970-1979), 75; redlining,
    62,64,98,99,102,150-51
Chile, human rights violations in,
    31,46-47,143,167-68
  background, 46
  National Council of Churches
    involvement, 119
  shareholder resolutions filed:
    Chrysler Corp., 119; Ford Motor Co.,
    119; GM Corp., 46-48,92-93,97,119,
    143; International Telephone & Telegraph
    Corp., 47-48,143; number (1970-1979),
    72; Superior Oil Co., 47-48, 143
  United Presbyterian Church
    involvement, 119
Christian Church
  on Christian investing, 21
  involvement:
    apartheid, 35-39,44,91,94,96,99,100;
    corporate payments overseas, 57-58,
    93,95,96,97,99,100; developing countries,
    53,96,99,146; human rights
    (Chile), 48,93,94,96,97,99; women's
    issues, 66,67,96,100,151-52
  press release usage, 121
  shareholder resolutions, number filed
    (1970-1979), 74
Christian investing. *See* investing, Christian
Chrysler Corp.
  shareholder resolutions filed:
    Chile, 119; number (1970-1979), 75;
    South Africa, 38,89,119
Church of the Brethren
  on Christian investing, 20-21,38
  involvement:
    apartheid, 103; infant formula distribution,
    56,102; nuclear weapons production,
    70,104; television advertising,
    67,68,104,121,152; television violence,
    70,97,98
  shareholder resolutions, number filed
    (1970-1979), 74
Church of Christ, 81
  involvement:
    Portuguese colonialism, 81
Church, Frank, 119
Church League of America, 130-31
Church Project on Equal Employment
  Opportunity, 87
Church Project on Southern Africa, 83
Citibank
  shareholder resolutions filed:
    South African loans, 115,116
Citicorp
  shareholder resolutions filed:
    number (1970-1979), 75; South African
    loans, 35-37,85-86,96
Civil Rights Act of 1964, 11
Clean Air Act of 1963, 11
Coca-Cola Co.
  shareholder resolutions filed:
    labor practices in Guatemala, 49-50,
    97,100,102,120; number (1970-1979), 75
Colgate-Palmolive Co.
  shareholder resolutions filed:
    apartheid (South Africa), 38-39; number
    (1970-1979), 75; response to, 152;
    women in advertising, 69,93,152-53
colonialism, in South Africa, 31,44-46,
    87,142-43,173
  shareholder resolutions filed, 142-43:
    response to, 142-43
  summarized, 167
  United Church of Christ involvement, 81.
    See also Angola, colonialism; Guinea-
    Bissau, colonialism; Mozambique,
    colonialism
Colt Industries Corp., 1
Committee for Economic Development, 13
Committee on Social Responsibility
  in Investment, 20,160
Community Reinvestment Act, 63,151,171
Conant, Roger R., 155
Conference Board Record, on corporate
  social responsibility, 3,12,134,136
Connecticut General Insurance Corp.
  shareholder resolutions filed:
    number (1970-1979), 75; redlining,
    63,64,104,117
Connor, John T., 79
Conoco, Inc.
  shareholder resolutions filed:
    apartheid (Namibia), 40-41,85-88;
    number (1970-1979), 75; strip mining,
    65-66,88,93
Consumer Products Safety Act of 1972, 11
Continental Illinois National Bank
  & Trust Co. of Chicago
  shareholder resolutions filed:
    apartheid (South Africa), 36-37,99,102,120;
    number (1970-1979), 75
Continental Oil Company. *See* Conoco, Inc.
Control Data Corp.
  apartheid, dialogue on, 163-64
  shareholder resolutions filed:
    apartheid (South Africa), 36-37,
    91,99,102,117; number of (1970-
    1979), 76; South Korea, 51
corporate environmental responsibility,
  business view of, 207 n.1

corporate payments overseas, 31,56-58, 72,148,183
  shareholder resolutions filed:
    American Home Products Corp., 57; Castle & Cooke, Inc., 58; Exxon Corp., 57,58; Ford Motor Co., 58; Gulf Oil Corp., 57; IT&T Corp., 57; Merck & Co., Corp., 57; Mobil Oil Corp., 58; Standard Oil Co. of California, 57; Tenneco Oil Co., 56-57
  summarized, 170
corporate philanthropy, 137-38
corporate policies, methods used to influence, 122
Corporate Policy Committee, 54
corporate social responsibility, 11,123-25
  challenge to business, 123-26
  church involvement, 14-21
  defined, 3-4,136-39
  emergence of, 8-14
  events affecting, 12-13
  United Presbyterian Church guidelines, 19-20
  views on:
    Bowen, Harold, 12; Chamber of Commerce, 137,157; Church League of America, 130; Cohn, Jules, 12-13; *Conference Board,* 3,12,134,136; Davis, Keith, 134; Dempsey, Bernard W., 12; Dilley, Steven, 136; Drotning, Phillip T., 12; Drucker, Peter, 134-35; Fenn, Dan, 136; Friedman, Milton, 132; Gray, Edmund R., 136-37; Humble, John, 134; IBM Corp. Committee, 115; Jensen, Michael and William Meckling, 129; Kandel, William, 13; Kastenholtz, E., 134; Kinard, Jerry, 134; Lank, Alden G., 137; Lark, Charles, 136; Leavitt, Theodore, 132-33; Manne, Henry G., 136; May, Elton, 11; moderate business, 134-39; Monsen, Joseph, 137; Moskowitz, Milton, 12,157; Rockefeller, J.D., 11.
  See also boycotts; direct contacts; shareholder resolutions
*Corporate Strategies for Social Performance,*186
Council of Economic Priorities, 165
Council for Financial Aid to Education, 138
Creative Investment Program, United Presbyterian Church, 122
Crocker National Bank
  shareholder resolutions filed:
    apartheid (South Africa), 39,100; number (1970-1979), 76

Davis, Keith, on social responsibility, 134

Deere & Co.
  shareholder resolutions filed:
    farm technology, appropriate, developing countries, 38,58-59,89,93; number (1970-1979), 76; response to, 148-49
Dilley, Steven, social responsibility defined, 136
direct contacts, other, 2,3,114-22,156, 165,176-78
  defined, 194 n.12
  summary of, 122
Disciples of Christ.
  See Christian Church, Disciples of Christ
Dominican Republic, human rights violations in
  background, 47
  shareholder resolutions filed:
    Gulf & Western Industries Corp., 48-49,91-93,95,97,103,144; number (1970-1979), 72; response to, 144; summarized, 168
Drucker, Peter, on corporate social responsibility, 134-35
Dun's Review, on church activism, 89

Eastman Kodak Co.
  shareholder resolutions filed:
    number (1970-1979), 76; South Africa, 37,38,86,99,102,119
Eilbirt, Henry and I. Robert Parket, study on church activism, 156
employment practices. *See* labor practices
energy crisis (U.S.), 31,58-59,72,87,149
  Presbyterian Church involvement, 117-18
  shareholder resolutions filed:
    Exxon Corp., 58-59,88,149; Gulf Oil Corp., 58-59,87-88; Kerr-McGee Oil Co., 118; response to, 149
  summarized, 170-71
  United Church of Christ involvement, 58-59,149
Engelhard Minerals & Chemicals Corp.
  shareholder resolutions filed:
    number (1970-1979), 76; South Africa, 35,88
environmental concerns
  business response to, 123-24
  corporate view of, 207 n.1
  public response to, historical, 124.
  See also strip mining
Episcopal Church, 81-84,118,120,160-61
  involvement:
    apartheid, 38-39,41,82,84,86,88,89, 91,94,96,97,99,100,101,102,103; colonialism, 47,88; equal employment opportunities (U.S.),

61,88,99; political contributions, 62-63,88,91,95,150; strip mining, 65-66, 84,86
shareholder resolutions, number filed (1970-1979), 74
equal employment opportunities (U.S.), 31-32,60-61,72,87,90,161,183
Church Project on, 87
Equal Pay Act of 1963, 11
shareholder resolutions filed:
CBS, 61; General Electric Co., 61,88,99; GM Corp., 20,89; IBM Corp., 61,88, 149-50; Kraft Corp., 61,77,89; Mobil Oil Corp., 61,101; Polaroid Corp., 61,64,89; Sears, Roebuck and Co., 61,89,91; J.P. Stevens Corp., 60,61; Xerox Corp., 60,61,89-91
United Methodist Church involvement, 60-61,120
United Presbyterian Church involvement, 120
Ethical Investor, The, 2,30
Ethics & Profits, 14
Exxon Corp.
Inuit people and, 118
shareholder resolutions filed:
energy crisis, 58-59, 88,149; Guinea-Bissau, 45,47,88; number (1970-1979), 76; political contributions, 57-58,94; South Africa, 102; strip mining, 66,88,96

Fair Labor Standards Act of 1938, 196 n.48
farm technology, appropriate, in developing countries, 31,58,92,148-49
shareholder resolutions filed:
Deere & Co., 38,58,76,89,93; number (1970-1979), 73; response to, 148-49 summarized, 170
Federal Communications Act of 1934, 196 n.48
Federal Council Commission on the Church and Social Services, 14-15
Federal Deposit Insurance Corporation (FDIC), purpose of, 196 n.48
Federal Fair Packaging and Labeling Act of 1966, purpose of, 196 n.48
Federal Food, Drug and Cosmetic Law (1938), purpose of, 196 n.48
Federal Power Act (1930), purpose of, 196 n.48
Federal Trade Commission (FTC), 13,152
Fenn, Dan, corporate social responsibility defined, 136
Filer, John, 156
Financial Executive, 134
First National Bank of Boston
shareholder resolutions filed:
loans to South Africa, 37,39,99, 104,116,117; number (1970-1979), 76; redlining, 62-69,99,102,150-51
First National Bank of Chicago
shareholder resolutions filed:
loans to South Africa, 103; number (1970-1979), 76
Firestone Corp.
shareholder resolutions filed:
South Africa, investments, 119
Foote Minerals Corp.
shareholder resolutions filed:
number (1970-1979), 76;
South Africa, 35,88
Ford Motor Co.
shareholder resolutions filed:
Chile, 119; number (1970-1979), 76; Philippines, 51-52,87-88; political contributions overseas, 58,94; response to, 145-46; South Africa, 36,38,96, 103,117,119
South Africa, affirmative actions, 161
Fortune, 6,12
Franklin, James R., 110
free enterprise system. *See* business, free enterprise system
Friedman, Milton
on corporate responsibility, 132
on traditional position of business, 2,131

Gale, Horace, on shareholder's responsibilities, 19
General Assembly Mission Council (UPC), 20
General Electric Co.
shareholder resolutions filed:
apartheid (South Africa), 35,36,85,86, 96,117,119; equal employment opportunities, 61,88,99; human rights, 99; labor practices, 149-50; military sales, foreign, 54-55,96,99; nuclear weapons production, 69,70,104; number (1970-1979), 76; response to, 146-47,153-54
General Foods Corp., nutrition policy, 160
General Motors Corp. (GM), 55,80,81, 116,117,159-60
Campaign GM, 79-80,120,126-27,173
shareholder resolutions filed:
Chile, 48,92,93,97,119; equal employment opportunities, 20,61,89; number (1970-1979), 76; South Africa, 35, 38,39,80,83,84,103,119,140-41; South Africa, affirmative action in, 160-61
Getty Oil Co.
shareholder resolutions filed:
apartheid (Namibia), 41,88,91; number (1970-1979), 76
Gillette Co.

shareholder resolutions filed:
apartheid (South Africa), 38,89; number (1970-1979), 76
Glass-Stengall Act (1933), purpose of, 196 n.48
Goodyear Tire & Rubber Co.
shareholder resolutions filed:
apartheid (South Africa), 35,36,83,84, 96,119; number (1970-1979), 76
Gray, Edmund R., on social responsibility, 136-37
Guatemala
human rights violations, 72
labor practices, 31,49-50,144-45,168
shareholder resolutions filed:
Coca Cola Co., 49-50,97,100,102,120, 144-45
United Presbyterian Church involvement, 144-45
Guerrant, David E., 113-14
Guinea-Bissau, colonialism
shareholder resolutions filed, 45-47,88
United Presbyterian Church involvement, 81.
See also colonialism, in South Africa
Gulf Oil Corp.
boycott, 44- 45,105-8,174-75
shareholder resolutions filed:
Angola, 47,83,88,204 n.111; apartheid, 81-84; energy crisis, 58-59,87-88, 149; number (1970-1979), 76; political contributions overseas, 57,94,120; South Korea, 160
Gulf & Western Industries Corp.
shareholder resolutions filed:
apartheid (South Africa), 39,97; Dominican Republic, 48-49,91-93, 95,97, 103,144; number filed (1970-1979), 76

Haas, Walter A., 156
Haendel, Dr. Mark S., 112-13
Hammurabi Code, 8,195 n.31
Hartford Insurance Co.
shareholder resolutions filed:
redlining activities, 160
Harvard Business Review, 132-33,159
Heidrick and Struggler, study on minorities, 158
Home Mortgage Disclosure Act of 1975, 63
Hudson, Frank, 155
Human Problems of an Industrial Civilization, The, 11-12
human rights violations, 87,92,99,161,180
United Church of Christ involvement, 46-47.
See also Chile, human rights violations in; Dominican Republic, human rights violations in; Guatemala, human rights violations in; Philippines, human rights violations in
Humble, John, on social responsibility, 134

Industry Week, on church activism, 84
infant formula, developing nations, 31,55-56, 92,98,147-48,169-70
Nestle involvement. *See* Nestle boycott
pro/con, 112-14
shareholder resolutions filed:
American Home Products Corp., 50,56, 90,94,96,99,102,117;
Bristol-Myers Co., 56,93,102,117,147; number (1970-1979), 72;
Infant Formula Action Coalition, 111,176
Interfaith Center on Corporate Responsibility, 1-2,19,29,35,89,111,115,118,119,163-65, 176,183
defined, 4-5
Dominican Republic involvement, 48,128
International Business Machines Corp. (IBM)
Committee on Social Responsibility, 115
shareholder resolutions filed:
equal employment opportunities, 61,88; human rights, 161; number (1970-1979), 76; response to, 149-50, South Africa, computer sales, 35,37, 38,83-86,88, 90,91,94,99, 119
South Africa, affirmative action, 160
Internal Revenue Act of 1935, purpose of, 196 n.48
International Court of Justice, on apartheid (Namibia), 40
International Harvester Corp.
shareholder resolutions filed:
number (1970-1979), 77; South Africa, 38,89,119
International Telephone & Telegraph Corp. (ITT)
shareholder resolutions filed:
apartheid (South Africa), 38,39,73, 86,91,94; Chile, 47,48,89,94,96,99, 103,119,143,160; number (1970-1979), 77; political contributions overseas, 57,96
Interstate Commerce Act of 1887, 11
Inuit people, and Exxon Corp., 118
investing
American Baptist Church views on, 20
Christian, 18-21
Committee on Social Responsibility in, 20,160
Creative Investment Program, 122

Gale, Horace, view on shareholder responsibility, 19
Invester Responsibility Research Center, 165
Investment Policy Guidelines, 19-20
Jesuit Advisory Committee on Investor Responsibility, 159
shareholder's power, 31
United Church of Christ, 20
United Methodist Church, 20
United Presbyterian Church, 119-21, 122,160.
See also activism, church

Jaffe, Sidney, 131
Jelliffer, Dr. Derrick, 110,111
Jensen, Frank L., 116
Jensen, Michael and William Meckling, on social activism, 129
Jesuit Advisory Committee on Investor Responsibility, 159
Job Safety and Health Act of 1970, 11

Kastenholz, E., on social responsibility, 134
Kennecott Corp.
shareholder resolutions filed:
number (1970-1979), 77; South Africa, 36,39,94,96,101; strip mining, 64-66, 81,82
Kerr-McGee Oil Co.
shareholder resolutions filed:
energy crisis, 118
Kinard, Jerry, on social responsibility, 134
Kirchoff, I. H., 7
Kodak. *See* Eastman Kodak Co.
Korea. *See* South Korea
Kraft Corp.
shareholder resolutions filed:
equal employment opportunity, 69,89; number (1970-1979), 77
Kreps, Juanita, on shareholder resolutions, 11,156

labor practices
American Baptist Mission Society, 120
National Council of Churches involvement, 120,150
shareholder resolutions filed:
General Electric Co., 149-50; number (1970-1979), 72; Phillips Petroleum Co., 91; United States Steel Corp., 120; Xerox Corp., 149-50
United Methodist Church involvement, 95,150.
See also Guatemala, labor practices; South Korea, wages and working conditions; J. P. Stevens Corp., labor practices
laissez-faire. *See* business
Lank, Alden G., on social responsibility, 137
Lark, Charles, on social responsibility, 136
Leavitt, Theodore, on social responsibility, 132-33
Lobbying the Corporation, 155
Lutheran Church in America
on Christian investing, 21
involvement:
Chile, 48,103; South Africa, 36-39, 96,99,103,104,115,116
shareholder resolutions, number filed (1970-1979), 74

Manne, Henry G., on social responsibility, 136
Manufacturers Hanover Trust Co.
shareholder resolutions filed:
number (1970-1979), 77; South Africa, 36-38,96,100,103,115,117
Margolis, David I., 1
Masonite Corp.
shareholder resolutions filed:
South African investments, 119
McDonald's Corp.
shareholder resolutions filed:
number, 77; response, 153; television violence issue, 79,97
Merhman, Jerrold, 110
Motorola Corp.
shareholder resolutions filed:
number (1970-1979), 77; South Korea, 50-51,90-91,94,145
Mozambique, colonialism, 46-47,75
shareholder resolutions filed:
Bethlehem Steel Corp., 74,88
United Presbyterian Church involvement, 81.
See also colonialism
Multinational corporations
criticisms of, 189
defined, 207 n.3
potential benefits to developing countries, 189-91
Senate Subcommittee on, 119
Worldwide Council of Churches campaign against, 128
Murphy, Thomas A., 160

Nader, Ralph, 14
Namibia, apartheid in
history, 39-40
International Court of Justice on, 40
shareholder resolutions filed:
AMAX Corp., 40; Conoco Corp., 40, 85-86,88; Gillette Co., 38,76,89;

Goodyear Tire & Rubber Co., 35-36, 76,83,96,119; Phillips Petroleum Co., 11,38,40,85-86,88,91,103; response to, 141; Standard Oil Co. of California, 41,88,91
United Church of Christ involvement, 161
United Nations actions, 40,141
National Alliance of Businessmen, 138
National Cash Register Corp. (NCR)
shareholder resolutions filed:
  South African investments, 119
National Council of Churches of Christ (USA), 3,12,16,19,29,45,165,177
on Christian investing, 21
defined, 4
involvement:
  apartheid, 35-39,86,89,91,94,97,99, 100,103,104,120; Chile, 119; colonialism, 47,88; Dominican Republic, 91,93,95,97,103; equal employment opportunities, 88; labor practices (U.S.), 120,150; military sales, foreign, 53-55,99; Philippines, 51,52,88,145
shareholder resolutions, number filed (1970-1979), 74
National Environment Policy Act of 1969, purpose of, 196 n.48
National Industry Recovery Act (1933), purpose of, 196 n.48
National Labor Relations Act of 1935, purpose of, 108,196 n.48
National Labor Relations Board, 175
National Traffic and Motor Vehicle Safety Act of 1966, purpose of, 196 n.48
Natural Gas Act of 1938, purpose of, 196 n.48
NBC, advertising issues, 115
Nederduitse Gereformeerde Kerk, 186-87
Nestle Co. boycott, 55,105,110-14,147-48, 174-76
  Guerrant, David E., 113-14
  churches supporting, 111
  United Nations involvement, 111
Newmont Mining Corp.
shareholder resolutions filed:
  apartheid (South Africa), 35,40,41, 85-86,88,91,97,100,117,161; number (1970-1979), 77
Nickel, Herman, 6
Norris, William C., 163-64
Norris-Laguardia Act (1932), purpose of, 196 n.48
nuclear weapons production, 32,153-54,174
shareholder resolutions filed:
  General Electric Co., 69,70,104; Monsanto Co., 68-70; number (1970-1979), 72; response to, 153-55; Union Carbide Corp., 69-70,104,153-54
summarized, 173
nutrition, children's, impact of television advertisements on, 32,67,68,121,152
Church of the Brethren involvement, 67-68
shareholder resolutions filed:
  number (1970-1979), 73; Pillsbury Co. (Burger King), 67,68,152,164; response to, 152
summarized, 172-73

Ohio Conference of United Church of Christ
  Gulf Oil Corp. boycott, 81
Otis Elevator Co.
shareholder resolutions filed:
  South African investments, 119

Pan-American Health Organization, 111
Pfizer Corp.
shareholder resolutions filed:
  number (1970-1979), 77; South Africa, 38,89
Phelps Dodge Corp.
shareholder resolutions filed:
  apartheid (South Africa), 36,97; number (1970-1979), 77
philanthropy, corporate, 137-38
Philippines
  background, 41
  human rights violations in, 51,52,72,145-46
  National Council of Churches involvement, 51-52,145
  shareholder resolutions filed, 51-52,72, 87-88,145-46
  United Church of Christ involvement, 41,42,145
Phillips Petroleum Co.
shareholder resolutions filed:
  apartheid (Namibia), 38,40,41,85,86,88, 91,103; labor practices, 91; number (1970-1979), 77; political activities/ contributions, 62,63,87,88,91,94, 150,161
Pillsbury Co.
shareholder resolutions filed:
  children's nutrition and television advertisements, 68,152,164; number filed (1970-1979), 77; sponsorship, television violence, 70,97,153
Pittston Co.
shareholder resolutions filed:
  number filed (1970-1979), 78; strip mining, 66,94,97,161
Polaroid Corp.
shareholder resolutions filed:
  equal employment, 61,89; number (1970-1979), 78

Index 241

policy statements, defined, 16
political contributions overseas, 56-58,92,98
 shareholder resolutions filed:
  3M Corp., 87,88; Exxon Corp., 93,95; Ford Motor Co., 95; Gulf Oil Corp., 94,120; Merck & Co., 94; Tenneco Oil Co., 97,100,117
political contributions (U.S.), 62,63,98,150
 Episcopal Church involvement, 150
 shareholder resolutions filed:
  3M Corp., 62,63,87,88,150,161; Phillips Petroleum Co., 62,63,87,88,90,91, 95,150,161; response to, 150
 summarized, 171
Pope, Liston, 187-88
Portugal. See colonialism, in South Africa
Presbyterian Church (U.S.)
 involvement:
  nuclear weapons production, 104; South Africa, 96,99,102; television violence, 70,104
 shareholder resolutions filed (1970-1979), 74
Presidential Campaign Committee, 150
Procter & Gamble Co.
 shareholder resolutions filed:
  number (1970-1979), 78; response to, 152-53; television violence, 70,98; women in advertising, 69,90,91,115
Project for Corporate Responsibility. See Campaign GM
Protestant churches
 defined, 11,193
 social ministry defined, 6
proxy statement, defined, 4
Public Utility Holding Company Act of 1935, purpose of, 196 n.48
Purcell, Theodore V., 159,182-83
Pure Food and Drug Act of 1906, 11

RCA (NBC), 115
redlining/reinvestment (U.S.), 32,62-64, 72,160,174
 shareholder resolutions filed:
  Allstate Insurance Co., 160; Chemical Bank, 62,64,98,99,102,150-51; Connecticut General Insurance Corp., 63, 64,107,117,160; First National Bank of Boston, 62,64,99,102,150-51; Hartford Insurance Co., 160; number (1970-1979), 72; response to, 150-51
 United Methodist Church involvement, 62-64,98-99,102,150-51
Reformed Church in America
 involvement:
  apartheid, 88,89,91,94,96,97,100,103; infant formula, 56,96; South Korea, 94,145

 shareholder resolutions filed (1970-1979), 74
Rhodesia, apartheid in, 34,40-44
 church involvement, 42,43,116
 history, 34,40-42
 shareholder resolutions filed, 35-43:
  Mobil Oil Corp., 42-44,96,99,100, 103,121,142; response to, 141-42; Standard Oil Co. of California, 43,44, 99,100,103; Texaco Corp., 44,99, 100,103; Union Carbide Corp., 43,44, 92,141-42;
 summarized, 171-72
 Unilateral Declaration of Independence, 42
 United Church of Christ involvement, 42-43
 United Nations involvement, 34,42,141
Robinson-Patman Act (1936), 196 n.48
Roche, James, 80,81

Schomer, Dr. Howard, 46-47,53,92-93, 97,117,119,143
Schwartz, Donald, 127
Sears, Roebuck and Co.
 shareholder resolutions filed:
  equal employment opportunity, 61,89,91; number (1970-1979), 78; response to, 153; television violence, 70,104
Securities Act of 1933, purpose of, 196 n.48
Securities Exchange Act of 1934, purpose of, 196 n.48
Securities and Exchange Commission (SEC), 1,98,118,120,148,155,165,171,176,177
 view of church activism, 154
selective patronage. See boycotts
Senate Subcommittee on African Affairs, 118
Senate Subcommittee on Multinational Corporations, 119
shareholder resolutions
 activities, annual, summarized (1970-1979), 71-104,173-79
 business opinion of, 79,123-33,139, 151,162,178-83,207 n.1
 church involvement, rationale, 30-32
 defined, 2-4
 history of, 29-30
 Kreps, Juanita, view of, 156
 major issues, 31-32,166
 number filed, 166
 Purcell, Theodore, on, 159
 response to specific, 139-54
 SEC view of, 154
 specific accomplishments of, 160-62
 summarized, 178
Sheetz, Father Thomas E., 48
Sherman Antitrust Act of 1890, 11
Silent Spring, 12

small farm technology. *See* farm technology, appropriate, in developing countries
Smith, Adam, 9-10,132,179
Smith, Rev. Mr. Timothy, 128,163-64
Social Creed of Churches, The, 15-16
social gospel, 5,16,17
social issues, 32-70
  choice of, examined, 183-84
  defined, 4,194 n.13
Social Responsibilities of the Businessman, 12
social responsibility. *See* corporate social responsibility
social statements. *See* policy statements, defined
South Africa, Republic of, apartheid in, 31-39,83,85,87,89,90,92,115,118,160,173, 180,183,186,187
  bank and corporate reinforcement of, 33
  Churchmen for South Africa, 83
  Church Project on U.S. investments in, 83
  early protest against (1960s), 32-33
  history, 33
  Lutheran Church involvement, 115,116
  reasoning against, 32
  shareholder resolutions filed:
    3M Corp., 37-39,86,104,119; Bank of America National Trust & Savings Assn., 37,102,117; Borg-Warner Corp., 39,75,103; Burlington Industries, 119; Burroughs Corp., 38,39, 86,88,103; Carnation Corp., 119; Caterpillar Tractor Co., 35,37,85,86,102; Chase Manhattan Bank, 115; Chrysler Corp., 38,89,119; Citibank, 115,116; Citicorp, 35-37,85,86,96; Colgate-Palmolive Co., 38,89; Continental Bank, 36,37,99,102; Continental Illinois National Bank, 120; Control Data Corp., 36,37,91,99,102,117, 163-64; Crocker National Bank, 39, 100,120; Deere & Co., 38; Eastman Kodak Co., 37,38,86,99,102,119; Engelhard Minerals & Chemicals Corp., 35,123,124; Exxon Corp., 37,102; Firestone Corp., 119; First National Bank of Boston, 37,39,99,104,116,117; First National Bank of Chicago, 37; Foote Minerals Corp., 35,76,88; Ford Motor Co., 36,38,96,103,117,119,161; General Electric Co., 8,35,36,96,117, 119; General Motors Corp., 35,38, 39,80-83,97,98,103,119,160; Gillette Co., 38,85,86; Goodyear Tire & Rubber Co., 35,36,140-41; Gulf Oil Corp., 81-82; Gulf & Western Industries Corp., 39,97; International Business Machines Corp., 35,37,38,83, 85,86,88,90,91,94,99,119,160; International Harvester Co., 38,77,89,119; International Telephone & Telegraph Corp., 38,39,73,86,91,94; Kennecott Corp., 36,39,64-66,81,82,94,96,101; Manufacturers Hanover Trust Co., 36-38,77,96,100,103,115,117; Masonite Corp., 119; Mobil Oil Corp., 35,38, 72,83,85,86,119; Morgan Guaranty Trust Co., 36-38,77,96,100,103,105; National Cash Register Corp., 105,119; National Council of Churches, 120; Newmont Mining Corp., 35,40,41, 77,85-86,88,91,97,100,117,161; Otis Elevator Co., 119; Pfizer Corp., 38, 77,89; Phelps Dodge Corp., 36,77,97; Phillips Petroleum Co., 38; Southern Co., 35-37,78,90,91,94,97,100; Sperry Rand Corp., 38,78,103; Standard Oil Co. of California, 36,94,97; Texaco Corp., 36-38,78,86,94,100,117; Union Carbide Corp., 35-38,88,91,97,100,103; U.S. Steel Corp., 37,38,100,103; Wells Fargo & Co., 38,78; Weyerhaeuser Co., 39,78; Xerox Corp., 38,86;
  United Church of Christ involvement, 121
  Worldwide Council of Churches involvement, 120-21
South Africa, colonialism, 44-46,72. *See also* Angola, colonialism; Guinea-Bissau, colonialism; Mozambique, colonialism
South Africa Review Committee, 101
South Korea, wages and working conditions, 50-51,72,145,149-50
  shareholder resolutions filed:
    Gulf Oil Corp., 160; Motorola Corp., 50-51,90-91,145; response to, 145, 149-50;
    summarized, 59,168
  United Church of Christ involvement, 145
South West Africa. *See* Namibia, apartheid in
Southern Co.
  shareholder resolutions filed:
    number (1970-1979), 78; South Africa, 35,36,90,91,94,100
Sperry Rand Corp.
  shareholder resolutions filed:
    apartheid (South Africa), 38,103; number (1970-1979), 78
Standard Brands, nutritional responsibility policies, 160
Standard Oil Co. of California
  shareholder resolutions filed:
    apartheid, 36,41,43,44,88,91,94,97,

99,100,103; number (1970-1979), 78;
political contributions overseas, 57;
strip mining, 66,94
Stanford Research Institute, 14
Steiner, George, 3-4, 136
J. P. Stevens Corp.
Amalgamated Clothing & Textile Workers Union, 109,175
boycott, 105,108-10,174-75:
charges against, 109; supporting churches, 109
shareholder resolutions filed:
equal employment opportunities, 60,61, 97,100; labor practices, 95,97,100; response to, 149-50
strip mining, 32,64-66,72,87,90,92,115,183
Episcopal Church involvement, 64,66
shareholder resolutions filed:
AMAX Corp., 64-66; American Electric Power Co., 66,91,93; Conoco, Inc., 65,66,88,93; Exxon, Corp., 66,88,96; Kennecott Corp., 64-66; Pittston Co., 79,94,97,161; response to, 151; Standard Oil Co. of California, 66,94
summarized, 172
United Church of Christ involvement, 65,66
Sullivan, Dr. Leon, 126,159
Superior Oil Co.
shareholder resolutions filed:
Chile, 47,48,103,143; number (1970-1979), 78

television advertising. *See* television violence; nutrition, children's, impact of television advertisements on; women's issues, advertising, stereotypical images of women in
television violence, 68,70,72,121,152
shareholder resolutions filed:
ABC, 115; CBS, 115; McDonald's Corp., 70,77,97; NBC, 115; Pillsbury Co., 70,97,153; Procter & Gamble Co., 70; response, 153; Sears, Roebuck & Co., 70,104,153,163
summarized, 173
United Methodist Church involvement, 115
Tenneco
shareholder resolutions filed:
number (1970-1979), 78; political contributions overseas, 57,97,100,117
Texaco Corp.
shareholder resolutions filed:
number filed (1970-1979), 78; Rhodesia, 44,99,100,103; South Africa, 36-38, 86,94,97,100,117

Thompson, May, 13
Thompson, William, 163-64
Tilman Act of 1907, 11
transnational corporation. *See* multinational corporations
Truth-in-Packaging Act, purpose of, 196 n.48
truth-in-securities rule, 196 n.48

Unilateral Declaration of Independence, Rhodesia, 141
Union Carbide Corp.
shareholder resolutions filed:
nuclear weapons production, 69,70, 104,153-54; number (1970-1979), 78; response, 155; Rhodesia, 43-44,92,94, 141-42; South Africa, 35-38,88,91, 97,100,103
United Church of Christ
activism, 114,166
Christian investing, 20
involvement, 117-20:
advertising, women in, 69,93,152-53; apartheid, 35-39,41-44,84,86,88,90, 91,94,96,97,99,100,102,103,104; Chile, 46-48,93; colonialism, 47,84,88; corporate payments overseas, 56-58, 94,95,97,100,104,119; developing countries, 53,96,99; energy crisis (U.S.), 58-59,88,149; equal employment opportunity, 61,86,88,100; infant formula, 56,93,102; military sales, foreign, 53-55,96,99; nuclear weapons production, 70,104; number (1970-1979), 73; Philippines, 51,52, 88,145; South Korea, 41,91,94,145; strip mining, 65-66,88,94;
shareholder resolutions, number filed (1970-1979), 73
United Methodist Church
activism, 166
Christian investing, 20
involvement:
advertising, women in, 69,104,115; apartheid, 35-39,41,86,88,89,92,94, 96,97,99,100,103; Chile, 93,97; colonialism, 47,88; corporate payments overseas, 57,94; equal employment opportunities, 61,89,91,92,95,97, 100,150; infant formula distribution, 56,94,96,99,102; military sales, foreign, 53-55,96; nuclear weapons production, 70,104; redlining, 62-64,98-100,102, 104,150-51; strip mining, 66,91; television violence, 115;
shareholder resolutions, number filed (1970-1979), 73

United Nations
　Food & Agricultural Organization, 111
　Rhodesia, economic sanctions against, 34,42, 141
　Security Council, 40
United Presbyterian Church
　Committee on Social Responsibility, 20,160
　Creative Investment Program, 122
　involvement, 90,152:
　　advertising, women in, 69,91; apartheid, 35-39,86,88,89,91,96,99,100,102,103; boycotts, 104-6; Chile, 48,119; colonialism, 47,81,88; energy crisis, 117-18; equal employment opportunities, 69,89,120; Guatemala, 49-50, 97,100,144-45; infant formula distribution, 56, 94,96, 99, 102; nuclear weapon production, 70,104; strip mining, 66,93,96
　shareholder resolutions, number filed (1970-1979), 74
urban community revitalization issue. *See* redlining/reinvestment (U.S.)
U.S. Steel Corp.
　shareholder resolutions filed:
　　employment practices, 120; number (1970-1979), 78; South Africa, 37, 38,100,103

violence in television programs. *See* television violence

Ward, Harry F., 15
Water Quality Improvement Act of 1970, 11
Wells Fargo & Co.
　shareholder resolutions filed:
　　apartheid (South Africa), 38; number (1970-1979), 78
Weyerhaeuser Co.
　shareholder resolutions filed:
　　apartheid (South Africa), 39; number (1970-1979), 78
Wheeler-Lea Act (1938), 196 n.48
White, Frank, 163-64
women's issues
　advertising, stereotypical images of women in, 32,68,69,90,91,92,115,121,152
　shareholder resolutions filed:
　　ABC, 115; CBS, 69,97,104,115; Colgate-Palmolive Co., 152-53; NBC, 115; number (1970-1979), 72; Procter & Gamble Co., 69,90,91,115; response to, 152-53;
　summarized, 72,171
　United Church of Christ involvement, 93,152-53
　United Methodist Church involvement, 115. *See also* American Fletcher Corp.; equal employment opportunities (U.S.)
World Health Assembly, 111
Worldwide Council of Churches
　campaign against multinationals, 128
　South Africa involvement, 120-21

Xerox Corp.
　shareholder resolutions filed, 78:
　　equal employment opportunity, 60,61, 89-91; labor practices, 149-50; number (1970-1979), 78; South Africa, 38,86